ST(P) MATHEMATICS 4A

ST(P) MATHEMATICS series:

ST(P) 1A
ST(P) 1B
ST(P) 1A Teacher's Notes and Answers
ST(P) 1B Teacher's Notes and Answers

ST(P) 2A
ST(P) 2B
ST(P) 2A Teacher's Notes and Answers
ST(P) 2B Teacher's Notes and Answers

ST(P) 3A
ST(P) 3B
ST(P) 3A Teacher's Notes and Answers
ST(P) 3B Teacher's Notes and Answers

ST(P) 4A
ST(P) 4B
ST(P) 4A Teacher's Notes and Answers
ST(P) 4B Teacher's Notes and Answers

ST(P) 5A (with answers)
ST(P) 5B (with answers)

ST(P) 5C
ST(P) 5C Copy Masters
ST(P) 5C Teacher's Notes and Answers

ST(P) Resource Book

ST(P) MATHEMATICS 4A

L. Bostock, B.Sc.

S. Chandler, B.Sc.

A. Shepherd, B.Sc.

E. Smith, M.Sc.

Second Edition

Stanley Thornes (Publishers) Ltd

First published in 1986
Second edition published 1992 by:
Stanley Thornes (Publishers) Ltd
Ellenborough House
Wellington Street
CHELTENHAM GL50 1YW

97 98 99 00 / 10 9 8 7 6

A catalogue record for this book is available from the British Library

ISBN 0 7487 1501 0

Typeset by Tech-Set, Gateshead, Tyne & Wear
Printed and bound in Great Britain at Redwood Books, Trowbridge

CONTENTS

INTRODUCTION

This book continues the work in 3A and is intended for use with pupils working towards level 9/10 of the national curriculum.

The contents of this book complete coverage of levels 8 and 9 of the national curriculum. Remaining topics in level 10 are covered in Book 5A.

There are plenty of straightforward questions and exercises are divided into three types.

The first type, identified by plain numbers, e.g. **12.**, are considered necessary for consolidation.

The second type, identified by a single underline, e.g. **12.**, are extra, but not harder, questions for extra practice or for later revision.

The third type, identified by a double underline, e.g. **12.**, are more demanding questions.

Multiple choice questions are included for the first time in the A series. These can provide useful self-test questions to confirm understanding. They also provide the basis for useful class discussions. At the end of the book there are some general revision exercises of examination type questions.

ACKNOWLEDGEMENTS

The authors and publishers would like to thank the following for permission to include material.

The Financial Times: for the Exchange Cross Rates table on page 293.

British Rail: for the timetable on page 381.

1 ALGEBRAIC FRACTIONS

ADDITION AND SUBTRACTION

In Book 3A, Chapter 23, we simplified algebraic fractions of the form

$$\frac{x}{4} - \frac{x+3}{3}$$

In this chapter we revise that work and extend it.

EXERCISE 1a

Simplify $\dfrac{2x-1}{5} - \dfrac{x+2}{4}$

$$\frac{(2x-1)}{5} - \frac{(x+2)}{4} = \frac{4(2x-1) - 5(x+2)}{20}$$

$$= \frac{8x - 4 - 5x - 10}{20}$$

$$= \frac{3x - 14}{20}$$

Simplify:

1. $\dfrac{x+1}{3} + \dfrac{x+2}{4}$

2. $\dfrac{2x-1}{4} + \dfrac{x-3}{5}$

3. $\dfrac{4x+3}{5} + \dfrac{x-2}{2}$

4. $\dfrac{x-2}{6} - \dfrac{x-3}{7}$

5. $\dfrac{3x+2}{3} - \dfrac{2x-1}{4}$

6. $\dfrac{x+3}{2} + \dfrac{x+1}{5}$

7. $\dfrac{x+1}{3} + \dfrac{x-2}{4}$

8. $\dfrac{2x-3}{5} + \dfrac{3x+1}{2}$

9. $\dfrac{x+2}{3} - \dfrac{x-2}{4}$

10. $\dfrac{5x-2}{6} - \dfrac{3x-2}{5}$

11. $\dfrac{2x+3}{3} + \dfrac{3x-4}{6}$

12. $\dfrac{5x-2}{12} - \dfrac{x-5}{4}$

1

Simplify $\dfrac{5}{2x+3} - \dfrac{2}{5x}$

$$\frac{5}{2x+3} - \frac{2}{5x} = \frac{5(5x)-2(2x+3)}{5x(2x+3)}$$

$$= \frac{25x-4x-6}{5x(2x+3)}$$

$$= \frac{21x-6}{5x(2x+3)}$$

$$= \frac{3(7x-2)}{5x(2x+3)}$$

Simplify:

13. $\dfrac{2}{x} + \dfrac{5}{4x}$

16. $\dfrac{4}{x-4} - \dfrac{2}{x+3}$

19. $\dfrac{3}{4a} - \dfrac{2}{3a}$

14. $\dfrac{1}{5a} - \dfrac{2}{13a}$

17. $\dfrac{3}{x+2} + \dfrac{5}{2(x+2)}$

20. $\dfrac{5}{x+3} + \dfrac{2}{x-1}$

15. $\dfrac{2}{x+3} + \dfrac{3}{x+4}$

18. $\dfrac{3}{x} + \dfrac{4}{3x}$

21. $\dfrac{8}{x+7} - \dfrac{3}{x-4}$

Sometimes we factorise the denominators first so that we can choose the simplest common denominator.

EXERCISE 1b

Simplify $\dfrac{2}{x^2-9} - \dfrac{3}{x+3}$

$$\frac{2}{x^2-9} - \frac{3}{x+3} = \frac{2}{(x+3)(x-3)} - \frac{3}{(x+3)}$$

$$= \frac{2-3(x-3)}{(x+3)(x-3)}$$

$$= \frac{2-3x+9}{(x+3)(x-3)}$$

$$= \frac{11-3x}{(x+3)(x-3)}$$

Simplify:

1. $\dfrac{3}{x+1} + \dfrac{2}{x^2-1}$

2. $\dfrac{5}{x^2-4} + \dfrac{3}{x+2}$

3. $\dfrac{3}{x^2-16} - \dfrac{4}{x-4}$

4. $\dfrac{4}{x-3} - \dfrac{1}{x^2-9}$

5. $\dfrac{2}{x+2} - \dfrac{x-4}{x^2-4}$

6. $\dfrac{7}{x^2-1} + \dfrac{2}{x-1}$

7. $\dfrac{3}{x+5} - \dfrac{2}{x^2-25}$

8. $\dfrac{5}{x^2-49} - \dfrac{9}{x-7}$

9. $\dfrac{4}{x+4} + \dfrac{3}{x^2-16}$

10. $\dfrac{1}{2x} + \dfrac{x-3}{x^2-2x}$

11. $\dfrac{2}{3x} + \dfrac{x-5}{x(x+3)}$

12. $\dfrac{3}{x^2-9} + \dfrac{5}{x+3}$

There are times when the fraction that results from reducing several fractions to a single fraction can be simplified further because there is a factor that is common to the numerator and the denominator.

EXERCISE 1c

Reduce $\dfrac{2x}{x^2-4} - \dfrac{1}{x-2}$ to a single fraction in its lowest terms.

(The first step is to factorise the denominator.)

$$\frac{2x}{x^2-4} - \frac{1}{x-2} = \frac{2x}{(x+2)(x-2)} - \frac{1}{x-2}$$

$$= \frac{2x-(x+2)}{(x+2)(x-2)}$$

$$= \frac{2x-x-2}{(x+2)(x-2)}$$

$$= \frac{(x-2)}{(x+2)(x-2)}$$

$$= \frac{1}{x+2}$$

Simplify:

1. $\dfrac{1}{x+1} + \dfrac{2}{x^2-1}$

9. $\dfrac{6}{x^2-9} + \dfrac{1}{x+3}$

2. $\dfrac{1}{2+x} + \dfrac{2x}{4-x^2}$

10. $\dfrac{1}{x-3} + \dfrac{1}{x^2-7x+12}$

3. $\dfrac{6}{x^2-2x-8} + \dfrac{1}{x+2}$

11. $\dfrac{3}{x^2-x-2} + \dfrac{1}{x+1}$

4. $\dfrac{3}{x^2+5x+4} + \dfrac{1}{x+4}$

12. $\dfrac{1}{x^2-4x+3} + \dfrac{1}{x^2-1}$

5. $\dfrac{2}{x+1} + \dfrac{4}{x^2-1}$

13. $\dfrac{9}{x^2+x-2} - \dfrac{3}{x-1}$

6. $\dfrac{1}{x-1} - \dfrac{x+2}{2x^2-x-1}$

14. $\dfrac{10}{2x^2-3x-2} - \dfrac{2}{x-2}$

7. $\dfrac{8}{x^2-2x-15} - \dfrac{1}{x-5}$

15. $\dfrac{x}{x^2+6x+8} + \dfrac{1}{x+2}$

8. $\dfrac{2}{x^2+4x+3} - \dfrac{1}{x^2+5x+6}$

16. $\dfrac{1}{x^2+9x+20} + \dfrac{2}{x^2+6x+8}$

MIXED QUESTIONS

EXERCISE 1d

Simplify:

1. $\dfrac{3x+2}{3} + \dfrac{x+1}{4}$

5. $\dfrac{3}{x^2-2x-8} - \dfrac{5}{x^2-5x+4}$

2. $\dfrac{5x-3}{5} - \dfrac{3x-2}{4}$

6. $\dfrac{2}{x+5} + \dfrac{14}{x^2+3x-10}$

3. $\dfrac{5}{6x} - \dfrac{2}{3x}$

7. $\dfrac{1}{x^2-7x+12} + \dfrac{1}{x^2-5x+6}$

4. $\dfrac{6}{x-2} - \dfrac{4}{x^2-4}$

8. $\dfrac{1}{2x^2+3x-2} - \dfrac{1}{3x^2+7x+2}$

SOLVING EQUATIONS WITH FRACTIONS

Remember that if we alter one side of an equation we must alter the other side in the same way. If an equation contains fractions we can remove them by multiplying both sides by the LCM of the denominators.

EXERCISE 1e

> Solve the equation $\dfrac{x}{2} + \dfrac{x}{8} = 10$
>
> $$\frac{x}{2} + \frac{x}{8} = 10$$
>
> Multiply both sides by 8 $$8 \times \frac{x}{2} + 8 \times \frac{x}{8} = 8 \times 10$$
>
> $$4x + x = 80$$
> $$5x = 80$$
> $$x = 16$$

Solve the following equations.

1. $\dfrac{x}{6} + \dfrac{x}{3} = 3$ **4.** $\dfrac{5x}{4} - \dfrac{2x}{3} = 7$ **7.** $\dfrac{2x}{5} - \dfrac{x}{3} = \dfrac{4}{3}$

2. $\dfrac{x}{4} - \dfrac{x}{8} = 1$ **5.** $\dfrac{x}{4} + \dfrac{x}{6} = 10$ **8.** $\dfrac{3x}{2} - \dfrac{4x}{7} = 13$

3. $\dfrac{2x}{3} + \dfrac{x}{5} = \dfrac{13}{3}$ **6.** $\dfrac{x}{5} - \dfrac{x}{10} = 2$ **9.** $\dfrac{5x}{3} - \dfrac{3x}{4} = \dfrac{11}{6}$

> Solve the equation $\dfrac{4}{5} - \dfrac{2}{x} = \dfrac{2}{15}$
>
> $$\frac{4}{5} - \frac{2}{x} = \frac{2}{15}$$
>
> Multiply both sides by $15x$
>
> $$^{3}\cancel{15x} \times \frac{4}{\cancel{5}_{1}} - 15\cancel{x} \times \frac{2}{\cancel{x}_{1}} = {}^{1}\cancel{15}x \times \frac{2}{\cancel{15}_{1}}$$
>
> $$12x - 30 = 2x$$
> $$10x - 30 = 0$$
> $$10x = 30$$
> $$x = 3$$

Solve the following equations.

10. $\dfrac{1}{2} - \dfrac{1}{x} = \dfrac{1}{4}$

14. $\dfrac{1}{2} - \dfrac{1}{x} = \dfrac{1}{6}$

11. $\dfrac{3}{2x} + \dfrac{5}{24} = \dfrac{7}{12}$

15. $\dfrac{2}{x} + \dfrac{1}{4} = \dfrac{11}{12}$

12. $\dfrac{3}{x} - \dfrac{1}{2x} = 5$

16. $\dfrac{2}{3x} - \dfrac{1}{2x} = \dfrac{1}{2}$

13. $\dfrac{7}{4x} - \dfrac{1}{2} = \dfrac{3}{8}$

17. $\dfrac{17}{7x} - \dfrac{5}{7} = \dfrac{1}{2}$

Solve the equation $\dfrac{x-2}{5} - \dfrac{x-5}{3} = \dfrac{1}{15}$

$$\frac{(x-2)}{5} - \frac{(x-5)}{3} = \frac{1}{15}$$

Multiply both sides by 15

$$\frac{^3\cancel{15}}{1} \times \frac{(x-2)}{\cancel{5}_1} - \frac{^5\cancel{15}}{1} \times \frac{(x-5)}{\cancel{3}_1} = \frac{^1\cancel{15}}{1} \times \frac{1}{\cancel{15}_1}$$

$$3(x-2) - 5(x-5) = 1$$
$$3x - 6 - 5x + 25 = 1$$
$$-2x + 19 = 1$$
$$19 = 1 + 2x$$
$$18 = 2x$$
$$9 = x$$

Solve the following equations.

18. $\dfrac{x-2}{2} + \dfrac{x}{3} = \dfrac{3}{2}$

22. $\dfrac{x-1}{3} + \dfrac{x}{4} = \dfrac{5}{6}$

19. $\dfrac{x-1}{9} + \dfrac{3x-7}{4} = \dfrac{13}{18}$

23. $\dfrac{2x-1}{4} + \dfrac{x-3}{5} = \dfrac{11}{20}$

20. $\dfrac{3x-2}{5} - \dfrac{x-1}{2} = \dfrac{3}{10}$

24. $\dfrac{2x-3}{6} - \dfrac{x-3}{2} = \dfrac{1}{3}$

21. $1 - \dfrac{3x+7 \cdot}{2} = \dfrac{x+4}{4}$

25. $\dfrac{1}{2} - \dfrac{x-2}{5} = \dfrac{2x-3}{10}$

Sometimes a fractional equation leads to a quadratic equation which will factorise.

EXERCISE 1f

Solve the equation $\dfrac{6}{x} + \dfrac{1}{x-5} = 2$

$$\frac{6}{x} + \frac{1}{x-5} = 2$$

Multiply both sides by $x(x-5)$

$$x(x-5)\left[\frac{6}{x} + \frac{1}{x-5}\right] = x(x-5)\times 2$$

$${}^{1}\!\!\!\not{x}(x-5)\times\frac{6}{\not{x}_{1}} + x\not{(x-5)}\times\frac{1}{\not{x-5}_{1}} = 2x(x-5)$$

$$6(x-5) + x = 2x(x-5)$$

$$6x - 30 + x = 2x^2 - 10x$$

$$7x - 30 = 2x^2 - 10x$$

$$0 = 2x^2 - 17x + 30$$

$\therefore$ $\qquad\qquad\qquad 2x^2 - 17x + 30 = 0$

$$(2x - 5)(x - 6) = 0$$

$\therefore$ $\quad$ either $\quad 2x - 5 = 0 \quad$ or $\quad x - 6 = 0$

$$2x = 5 \quad \text{or} \quad x = 6$$

$\therefore$ $\qquad\qquad\qquad x = 2\tfrac{1}{2} \quad \text{or} \quad x = 6$

Solve the following equations, each of which leads to a quadratic equation that factorises.

1. $\dfrac{5}{x+3} - \dfrac{1}{x} = \dfrac{1}{2}$

2. $\dfrac{1}{x} - \dfrac{1}{x+1} = \dfrac{1}{20}$

3. $\dfrac{x+5}{x} = x - 3$

4. $\dfrac{2}{x+4} + \dfrac{3}{x} = 1$

5. $\dfrac{3}{x-1} - \dfrac{x}{3} = \dfrac{1}{2}$

6. $\dfrac{8}{x} + \dfrac{1}{x-5} = 1$

7. $x + \dfrac{3}{x+4} = 0$

8. $\dfrac{2}{x} - \dfrac{1}{x+2} = \dfrac{1}{3}$

9. $\dfrac{3}{x} + \dfrac{2}{x-1} = 2$

10. $\dfrac{5}{x+1} + \dfrac{2}{x+6} = \dfrac{6}{5}$

11. $\dfrac{2}{x+1} + \dfrac{3}{x+4} = \dfrac{2}{3}$

12. $\dfrac{4}{x-8} + \dfrac{3}{x-2} = \dfrac{1}{2}$

13. $\dfrac{3}{x+2} - \dfrac{1}{x+1} = 8$

14. $\dfrac{1}{x-3} - \dfrac{3}{x-4} = \dfrac{1}{2}$

15. $\dfrac{3}{5-x} - \dfrac{3}{4} = \dfrac{1}{x+2}$

16. $\dfrac{x+2}{4} - \dfrac{3}{x-5} = 1\tfrac{1}{2}$

2 CONGRUENT TRIANGLES

CONGRUENT FIGURES

Two figures are congruent if one figure is an exact copy of the other. If the figures are drawn on squared paper it is easy to determine if they are congruent. If the shapes are drawn accurately on plain paper, we can use tracing paper to see whether they appear to be congruent but we need precise information about the lengths of sides and the sizes of angles to determine whether they really are congruent.

CONGRUENT TRIANGLES

Triangles are simple figures and not very much information is needed to determine whether one triangle is an exact copy of another triangle

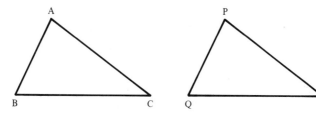

If $\triangle$s $\dfrac{\text{ABC}}{\text{PQR}}$ are congruent it follows that

$$\left. \begin{array}{l} \text{AB} = \text{PQ} \\ \text{AC} = \text{PR} \\ \text{BC} = \text{QR} \end{array} \right\} \quad \text{and} \quad \left\{ \begin{array}{l} \hat{\text{A}} = \hat{\text{P}} \\ \hat{\text{B}} = \hat{\text{Q}} \\ \hat{\text{C}} = \hat{\text{R}} \end{array} \right.$$

To make an exact copy of these triangles we do not need to know the lengths of all three sides and the sizes of all three angles: three measurements are usually enough and we now investigate which three measurements are suitable.

EXERCISE 2a

In each of the following questions make a rough sketch of $\triangle$ABC. Construct a triangle with the same measurements as those given for $\triangle$ABC. Is your construction an exact copy of $\triangle$ABC? (Try to construct a different triangle with the given measurements.)

1. △ABC, in which AB = 8 cm, BC = 5 cm, AC = 6 cm.

2. △ABC, in which $\widehat{A}$ = 40°, $\widehat{B}$ = 60°, $\widehat{C}$ = 80°.

3. △ABC, in which AB = 7 cm, BC = 12 cm, AC = 8 cm.

4. △ABC, in which $\widehat{A}$ = 20°, $\widehat{B}$ = 40°, $\widehat{C}$ = 120°.

5. What extra information do you need about △ABC in questions 2 and 4 in order to make an exact copy?

THREE PAIRS OF SIDES

From the last exercise you should be convinced that an exact copy of a triangle can be made if the lengths of the three sides are known. Therefore,

> two triangles are congruent if the three sides of one triangle are equal to the three sides of the other triangle.

However if the three angles of one triangle are equal to the three angles of another triangle they may not be congruent (but they are similar).

EXERCISE 2b

Decide whether the following pairs of triangles are congruent. Give brief reasons for your answers.

a)

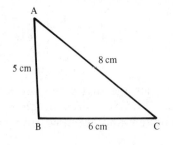

$$\left. \begin{array}{l} AB = PQ \\ BC = QR \\ AC = PR \end{array} \right\} \quad \therefore \quad \triangle s \; \begin{array}{l} ABC \\ PQR \end{array} \; \text{are congruent} \quad (3 \text{ sides})$$

(Notice that we write corresponding vertices one under the other.)

b)

 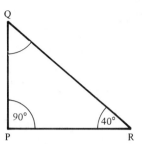

In △ABC, $\widehat{A} = 80°$ (angles of △)

In △PQR, $\widehat{Q} = 50°$ (angles of △)

∴   △ABC and △PQR are not congruent.

c)

In △ABC, $\widehat{C} = 40°$ (angles of △)

In △PQR, $\widehat{Q} = 90°$ (angles of △)

∴ △s $\dfrac{ABC}{PQR}$ are similar, but probably not congruent.

In questions 1 to 6 state whether or not the two triangles are congruent. Give a brief reason for your answers. All lengths are in centimetres:

1.

2.

3.

4.

5.

6.

Give brief reasons for your answers to questions 7 to 10.

7.

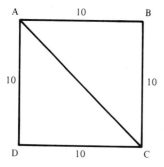

Are △ADC and △ABC congruent?

8.

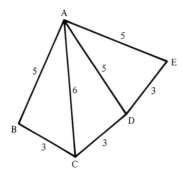

Which triangles are congruent?

9.

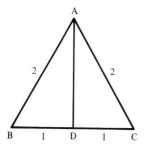

Are △ABD and △ACD congruent?

10.

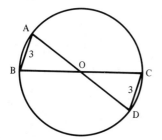

The point O is the centre of the circle and the radius is 5 cm. Are △ABO and △CDO congruent?

TWO ANGLES AND A SIDE

To make an exact copy of a triangle we need to know the length of at least one side.

EXERCISE 2c

1. Construct $\triangle ABC$, in which   AB = 6 cm, $\widehat{A}$ = 30°, $\widehat{B}$ = 60°.

2. Construct $\triangle PQR$, in which   PR = 6 cm, $\widehat{P}$ = 30°, $\widehat{Q}$ = 60°.

3. Construct $\triangle LMN$, in which   LM = 6 cm, $\widehat{L}$ = 30°, $\widehat{M}$ = 60°.

4. Construct $\triangle XYZ$, in which   YZ = 6 cm, $\widehat{X}$ = 30°, $\widehat{Y}$ = 60°.

5. How many of the triangles that you have constructed are congruent?

6. How many different triangles can you construct from the following information: one angle is 40°, another angle is 70° and the length of one side is 8 cm?

Now you can see that we are able to make an exact copy of a triangle if we know the sizes of two of its angles and the length of one side, provided that we place the side in the same position relative to the angles in both triangles, i.e.

> two triangles are congruent if two angles and one side of one triangle are equal to two angles and the *corresponding* side of the other triangle.

EXERCISE 2d

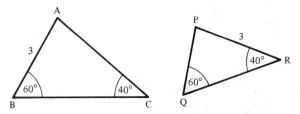

Decide whether these triangles are congruent. Give a brief reason for your answer.

$\triangle$s $\dfrac{ABC}{PQR}$ are similar   (angles equal)

but not congruent   (AB and PQ are corr. sides and are *not* equal).

In questions 1 to 8 state whether or not the two triangles are congruent. Give brief reasons for your answers. All lengths are in centimetres.

1.

2.

3.

4.

5.

6.

7.

8.

9.

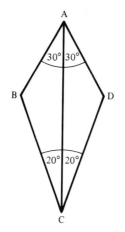

Are △ABC and △ADC congruent?

10.

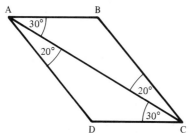

Are △ABC and △ADC congruent?

TWO SIDES AND AN ANGLE

We are now left with one more possible combination of three measurements: if we know the lengths of two sides and the size of one angle in a triangle, does this fix the size and shape of the triangle?

EXERCISE 2e

Can you make an exact copy of the following triangles from the information given about them? (Try to construct each triangle.)

1. △ABC, in which AB = 8 cm, BC = 5 cm, $\hat{B}$ = 30°.

2. △XYZ, in which XY = 8 cm, XZ = 5 cm, $\hat{Y}$ = 30°.

3. △PQR, in which $\hat{Q}$ = 60°, PQ = 6 cm, QR = 8 cm.

4. △LMN, in which LM = 8 cm, $\hat{M}$ = 20°, LN = 4 cm.

5. △DEF, in which DE = 5 cm, $\hat{E}$ = 90°, EF = 6 cm.

Now it is possible to see that we can make an exact copy of a triangle if we know the lengths of two sides and the size of one angle, provided that the angle is between those two sides. Therefore,

> two triangles are congruent if two sides and the *included* angle of one triangle are equal to two sides and the *included* angle of the other triangle.

If the angle is not between the two known sides, then we cannot always be sure that we can make an exact copy of the triangle. We will now investigate this case further.

EXERCISE 2f

Can you make an exact copy of each of the following triangles from the information given about them?

1. △ABC, in which AB = 6 cm, $\hat{B} = 90°$, AC = 10 cm.

2. △PQR, in which PQ = 8 cm, $\hat{Q} = 40°$, PR = 6.5 cm.

3. △XYZ, in which XY = 5 cm, $\hat{Y} = 90°$, XZ = 13 cm.

4. △LMN, in which LM = 5 cm, $\hat{M} = 60°$, LN = 4.5 cm.

5. △DEF, in which DE = 7 cm, $\hat{E} = 90°$, DF = 10 cm.

6. △RST, in which RS = 5 cm, $\hat{S} = 120°$, RT = 8 cm.

7. Can you calculate any further information about any of the triangles in questions 1 to 6?

From question 7 you can see that, when the given angle is 90° the length of the remaining side of the triangle can be calculated.

Therefore, if we are told that one angle in a triangle is a right angle and we are also given the length of one side and the hypotenuse, then this information fixes the shape and size of the triangle since it is equivalent to knowing the lengths of the three sides.

> Two triangles are congruent if they both have a right angle, and the hypotenuse and a side of one triangle are equal to the hypotenuse and a side of the other triangle.

EXERCISE 2g

In questions 1 to 8 state whether or not the two triangles are congruent. Give brief reasons for your answers. All lengths are in centimetres.

1.

2.

3.

4.

5.

6.

7.

8.

9.

Are △ABD and △ACD congruent ?

10.

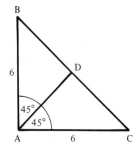

Are △ABD and △ACD congruent ?

Summing up, two triangles are congruent if:

either   the three sides of one triangle are equal to the three sides of the other triangle (S S S)

or   two angles and a side of one triangle are equal to two angles and the corresponding side of the other triangle (A A S)

or   two sides and the included angle of one triangle are equal to two sides and the included angle of the other triangle (S A S)

or   two triangles each have a right angle, and the hypotenuse and a side of one triangle are equal to the hypotenuse and a side of the other triangle (R H S).

EXERCISE 2h

State whether or not each of the following pairs of triangles are congruent. Give brief reasons for your answers. All measurements are in centimetres.

1.

2.

3.

4.

5.

6.

7.

8.

9.

10.

11.

12.

13.

14.

15.

 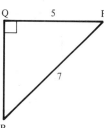

PROBLEMS

We do not need to know actual measurements to prove that triangles are congruent. If we can show that a correct combination of sides and angles are the same in both triangles, the triangles must be congruent.

EXERCISE 2i

In a quadrilateral ABCD, AB = DC and AD = BC. The diagonal BD is drawn. Prove that △ABD and △CDB are congruent.

(Mark on your diagram all the information given and any further facts that you discover. The symbol ⌒ on BD indicates that it is common to both triangles.)

In △s ABD, CDB   AB = CD   (given)

                     AD = CB   (given)

                     DB is the same for both triangles

∴   △s $\frac{ABD}{CDB}$ are congruent (S S S).

1.

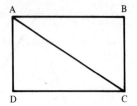

ABCD is a rectangle. Prove that △ABC and △CDA are congruent.

2.

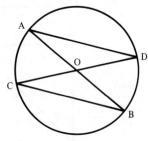

AB and CD are diameters of the circle and O is the centre. Prove that △AOD and △COB are congruent.

3.

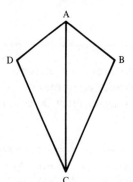

ABCD is a kite in which AD = AB and CD = BC. Prove that △ADC and △ABC are congruent.

4.

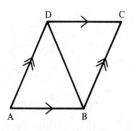

ABCD is a parallelogram. Prove that △ABD and △CDB are congruent.

5.

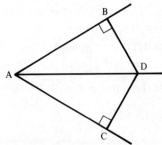

AD bisects BÂC, DB is perpendicular to AB and DC is perpendicular to AC. Prove that △ABD and △ACD are congruent.

6.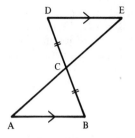

Prove that △ABC and △EDC are congruent.

7.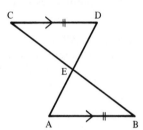

CD and AB are equal and parallel. Prove that △ABE and △DCE are congruent.

8.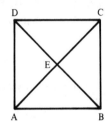

ABCD is a square. Show that △s ABE, BCE, CDE and DAE are all congruent.

9.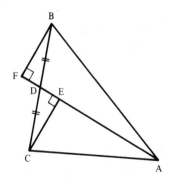

D is the midpoint of BC. CE and BF are perpendicular to AF. Find a pair of congruent triangles.

10.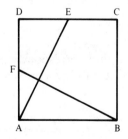

ABCD is a square. E is the midpoint of DC and F is the midpoint of AD. Show that △ADE and △BAF are congruent.

11.

ABC is an isosceles triangle in which AB = AC. D is the midpoint of AB and E is the midpoint of AC. Prove that △BDC is congruent with △CEB.

12. ABCD is a rectangle and E is the midpoint of AB. Join DE and CE and show that △ADE is congruent with △BCE.

13. ABCD is a rectangle. E is the midpoint of AB and F is the midpoint of DC. Join DE and BF and show that △ADE is congruent with △CBF.

USING CONGRUENT TRIANGLES

Once two triangles have been shown to be congruent it follows that the other corresponding sides and angles are equal. This gives a good way of proving that certain angles are equal or that certain lines are the same length.

EXERCISE 2j

ABCD is a square and AE = DF.
Show that DE = CF.

In △s DAE and CDF

$$AE = DF \quad (\text{given})$$
$$DA = CD \quad (\text{sides of a square})$$
$$D\hat{A}E = C\hat{D}F \quad (\text{angles of a square are } 90°)$$

∴ △s $\begin{matrix} DAE \\ CDF \end{matrix}$ are congruent (S A S)

(We have written the triangles so that corresponding vertices are lined up. We can then see the remaining corresponding sides and angles.)

∴ DE = CF

1.

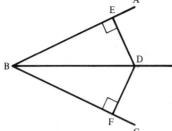

BD bisects A$\widehat{B}$C. BE and BF are equal. Show that triangles BED and BFD are congruent and hence prove that ED = FD.

2.

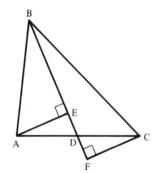

D is the midpoint of AC. AE and CF are both perpendicular to BF. Show that triangles AED and CFD are congruent and hence prove that AE = CF.

3.

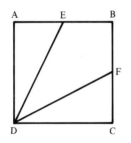

ABCD is a square and E and F are the midpoints of AB and BC. Show that △ADE is congruent with △CDF and hence prove that DE = DF.

4.

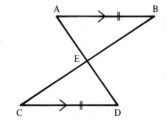

AB and CD are parallel and equal in length. Show that △AEB and △DEC are congruent and hence prove that E is the midpoint of both CB and AD.

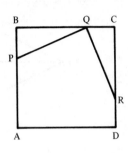

ABCD is a square and P, Q and R are points on AB, BC and CD respectively such that AP = BQ = CR.

Show that $P\hat{Q}R = 90°$.

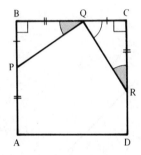

(We will first prove that $\triangle PBQ$ and $\triangle QCR$ are congruent.)

In $\triangle PBQ$ and $\triangle QCR$

$$BQ = CR \hspace{3cm} \text{(given)}$$

$$P\hat{B}Q = Q\hat{C}R = 90° \hspace{2cm} \text{(angles of a square)}$$

also $\hspace{1cm} PB = QC \hspace{0.3cm} \begin{cases} AB = AC & \text{(sides of a square)} \\ AP = BQ & \text{(given)} \end{cases}$

$\therefore \hspace{0.3cm} \triangle s \begin{matrix} PBQ \\ QCR \end{matrix}$ are congruent. $\hspace{2cm}$ (SAS)

$\therefore \hspace{3cm} B\hat{Q}P = Q\hat{R}C$

In $\triangle QRC \hspace{1cm} Q\hat{R}C + C\hat{Q}R = 90° \hspace{1cm} \text{(angles of triangle)}$

$\therefore \hspace{2cm} B\hat{Q}P + C\hat{Q}R = 90°$

But $\hspace{1cm} B\hat{Q}P + P\hat{Q}R + C\hat{Q}R = 180° \hspace{1cm} \text{(angles on st. line)}$

$$P\hat{Q}R = 90°$$

5.

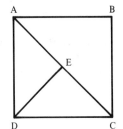

ABCD is a square and E is the midpoint of the diagonal AC. First show that triangles ADE and CDE are congruent and hence prove that DE is perpendicular to AC.

6.

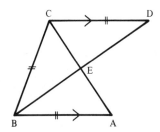

CD is parallel to BA and

$$CD = CB = B$$

Show that △CDE is congruent with △BAE and hence that CA bisects BD.

7. Using the same diagram and the result from question 6, show that △BEC is congruent with △CED. Hence prove that CA and BD cut at right angles.

8.

Triangle ABC is isosceles, with AB = AC. BX is perpendicular to AC and CQ is perpendicular to AB. Prove that BX = CQ. (Find a pair of congruent triangles first.)

9.

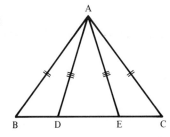

In the diagram, AB = AC and AD = AE. Prove that BD = EC.

(Consider triangles ABD and ACE.)

10. AB is a straight line. Draw a line AX perpendicular to AB. On the other side of AB, draw a line BY perpendicular to AB so that BY is equal to AX. Prove that $A\hat{X}Y = B\hat{Y}X$.

PROPERTIES OF PARALLELOGRAMS

In earlier books we investigated the properties of parallelograms by observation and measurement of a few particular parallelograms. Now we can use congruent triangles to prove that these properties are true for all parallelograms.

A parallelogram is formed when two pairs of parallel lines cross each other.

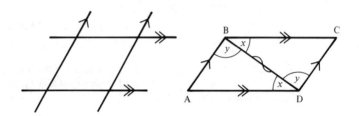

In the parallelogram ABCD, joining BD gives two triangles in which

> the angles marked x are equal (they are alternate angles with respect to parallels AD and BC);

> the angles marked y are equal (they are alternate angles with respect to parallels AB and DC);

> and BD is the same for both triangles.

$\therefore$ $\triangle$s $\begin{matrix} \text{BCD} \\ \text{DAB} \end{matrix}$ are congruent   (AAS)

$\therefore$ BC = AD   and   AB = DC

i.e.   the opposite sides of a parallelogram are the same length.

Also from the congruent triangles

$$\hat{A} = \hat{C}$$

and $$\hat{ABC} = \hat{CDA} \quad (x+y = y+x)$$

i.e.   the opposite angles of a parallelogram are equal.

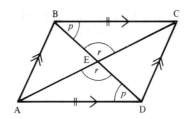

Drawing both diagonals of the parallelogram gives four triangles.

Considering the two triangles BEC, DEA

$$BC = AD \quad (\text{opp. sides of } \| \text{gram})$$

$$E\widehat{B}C = E\widehat{D}A \quad (\text{alt. } \angle s)$$

$$B\widehat{E}C = A\widehat{E}D \quad (\text{vert. opp. } \angle s)$$

∴   △s $\dfrac{\text{BEC}}{\text{DEA}}$ are congruent   (A A S)

∴ $$BE = ED \quad \text{and} \quad AE = EC$$

i.e.   the diagonals of a parallelogram bisect each other.

The diagrams below summarise these properties.

It is equally important to realise that, in general,

the diagonals are *not* the same length,

the diagonals do *not* bisect the angles of a parallelogram.

In the exercise that follows, you are asked to investigate the properties of some of the other special quadrilaterals.

EXERCISE 2k

1.

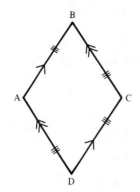

ABCD is a rhombus (a parallelogram in which all four sides are equal in length). Join AC and show that △ABC and △ADC are congruent. What does AC do to the angles of the rhombus at A and C? Does the diagonal BD do the same to the angles at B and D?

2.

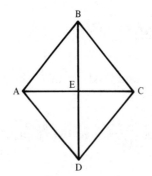

ABCD is a rhombus. Use the results from question 1 to show that △s ABE an BCE are congruent. What can you now say about the angles AEB and BEC?

3.

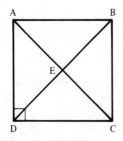

ABCD is a square (a rhombus with right-angled corners). Use the properties of the diagonals of a rhombus to show that △AED is isosceles. Hence prove that the diagonals of a square are the same length.

Are the two diagonals of *every* rhombus the same length?

4.

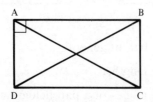

ABCD is a rectangle (a parallelogram with right-angled corners). Prove that △s ADB and DAC are congruent. What can you deduce about the lengths of AC and DB?

5.

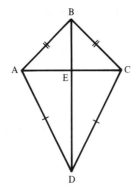

ABCD is a kite in which AB = BC and AD = DC.

Does the diagonal BD bisect the angles at B and D?
Does the diagonal AC bisect the angles at A and C?
Is E the midpoint of either diagonal?
What can you say about the angles at E?

6.

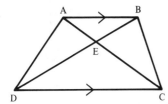

ABCD is a trapezium: it has just one pair of parallel sides. Are there any congruent triangles in this diagram?

7.

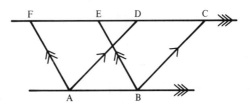

In the diagram, ABCD and ABEF are parallelograms. Show that △s ADF and BCE are congruent.

By considering the shape ABCF and then removing each of the triangles AFD and BEC in turn, what can you say about the areas of the two parallelograms?

USING PROPERTIES OF SPECIAL QUADRILATERALS

In question 7 you proved a property of two parallelograms.

> Two parallelograms with the same base, and drawn between the same pair of parallel lines, are equal in area.

The diagrams below summarise the other results from Exercise 2k

rectangle

rhombus

square

kite

You can now use any of these facts in the following exercise.

EXERCISE 2l

1.

ABCD is a rectangle. The diagonals AC and DB cut at E. How far is E from BC?

2.

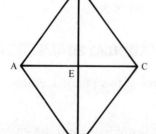

ABCD is a rhombus in which AC = 6 cm and BD = 8 cm. Find the length of AB.

3.

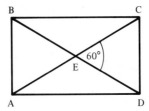

ABCD is a rectangle in which $C\widehat{E}D = 60°$. Find $E\widehat{C}D$.

4.

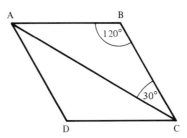

ABCD is a parallelogram in which $A\widehat{B}C = 120°$ and $B\widehat{C}A = 30°$. Show that ABCD is also a rhombus.

5. In a rectangle ABCD, $AB = 6\,cm$ and the diagonal BD is 10 cm. Make a rough sketch of the rectangle and then construct ABCD. Measure AD.

6. In a rhombus ABCD, the diagonal AC is 8 cm and the diagonal BD is 6 cm. Construct the rhombus and measure AB.

(Remember first to make a rough sketch.)

7. ABCD is a parallelogram in which the diagonal AC is 10 cm and the diagonal BD is 12 cm. AC and BD cut at E and $A\widehat{E}B = 60°$. Make a rough sketch of the parallelogram and then construct ABCD. Measure BC.

8. Construct a rhombus ABCD in which the sides are 5 cm long and the diagonal AC is 8 cm long. Measure the diagonal BD.

9. Construct a square ABCD whose diagonal, AC, is 8 cm long. Measure the side AB.

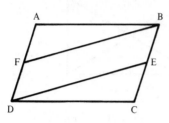

ABCD is a parallelogram. E is the midpoint of BC and F is the midpoint of AD.

Prove that BF = DE.

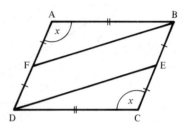

In △s ABF and CDE

$$AF = EC \qquad (\tfrac{1}{2} \text{ opp. sides of parallelogram})$$

$$AB = DC \qquad (\text{opp. sides of parallelogram})$$

$$\hat{FAB} = \hat{ECD} \qquad (\text{opp. angles of parallelogram})$$

∴   △s $\dfrac{\text{ABF}}{\text{CDE}}$ are congruent (SAS).

∴   BF = DE

10.

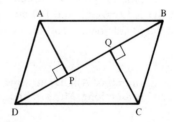

ABCD is a parallelogram. AP is perpendicular to BD and CQ is perpendicular to BD. Prove that AP = CQ.

11.

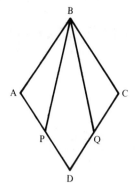

ABCD is a rhombus. P is the midpoint of AD and Q is the midpoint of CD.

Prove that BP = BQ.

12.

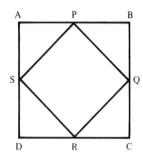

ABCD is a square and P, Q, R and S are the midpoints of AB, BC, CD and DA. Prove that PQRS is a square.

13.

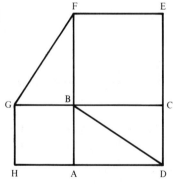

ABCD is a rectangle. ABGH and BCEF are squares. Show that GF = BD.

3 PRISMS AND PYRAMIDS

VOLUME OF A CUBOID

The volume of a cuboid = length × breadth × height.
The three measurements must be expressed in the same unit before multiplying.

EXERCISE 3a

Find the volume of a cuboid measuring 42 cm by 1.2 m by 382 mm. Give your answer in cubic metres.

$$42\,\text{cm} = 0.42\,\text{m}$$

$$382\,\text{mm} = 0.382\,\text{m}$$

$$\text{Volume} = 1.2 \times 0.42 \times 0.382\,\text{m}^3$$

$$= 0.1925\,\text{m}^3$$

$$= 0.193\,\text{m}^3 \quad \text{correct to 3 s.f.}$$

Find the volumes of the cuboids whose measurements are given in questions 1 to 5. Give your answers in the units indicated in the brackets.

1. 62 cm by 48 cm by 0.12 m   (cm³)
2. 1.3 cm by 62 mm by 1.7 cm   (cm³)
3. 420 cm by 500 cm by 620 cm   (m³)
4. 0.03 m by 0.16 m by 0.09 m   (cm³)
5. 1.6 cm by 1.5 cm by 7 mm   (mm³)
6. a) How many cubic centimetres are there in 1 m³?
   b) Express 4.23 m³ in cubic centimetres.
7. a) How many cubic millimetres are there in 1 cm³?
   b) Express 628 mm³ in cubic centimetres.

In questions 8 to 13, express the given volumes in the units indicated in brackets. Remember that 1 litre = 1000 cm^3

8. 4200 cm^3 (litres)

11. 432 000 cm^3 (m^3)

9. 0.048 m^3 (cm^3)

12. 7800 mm^3 (cm^3)

10. 75 000 000 cm^3 (m^3)

13. 42 cm^3 (mm^3)

Find the length of a cuboid of volume 18 cm^3 whose breadth is 5.2 cm and whose height is 12 mm.

$$\text{Height} = 12\,\text{mm}$$

$$= 1.2\,\text{cm}$$

$$\text{Volume} = \text{length} \times \text{breadth} \times \text{height}$$

$$18 = l \times 5.2 \times 1.2$$

$$\frac{18}{5.2 \times 1.2} = l$$

$$\therefore \qquad l = 2.884$$

The length is 2.88 cm   correct to 3 s.f.

Find the missing measurements for each of the following cuboids.

	Volume	Length	Breadth	Height
14.	128 cm^3	4.8 cm	2 cm	cm
15.	24 m^3	m	0.7 m	15 m
16.	32 cm^3	cm	8 cm	64 mm
17.	241 mm^3	2.2 cm	mm	5.2 mm
18.	cm^3	6.2 cm	0.3 m	190 mm

19. A block of metal measures 44 cm by 10 cm by 6 cm. It is melted down and formed into a cuboid which is 4 cm wide and 33 cm high. How long is the new block?

20. Rain falls on a flat roof measuring 3 m by 4 m and runs off into a rectangular tank which is 0.4 m long and 0.6 m wide. 1 cm of rain falls on the roof.

a) Find the volume of rain falling on the roof.

b) If the tank is empty to start with, how deep is the water in it when the rain stops ?

21.

The diagram shows the net for a cuboid. Find the volume of the cuboid.

VOLUME OF A PRISM

A solid whose cross-section is the same all through is called a *prism*.

The volume of a solid whose cross-section is the same all the way through is given by

$$\text{volume} = \text{area of cross-section} \times \text{length}$$

EXERCISE 3b

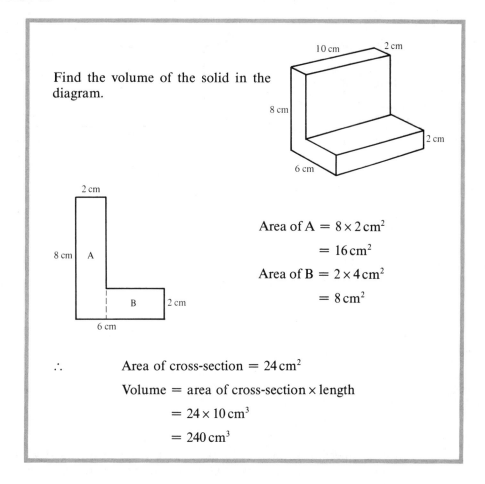

Find the volume of the solid in the diagram.

Area of A $= 8 \times 2\,\text{cm}^2$

$= 16\,\text{cm}^2$

Area of B $= 2 \times 4\,\text{cm}^2$

$= 8\,\text{cm}^2$

$\therefore$ Area of cross-section $= 24\,\text{cm}^2$

Volume $=$ area of cross-section $\times$ length

$= 24 \times 10\,\text{cm}^3$

$= 240\,\text{cm}^3$

Find the volumes of the solids illustrated in questions 1 to 6. In each case draw a diagram of the cross-section but do not draw a picture of the solid.

1.

2.

3.

5.

4.

6.

In each question from 7 to 10, find the volume of the solid whose cross-section and length are given. Give the answer in the unit indicated in brackets.

7.

Length = 1 m
(cm³)

8.

Length = 24 cm
(cm³)

9.   **10.**

60 cm

40 cm

50 cm   30 cm

Length = 4 m
(m³)

11 cm

8 cm

16 cm

Length = 16 cm
(cm³)

The volume of the solid shown in the diagram is 144 cm³ and the area of its cross-section is 14 cm². Find its length.

Let its length be l cm

$$\text{Volume} = \text{area of cross-section} \times \text{length}$$

$$144 = 14 \times l$$

$$l = \frac{144}{14}$$

$$= 10.28$$

i.e. the length is 10.3 cm   correct to 3 s.f.

11. The volume of a solid of uniform cross-section is 72 cm³. The area of its cross-section is 8 cm². Find the length of the solid.

12. The volume of a solid of uniform cross-section is 32 m³. Its length is 10 m. Find the area of its cross-section.

13.

The volume of the solid is 396 cm³.

Find   a) the area of the cross-section

b) the length of the solid.

14.

The cross-section of the solid is an isosceles triangle. The volume of the solid is 1200 cm³.

Find   a) the height of the triangle

b) the area of the cross-section

c) the length of the solid.

15.

The cross-section of the solid is a trapezium. The height of the trapezium is 10 cm and the volume of the solid is 7800 cm³.

Find the length of the solid.

16. A drop of oil of volume 2.5 cm³ is dropped on to a flat surface and spreads out to form a pool of even thickness and area 50 cm².

How thick is the oil   a) in centimetres   b) in millimetres ?

17.

A cuboid of metal measuring 6 cm by 8.2 cm by 9.5 cm is recast into the shape of a prism. The cross-section of the prism is shown in the diagram. How long is the prism ?

Water comes out of a pipe of cross-section 3.2 cm² at a speed of 0.5 m/s. How much water is delivered by the pipe in one second?

(Imagine 0.5 m of pipe being emptied in 1 second)

$$\text{Volume} = \text{area of cross-section} \times \text{length}$$
$$= 3.2 \times 50 \text{ cm}^3$$
$$= 160 \text{ cm}^3$$

∴ 160 cm³ of water is delivered in 1 second.

18. The cross-section of a pipe is 4.8 cm². If water comes out of the pipe at 30 cm/s, how much water is delivered in 1 second?

19. Water comes out of a pipe at 60 cm/s. The cross-section of the pipe is a circle of radius 0.5 cm.

How much water is delivered   a) in 1 second   b) in 1 minute?

20.

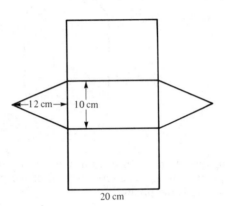

The diagram shows the net for a prism with an isosceles triangular cross-section.

Find   a) the lengths of the sides of the triangular cross-section
b) the area of the triangular ends
c) the volume of the prism.

21.

The diagram shows the side view of a swimming bath of width 25 m.

a) Find the volume of water in the bath when it is full. Give your answer in cubic metres.

b) The bath is emptied through a pipe whose cross-sectional area is 200 cm²; the water runs out at 1.5 m/s. What volume of water is removed in 1 second?

c) Find how long it would take to empty the bath if four similar pipes are used each removing water at the same steady rate as in (b).

VOLUME OF A PYRAMID

  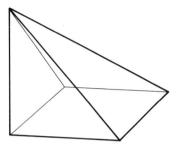

We can show that the volume of a pyramid is given by

$$\text{Volume} = \tfrac{1}{3} \text{ area of base} \times \text{perpendicular height}$$

EXERCISE 3c

Find the volume of the pyramid in the diagram. Its height is 7 cm and its base is a rectangle.

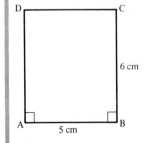

Area of base $= 5 \times 6 \, \text{cm}$

$= 30 \, \text{cm}^2$

Volume $= \tfrac{1}{3}$ area of base $\times$ perpendicular height

$= \tfrac{1}{\cancel{3}} \times \cancel{30}^{10} \times 7 \, \text{cm}^3$

$= 70 \, \text{cm}^3$

Find the volumes of the pyramids in questions 1 to 7.

1.

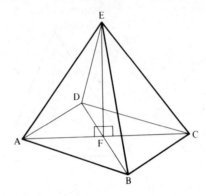

The base ABCD is a rectangle.
AB = 8 cm, BC = 4.5 cm and EF = 6 cm.

2.

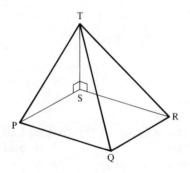

The base PQRS is a rectangle.
PQ = 20 cm, QR = 12 cm and TS = 8 cm.

3.

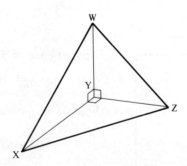

The base is a triangle XYZ.
$X\hat{Y}Z = 90°$, XY = 10 cm, YZ = 8 cm and WZ = 10 cm.

4. The base of a pyramid is a horizontal rectangle ABCD. The vertex E is vertically above A.
AB = 15 m, BC = 16 m and AE = 12 m.

5.

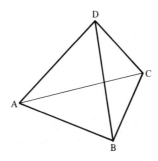

The base of the pyramid in △ABC whose area is 52 cm². The height of the pyramid is 6.8 cm.

6.

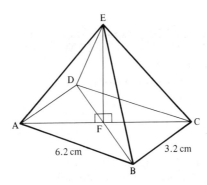

The base of the pyramid is a rectangle ABCD.
AB = 6.2 cm, BC = 3.2 cm and EF = 5.8 cm.

7. The base of a pyramid is a horizontal square PQRS. The diagonals of the square meet at T. The vertex U is vertically above T. PQ = 8 cm and PU = 12 cm.

8.

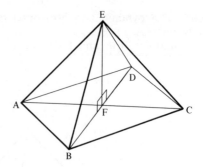

The base ABCD of the pyramid is a rectangle.
AB = 6 cm, BC = 8 cm and EC = 13 cm.

Find   a) AC and FC

b) the height of the pyramid

c) the volume of the pyramid.

9.

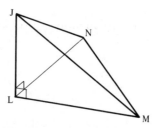

The base of the pyramid is triangle LMN.
$N\hat{L}M = 90°$, LN = 11 cm, LM = 12 cm and $J\hat{M}L = 32°$

Find   a) JL

b) the volume of the pyramid.

MASS

When we use a weighing machine such as a spring balance we measure the *weight* of a body, that is, the pull of the earth on the body.

This weight is proportional to the amount of material in the body, i.e. to the *mass* of the body. Scientists deal more often with the mass than with the weight.

We often make use in calculations of the mass of one unit of volume of the material of which a body is made.

For instance we may be told that the mass of 1 cm³ of silver is 10.5 g.

This is sometimes called the *density* of the material, i.e. the density of silver is 10.5 g/cm³.

EXERCISE 3d

> The volume of a cuboid of brass is $14.3\,cm^3$. The mass of $1\,cm^3$ of brass is $8.5\,g$. Find the mass of the cuboid.
>
> $$\text{Volume} = 14.3\,cm^3$$
> $$\text{Mass} \quad = 14.3 \times 8.5\,g$$
> $$= 121.55\,g$$
> $$= 122\,g \text{ correct to 3 s.f.}$$

Find the masses of the following objects. Check first that the units are consistent.

1. A block of wood of volume $105\,cm^3$. The mass of $1\,cm^3$ of the wood is $0.68\,g$.

2. The volume of aluminium used in making a saucepan is $40\,cm^3$. The mass of $1\,cm^3$ of aluminium is $2.65\,g$.

3. A cuboid of platinum measuring $0.6\,m$ by $4.8\,cm$ by $3.2\,cm$. The mass of $1\,cm^3$ of platinum is $21.5\,g$. Give your answer correct to 3 significant figures in   a) grams   b) kilograms.

4. A litre of milk. The mass of $1\,cm^3$ of milk is $0.98\,g$.

5. An ingot of gold of volume $32\,cm^3$. The density of the gold is $19.3\,g/cm^3$.

6. A cuboid of ice measuring $4\,cm$ by $15\,mm$ by $25\,mm$. The density of ice is $0.92\,g/cm^3$.

> Find the mass of $1\,cm^3$ of oak if a block of oak measuring $3\,cm$ by $12.8\,cm$ by $5\,cm$ has a mass of $153.6\,g$.
>
> $$\text{Volume} = 3 \times 12.8 \times 5\,cm^3$$
> $$= 192\,cm^3$$
> $$192\,cm^3 \text{ has mass } 153.6\,g$$
> $$1\,cm^3 \text{ has mass } \frac{153.6}{192}\,g$$
> $$= 0.8\,g$$

Find the mass of $1\,cm^3$ of the material referred to in each of questions 7 to 10.

7. A gold cup is made from $15\,cm^3$ of gold. The mass of the cup is $258\,g$.

8. The mass of two litres of petrol is $1380\,g$.

9. An ingot of copper in the form of a cuboid measuring $5.5\,cm$ by $3\,cm$ by $12\,cm$ has a mass of $1762.2\,g$.

10. The volume of beech in a kitchen table is $0.24\,m^3$ and its mass is $132\,kg$.

Find the density of the materials of which the bodies in questions 11 and 12 are made.

11. The volume of a china figure is $104\,cm^3$ and its mass is $260\,g$.

12. The volume of a slab of granite is $4200\,cm^3$ and its mass is $10.92\,kg$.

13. Find the volume of a piece of metal of mass $930\,g$. The mass of $1\,cm^3$ of the metal is $15\,g$.

14. The mass of $1\,cm^3$ of marble is $2.8\,g$. Find the volume of a marble statue whose mass is $6.86\,kg$.

15. A pyramid of copper has a square base of side $8\,cm$ and a height of $10.5\,cm$. The mass of $1\,cm^3$ of copper is $8.9\,g$. Find the mass of the pyramid.

16.

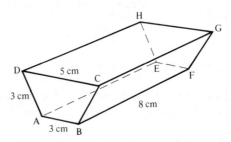

An ingot of gold is of uniform cross-section. ABCD is a trapezium with AB parallel to DC. $AB = 3\,cm$, $CD = 5\,cm$, $BF = 8\,cm$ and $AD = BC = 3\,cm$.

a) Find the height of the trapezium.

b) Find the volume of the ingot.

c) The mass of $1\,cm^3$ of the gold is $16\,g$. Find the mass of the ingot in
   i) grams   ii) kilograms.

d) If the gold is worth £7 per g, find the value of the ingot.

17.

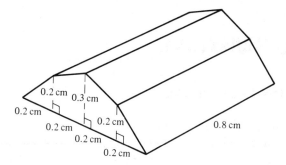

A diamond is cut in the shape of a solid of uniform cross-section as shown in the diagram.
The mass of $1\,cm^3$ of diamond is 3.5 g.

Find   a) the volume of the diamond
        b) the mass of the diamond.

EXERCISE 3e

In this exercise several alternative answers are given. Write down the letter that corresponds to the correct answer.

1. A wooden cuboid measures 4 cm by 7 cm by 5 cm. The mass of $1\,cm^3$ of the wood is 2.8 g.
The mass of the cuboid is

A 50 g **B** 392 g **C** 44.8 g **D** 131 g

2.

The volume of the solid of uniform cross-section is

A 24 000 cm^3 **B** 700 cm^3 **C** 4800 cm^3 **D** 12 000 cm^3

3. The base of a pyramid is a rectangle measuring 6 cm by 10 cm. Its height is 4 cm.
Its volume is

A 240 cm^3 **B** 80 cm^3 **C** 800 cm^3 **D** 120 cm^3

4. A cuboid of metal measuring 8 cm by 10 cm by 4 cm is melted down and made into a cuboid, two of whose measurements are 16 cm and 5 cm.
The third measurement of the new cuboid is

A 10 cm **B** 1 cm **C** 4 cm **D** 40 cm

4 FORMULAE

CONSTRUCTING FORMULAE

A formula can be thought of as a set of instructions for working out the value of a required quantity. Using this idea we can construct a formula for a given situation. For instance, to decide on the time needed to cook a turkey in foil we allow fifteen minutes per kilogram plus an extra ninety minutes.

If the turkey weighs $4\,\text{kg}$, then the cooking time is $(4 \times 15 + 90)$ minutes i.e. 150 minutes.

Expressing this in algebraic terms, if t minutes is the total time and the turkey weighs x kg then $t = 15x + 90$ or $t = 15(x + 6)$

If the time is T hours then we need an extra instruction to divide by 60, to change the unit from minutes to hours.

$$T = \frac{15(x + 6)}{60} \quad \text{i.e.} \quad T = \tfrac{1}{4}(x + 6)$$

Notice that there are no units in a formula. We must make sure that the units are consistent before we start making the formula.

EXERCISE 4a

> Susan is 12 years old this year. In x years time she will be y years old. Express y in terms of x.
>
> (In, say, 5 years time, Susan will be $(12 + 5)$ years old)
>
> $$y = 12 + x$$

1. Cakes cost $25\,\text{p}$ each and buns cost $15\,\text{p}$ each.
   a) Find the cost in pence of 2 cakes and 3 buns.
   b) Give a formula for the cost, C pence, of x cakes and y buns.

2. a) The two base angles of an isosceles triangle are $70°$ each. Find the third angle of the triangle.
   b) The two base angles of an isosceles triangle are $x°$ each. If the third angle is $y°$ find a formula for y in terms of x.

In questions 3 to 12, consider if necessary a numerical version, then give a formula connecting the given letters.

3. A number n is equal to the mean of two numbers a and b.

4. P is the perimeter of a rectangle of length l and breadth b.

5. The cost of m metres of cloth at p pence per metre is £c (be careful about the units).

6. The cost, £C, of hiring a car for n days is a fixed charge of £A plus £D per day.

7. I can buy p tenpenny tickets for £q.

8. When making tea for n people, the number, T, of teaspoonfuls is given by the rule 'one per person and one for the pot'.

9. The nth term of the sequence 1, 3, 5, 7, . . . is t.

10. In a class of c pupils, each pupil is given 3 pieces of paper and 10 spare sheets are put on the teacher's desk. The total number of pieces of paper is b.

11. The sum of x metres and y centimetres is z metres.

12. The sum of three consecutive whole numbers, the first of which is n, is S.

USING FORMULAE

EXERCISE 4b

If $P = ab + c$, find P when $a = 6$, $b = -2$ and $c = 3$

$$a = 6, \ b = -2, \ c = 3$$
$$P = ab + c$$
$$= 6 \times (-2) + 3$$
$$= -12 + 3$$
$$= -9$$

1. If $x = 3y + z$, find x when

a) $y = 3$ and $z = 6$ b) $y = 3.2$ and $z = 4.8$

2. If $p = q - \frac{1}{2}r$, find p when

a) $q = 14$ and $r = 30$ b) $q = 2.6$ and $r = 0.05$

3. If $M = \dfrac{6 + n}{l}$, find M if

a) $l = 32$ and $n = 14$ b) $l = 1.2$ and $n = 8.4$

4. If $F = \dfrac{9C}{5} + 32$, find F when

a) $C = 25$ b) $C = -6$

5. If $x = z(y - 3)$, find x if

a) $y = 12$ and $z = 7$ b) $y = 7.2$ and $z = 1.8$

The volume V cm^3 of a sphere of radius r cm is given by the formula $V = \frac{4}{3}\pi r^3$. If $\pi = 3.142$ and the radius is 2.4 cm, find the volume.

$$\pi = 3.142 \qquad r = 2.4$$

$$\text{Volume of sphere} = \tfrac{4}{3}\pi r^3$$

$$= \tfrac{4}{3} \times 3.142 \times 2.4^3 \text{ cm}^2$$

$$= 57.90 \text{ cm}^3$$

$$= 57.9 \text{ cm}^3 \quad \text{correct to 3 s.f.}$$

---

6. The surface area A cm^2 of a sphere of radius r cm is given by the formula $A = 4\pi r^2$. If $\pi = 3.142$ and the radius is 6 cm, find the surface area.

7. The time, T seconds, of the swing of a pendulum of length l metres is given by $T = 2\pi\sqrt{\dfrac{l}{9.8}}$. Find the time of swing of a pendulum of length 3.2 m. (Use $\pi = 3.142$)

8. The curved surface area A of a cone of radius r and slant height l is given by $A = \pi r l$. Find the curved surface area of a cone of radius 7 cm and slant height 15 cm. $\left(\text{Use } \pi = \dfrac{22}{7}\right)$

9. From a point x metres above the sea it is possible to see a distance of y metres where $y = 100\sqrt{1274x}$. Find the distance that can be seen from a height of 10 m.

10. The kinetic energy, E joules, of an object of mass m kg and moving with velocity v m/s is given by $E = \frac{1}{2}mv^2$. Find the kinetic energy of an object of mass 2.4 kg and velocity 3.2 m/s.

11. An object starts with a speed of u m/s and during t seconds its speed increases steadily to v m/s. The distance, s metre, travelled in this time is given by $s = \left(\dfrac{u+v}{2}\right)t$. If it starts at 4.2 m/s and reaches 6.8 m/s in 4.2 s, how far does it travel ?

We may use a formula to find the value of a letter other than the subject.

EXERCISE 4c

If $c = a(b+d)$, find b when $c = 20$, $a = 4$ and $d = 3$

$$c = 20 \qquad a = 4 \qquad d = 3$$
$$c = a(b+d)$$
$$20 = 4(b+3)$$
$$20 = 4b + 12$$
$$8 = 4b$$
$$2 = b$$

i.e. $b = 2$

1. If $A = \frac{1}{2}(a+b)h$, find
a) h when $A = 9$, $a = 2$ and $b = 1$
b) a when $A = 12$, $b = 3$ and $h = 4$

2. If $A = \pi r l$, find l if $A = 396$, $r = 14$ and $\pi = \dfrac{22}{7}$

3. If $x = 4z + y$, find z when
a) $x = 6$ and $y = 3$ b) $x = 9.8$ and $y = 2.6$

4. If $P = \dfrac{Q+4}{R}$ find

a) Q when $P = 7$ and $R = 3$ b) R when $P = 3$ and $Q = 3$

5. If $y = 12x^2z$ find z when

a) $x = 3$ and $y = 216$ b) $x = 0.5$ and $y = 4.8$

6. If $a = b(c+d)$ find

a) b when $a = 35.4$, $c = 4.2$ and $d = 1.7$

b) d when $a = 0.825$, $b = 1.5$ and $c = 0.3$

7. The total resistance, R, of two resistances r_1 and r_2 joined in parallel, is given by the formula $\dfrac{1}{R} = \dfrac{1}{r_1} + \dfrac{1}{r_2}$.

Find R if $r_1 = 4$ and $r_2 = 3$.

8. A stone is thrown vertically upwards into the air with velocity u m/s. After t seconds it is s metres high where $s = ut - 5t^2$.

Find u if the height of the stone is 8 m after 4 seconds.

9. The area, A cm^2, of a trapezium is given by the formula $A = \frac{1}{2}(a+b)h$ where a cm and b cm are the lengths of the parallel sides and h cm is the distance between them.

a) The area is 55 cm^2 and the parallel sides are of lengths 4 cm and 7 cm. Find the distance between the parallel sides.

b) One of the parallel sides is of length 25 cm, the area is 270 cm^2 and the distance between the parallel sides is 12 cm. Find the length of the other parallel side.

10. The size, $a°$, of an interior angle of a regular n-sided polygon is given by the formula $a = \dfrac{180(n-2)}{n}$. Find the number of sides of a regular polygon if the size of each interior angle is 150°.

11. The cost, £C, per person for a coach trip of a distance of x miles when there are n people in the party is given by $C = \dfrac{30+x}{n}$.

a) If the cost per person is £4.50 when there are 40 people, how many miles are covered?

b) If the cost per person is £2.50 when 100 miles are travelled, how many people are there in the party?

CHANGING THE SUBJECT OF A FORMULA

Instead of using a formula in its original form to find the value of a letter other than the subject, we might prefer to rearrange the formula so that the letter we want becomes the subject. This is better if we have to use the formula several times.

Take as an example $I = \dfrac{PTR}{100}$. If we have to find P for several different sets of values of I, T and R then it is useful to have a formula for P in terms of the other letters.

To rearrange the formula we treat it as an equation and solve it for P.

$$I = \frac{PTR}{100}$$

Multiply each side by 100 $\qquad 100 \times I = \cancel{100} \times \dfrac{PTR}{\cancel{100}}$

$$100I = PTR$$

Divide each side by TR $\qquad \dfrac{100I}{TR} = P$

$\therefore \qquad\qquad\qquad\qquad\qquad P = \dfrac{100I}{TR}$

In several of the following exercises there are a few numerical equations to remind us of the processes to use.

ONE OPERATION

EXERCISE 4d

Find x in terms of the other letters if
a) $ax = b$ $\qquad$ b) $x - a = b$

a) $\qquad\qquad\qquad\qquad\qquad ax = b$

Divide both sides by a $\qquad x = \dfrac{b}{a}$

b) $\qquad\qquad\qquad\qquad\qquad x - a = b$

Add a to each side $\qquad\qquad x = b + a$

In questions 1 to 10, find x in terms of the other letters or numbers.

1. $x + 4 = 6$

2. $7 + x = 2$

3. $x + a = 9$

4. $6x = q$

5. $p + x = q$

6. $mx = n$

7. $x - e = f$

8. $g = hx$

9. $g = x - h$

10. $k = h + x$

In questions 11 to 20 make the letter in the bracket the subject of the formula.

11. $p = q + r$ (r)

12. $r = s - t$ (s)

13. $r = s + t$ (t)

14. $y = xz$ (z)

15. $l + m = n$ (m)

16. $P = QR$ (Q)

17. $2s = a + b + c$ (a)

18. $C = 2\pi r$ (r)

19. $A = lb$ (b)

20. $v = u + at$ (u)

TWO OR MORE OPERATIONS

EXERCISE 4e

Make x the subject of the formula $c = ax + b$

(If you cannot see what to do, put some numbers in, e.g. $8 = 2x + 4$)

$$c = ax + b$$

Take b from each side $\quad c - b = ax$

Divide both sides by $a \quad \dfrac{c - b}{a} = x$

i.e. $\qquad\qquad\qquad x = \dfrac{c - b}{a}$

In each question from 1 to 10, find x in terms of the other letters or numbers.

1. $4x + 3 = 11$

2. $2x - 1 = 7$

3. $6 - 2x = 2$

4. $2(x + 1) = 5$

5. $px + q = r$

6. $c = d + bx$

7. $ax - b = c$

8. $a - bx = c$

9. $a(x + b) = c$

10. $2 = p(x - q)$

In each question from 11 to 20, make the letter in the bracket the subject of the formula.

11. $ab - d = c$ (d)

12. $ab - d = c$ (a)

13. $p(q + r) = 1$ (q)

14. $3(P - Q) = 2$ (P)

15. $s = 7t + u$ (t)

16. $l - mn = 2$ (l)

17. $l - mn = 2$ (m)

18. $4T = 2P + Q$ (P)

19. $m - pr = mr$ (p)

20. $x(y - z) = 2$ (y)

21. If $P = 4(a + b)$
    a) find P when $a = 4.2$ and $b = 7.1$
    b) find a when $P = 60$ and $b = 4$
    c) make a the subject of the formula.
    d) Use the formula found in (c) to find a when $P = 60$ and $b = 4$.
    Does your answer agree with (b)?

22. If $A = 3n(a + l)$
    a) find A when $n = 8$, $a = 3.2$ and $l = 39.2$
    b) find a when $A = 72$, $n = 6$ and $l = 6$
    c) make a the subject of the formula.
    d) Use the formula found in (c) to find a when $A = 72$, $n = 6$ and $l = 6$.
    Does your answer agree with (b)?

23. If $x = yz + z$
    a) find x when $y = 2.5$ and $z = 0.6$
    b) find y when $x = 36$ and $z = 24$
    c) make y the subject of the formula.
    d) Use the formula found in (c) to find y when $x = 36$ and $z = 24$.
    Does your answer agree with (b)?

COLLECTING LIKE TERMS

EXERCISE 4f

Make x the subject of the formula $ax + d = c + bx$

$$ax + d = c + bx$$

(Decide on which side to collect the x terms. In this case either side will do.)

Take bx from each side $\qquad ax - bx + d = c$

Take d from each side $\qquad ax - bx = c - d$

Take out the common factor $\qquad x(a - b) = c - d$

(This means that the number of xs is $(a - b)$)

Divide both sides by $(a - b)$ $\qquad x = \dfrac{c - d}{a - b}$

In questions 1 to 12, find x in terms of the other letters or numbers.

1. $3x + 6 = 5x + 1$ **5.** $ax = bx + c$ **9.** $a - bx = c + dx$

2. $7x - 4 = 2x - 1$ **6.** $ax - b = cx$ **10.** $a - bx = c - dx$

3. $6 + 2x = 8 - 3x$ **7.** $px - q = rx + q$ **11.** $p - qx = rx + sx$

4. $8 - 3x = 4 - x$ **8.** $s - tx = px$ **12.** $a + b = cx - d$

Make x the subject of the formula $x + ax = b$

$$x + ax = b$$
$$x(1 + a) = b$$
$$x = \dfrac{b}{1 + a}$$

In each question from 13 to 16, make x the subject of the formula.

13. $ax + x = c$ **15.** $x = cx - d$

14. $bx = x + 4$ **16.** $a(x + 1) = x(1 - a)$

In each question from 17 to 24, make the letter in the bracket the subject of the formula.

17. $pq = r - ps$ (p)

18. $ab + ac = d$ (a)

19. $ab - c = ad$ (a)

20. $ax + b = ay + c$ (a)

21. $pq + qr + rp = 0$ (p)

22. $a + b = ac$ (a)

23. $pr - p = qr + q$ (q)

24. $pr - p = qr + q$ (r)

In each question from 25 to 32, find x in terms of the other letters or numbers.

25. $2(x + 3) = 16$

26. $4(2x - 1) = 2x$

27. $3(x + 2) = 4(x - 1)$

28. $ax = b(x + 1)$

29. $a(x - b) = c$

30. $a(x + b) = bx$

31. $a(x + c) = b(x - c)$

32. $a(x + b) = c(x + d)$

In each question from 33 to 40, make the letter in the bracket the subject of the formula.

33. $p(q + r) = q$ (q)

34. $ab = c(b + a)$ (a)

35. $s(t + u) = t(u - s)$ (s)

36. $m(l - n) = n$ (n)

37. $p(q + r) = q$ (p)

38. $Q(R + P) = PR$ (R)

39. $ab = c(b + a)$ (b)

40. $s(t + u) = t(u - s)$ (u)

SQUARE ROOTS

If $x^2 = 25$ then x could be $+5$ or -5 because both $+5$ and -5 are square roots of 25.
We write $x = \pm 5$.
Only the positive square root is denoted by $\sqrt{25}$
so $\sqrt{25} = 5$.
Hence, if $x^2 = a$, then $x = \pm \sqrt{a}$.

In a problem we should always consider both square roots, as they may give two different correct answers to the question. Sometimes one of the square roots is meaningless; for instance if we are dealing with a problem about length we would probably find that only the positive root makes any sense.

Sometimes square roots can be found by inspection, even fractional square roots, e.g. $\sqrt{2\frac{1}{4}} = \sqrt{\frac{9}{4}} = \frac{3}{2}$. If the square roots are not obvious a calculator can be used.

CUBE ROOTS

Cube roots too can sometimes be found by inspection instead of by using a calculator. We can see that $\sqrt[3]{27}$ is 3 by guessing and testing. (We know $3 \times 3 \times 3 = 27$)

Even $\sqrt[3]{216}$ may be guessed: it is even and a multiple of 3, so try 6.

The cube root of a number is often much smaller than we might expect (e.g. $\sqrt[3]{512}$ is 8), so try small numbers first.

The cube root of a positive number is positive and of a negative number is negative. There is only one cube root of a number.

EXERCISE 4g

Find   a) $\sqrt{81}$ b) x if $x^2 = 81$ c) $\sqrt[3]{3\frac{3}{8}}$

a) $\sqrt{81} = 9$

b) $x^2 = 81$

  $x = \pm 9$

c) $\sqrt[3]{3\frac{3}{8}} = \sqrt[3]{\frac{27}{8}}$

  $= \frac{3}{2}$

  $= 1\frac{1}{2}$

Find, without using a calculator:

1. $\sqrt{64}$

2. $\sqrt[3]{125}$

3. $\sqrt{6\frac{1}{4}}$

4. $\sqrt{\frac{4}{9}}$

5. $\sqrt{20\frac{1}{4}}$

6. $\sqrt[3]{15\frac{5}{8}}$

7. $\sqrt{\frac{1}{64}}$

8. $\sqrt[3]{1\,000\,000}$

9. $\sqrt{1\,000\,000}$

Find x in questions 10 to 15.

10. $x^2 = 144$ **12.** $x^2 = 121$ **14.** $x^2 = 100$

11. $x^3 = 64$ **13.** $x^2 = 900$ **15.** $x^3 = -27$

FORMULAE INVOLVING SQUARES AND SQUARE ROOTS

EXERCISE 4h

> a) Find x if $4x^2 = 9$
>
> b) Make x the subject of the formula $ax^2 = b$
>
> a) $4x^2 = 9$
>
> $$x^2 = \frac{9}{4}$$
>
> Take the square root of each side.
>
> $$x = \pm\frac{3}{2}$$
>
> b) $ax^2 = b$
>
> $$x^2 = \frac{b}{a}$$
>
> Take the square root of each side.
>
> $$x = \pm\sqrt{\frac{b}{a}}$$

In questions 1 to 16 do not use a calculator.

Find x in terms of the other letters or numbers.

1. $6x^2 = 24$ **5.** $px^2 = q$

2. $9x^2 = 25$ **6.** $px^2 = q^2$

3. $3x^2 + 4 = 9$ **7.** $x^2 = p + q$

4. $x^2 = p$ **8.** $\dfrac{ax^2}{b} = c$

Find x in terms of a and b if

a) $a = b\sqrt{x}$ b) $a = \sqrt{bx}$

a) $a = b\sqrt{x}$

Square both sides

$$a^2 = b^2 x$$

$$\frac{a^2}{b^2} = x$$

i.e. $x = \dfrac{a^2}{b^2}$

b) $a = \sqrt{bx}$

Square both sides

$$a^2 = bx$$

$$\frac{a^2}{b} = x$$

i.e. $x = \dfrac{a^2}{b}$

Find x in terms of the other letters or numbers.

9. $\sqrt{x} = 4$ **13.** $p\sqrt{x} = q$

10. $3\sqrt{x} = 2$ **14.** $\sqrt{px} = r$

11. $\sqrt{3x} = 9$ **15.** $\sqrt{x} = p\sqrt{q}$

12. $\sqrt{x} = a$ **16.** $\sqrt{x+a} = 4$

In questions 17 to 24 make the letter in the bracket the subject of the formula.

17. $4p^2 = q$ (p) **21.** $\sqrt{A+B} = C$ (A)

18. $a = 2\sqrt{p}$ (p) **22.** $D = \sqrt{\dfrac{3h}{2}}$ (h)

19. $\sqrt{x+a} = b$ (a) **23.** $\sqrt{z} = \sqrt{a+b}$ (b)

20. $a^2 + b = c$ (a) **24.** $\sqrt{x^2 + a^2} = b$ (x)

25. If $z = 2(x^2 + y^2)$ find x when
     a) $z = 26$ and $y = 2$ b) $z = 82$ and $y = -4$

26. A stone is dropped from a tower and after t seconds it has fallen s metres where $s = 5t^2$. Find how long it takes to fall 45 m.

27. If $P = \sqrt{Q+R}$
     a) find P when $Q = 6$ and $R = 10$
     b) find Q when $P = 5$ and $R = 5$
     c) make Q the subject of the formula.
     d) Use the formula found in (c) to find Q when $P = 5$ and $R = 5$.
     Does your answer agree with (b)?

FRACTIONS

When solving a fractional equation or changing a formula involving fractions, it is most important that the fractions are removed *as soon as possible* by multiplying by the appropriate number or letter.

EXERCISE 4i

Make x the subject of the formula

a) $\dfrac{x}{a} + \dfrac{x}{b} = c$ b) $\dfrac{x}{a-b} = c$

    a) $\dfrac{x}{a} + \dfrac{x}{b} = c$

Multiply both sides by ab

$$\overset{1}{\cancel{ab}} \times \frac{x}{\cancel{a}_1} + a\cancel{b} \times \frac{x}{\cancel{b}_1} = ab \times c$$

$$bx + ax = abc$$

$$x(b+a) = abc$$

$$x = \frac{abc}{a+b}$$

    b) $\dfrac{x}{a-b} = c$

Multiply both sides by $(a-b)$

$$\overset{1}{\cancel{(a-b)}} \times \frac{x}{\cancel{a-b}_1} = (a-b) \times c$$

$$x = c(a-b)$$

In questions 1 to 12, find x in terms of the other letters or numbers. Remember to get rid of fractions first.

1. $\dfrac{x}{6} = 4$

2. $\dfrac{2x}{3} = 5$

3. $\dfrac{x}{2} + \dfrac{x}{3} = \dfrac{4}{3}$

4. $\dfrac{2x}{3} - \dfrac{x}{4} = 1$

5. $\dfrac{x}{p} = q$

6. $\dfrac{x}{p} - \dfrac{x}{q} = 1$

7. $\dfrac{ax}{p} = r$

8. $\dfrac{x}{p+q} = r$

9. $\dfrac{x}{a} + b = c$

10. $\dfrac{x+a}{b} = \dfrac{x-b}{a}$

11. $\dfrac{x}{a} = \dfrac{x+b}{a+b}$

12. $\dfrac{x}{a} + \dfrac{x}{b} = \dfrac{c}{a}$

In each question from 13 to 24, make the letter in the bracket the subject of the formula.

13. $I = \dfrac{PTR}{100}$ (R)

14. $A = \dfrac{n}{2}(a+l)$ (n)

15. $P = \dfrac{Q+R}{4}$ (Q)

16. $\dfrac{a}{3} = \dfrac{b}{2} - \dfrac{c}{4}$ (b)

17. $\dfrac{1}{x} = \dfrac{1}{a} + \dfrac{1}{b}$ (x)

18. $\dfrac{p}{x} + \dfrac{q}{x} + \dfrac{r}{x} = 1$ (x)

19. $\dfrac{s}{x} = \dfrac{r}{x} + t$ (x)

20. $a = 2\sqrt{\dfrac{p}{q}}$ (q)

21. $T = 2\pi\sqrt{\dfrac{l}{g}}$ (l)

22. $t = \dfrac{2Hh}{H+h}$ (H)

23. $a^2 + \dfrac{b}{X} + \dfrac{c}{bX} = 0$ (X)

24. $\dfrac{L}{M} = \dfrac{2a}{B-b}$ (B)

MIXED QUESTIONS

EXERCISE 4j

In each question, make the letter in the bracket the subject of the formula.

1. $v = u + at$ (t)

2. $A = \frac{1}{2}bh$ (h)

3. $a^2 = b^2 + c^2$ (c)

4. $A = \frac{1}{2}(a+b)h$ (h)

5. $\dfrac{1}{v} + \dfrac{1}{u} = \dfrac{1}{f}$ (f)

6. $A = \frac{1}{2}(a+b)h$ (a)

7. $s = \dfrac{t}{2}(u + v)$ (v)

8. $s = \dfrac{t}{2}(u + v)$ (t)

9. $\dfrac{1}{v} + \dfrac{1}{u} = \dfrac{1}{f}$ (u)

10. $v^2 = u^2 + 2as$ (a)

11. $A = \pi r^2 + \pi rh$ (h)

12. $v^2 = u^2 + 2as$ (u)

13. $v = \omega\sqrt{a^2 - x^2}$ (a)

14. $A = \pi r\sqrt{h^2 + r^2}$ (h)

15. $s = ut + \frac{1}{2}at^2$ (u)

16. $s = ut + \frac{1}{2}at^2$ (a)

17. $A = \frac{1}{2}pq \sin R$ (p)

18. $E = \frac{1}{2}m(v^2 - u^2)$ (u)

19. $T = 2\pi\sqrt{\dfrac{l}{g}}$ (g)

20. $A = P + \dfrac{PTR}{100}$ (R)

MIXED EXERCISES

EXERCISE 4k

1. If $Y = a + \dfrac{4}{c}$, find Y when $a = 6$ and $c = 5$.

2. If $T = \dfrac{d}{v - u}$, find v when $T = 2$, $d = 10$ and $u = 2$.

3. If $a = b\sqrt{c + d}$, find c in terms of a, b and d.

4. If $I = \dfrac{PTR}{100}$, find T in terms of I, P and R.

5. If $p = \sqrt{q^2 - r}$, find p when $q = -6$ and $r = -13$.

EXERCISE 4l

1. If $T = \dfrac{d}{v - u}$, find T when $v = 20$, $u = 6$ and $d = -7.7$.

2. If $p^2 = qr$, find p when $q = 9$ and $r = 4$.

3. If $T = \dfrac{d}{v - u}$, make d the subject of the formula.

4. If $4\sqrt{p} = q$, find p in terms of q.

5. If $a(b + c) = bc$, find b in terms of a and c.

EXERCISE 4m

In this exercise you are given several alternative answers. Write down the letter that corresponds to the correct answer.

1. If $P = Q - R^2$, $Q = 5$ and $R = 2$, then P is equal to

    A 9   **B** 49   **C** 1   **D** 9

2. If $z = \dfrac{x}{y}$, $z = 2.5$ and $y = 0.5$, then x is equal to

    A 5   **B** 0.2   **C** 1.25   **D** 3

3. If $cx + d = bx + a$, then x is equal to

    A $\dfrac{a-d}{c-b}$ **B** $\dfrac{b-c}{a+d}$ **C** $\dfrac{a+d}{b+c}$ **D** $\dfrac{c-b}{a-d}$

4. If $l = m\sqrt{n}$ then n is equal to

    A $\dfrac{l}{m}$ **B** $\dfrac{m^2}{l^2}$ **C** $\dfrac{l^2}{m^2}$ **D** $\dfrac{l^2}{m}$

5. If $\dfrac{1}{a} = \dfrac{1}{b} + \dfrac{1}{c}$ then a is equal to

    A $\dfrac{b+c}{bc}$ **B** $b+c$ **C** $\dfrac{1}{b+c}$ **D** $\dfrac{bc}{b+c}$

5 GRAPHS

THE PARABOLA

All the graphs in Book 3A, Exercise 14c came from equations of the form $y = ax^2 + bx + c$, and were curves of the same shape,

either   or

This shape is called a parabola.

In each case there is a turning point called a vertex.

When the x^2 term is *positive* the vertex is at the bottom and there is no highest value of y.

On the other hand when the x^2 term is *negative* the vertex is at the top and there is no lowest point.

The simplest equation whose graph is a parabola is $y = x^2$.

Another parabola whose equation is a little more complicated than $y = x^2$ is $y = x(x - 4)$.

We will plot the graph of this parabola for values of x from -1 to $+5$ at half-unit intervals.

To find the value of y for a given value of x we multiply the value of x by the value of $(x - 4)$. The table shows each value of x, the corresponding value of $x - 4$, and the resulting value of y.

x	-1	$-\frac{1}{2}$	0	$\frac{1}{2}$	1	$\frac{3}{2}$	2	$\frac{5}{2}$	3	$\frac{7}{2}$	4	$\frac{9}{2}$	5
$(x-4)$	-5	$-4\frac{1}{2}$	-4	$-3\frac{1}{2}$	-3	$-2\frac{1}{2}$	-2	$-1\frac{1}{2}$	-1	$-\frac{1}{2}$	0	$\frac{1}{2}$	1
y	5	$2\frac{1}{4}$	0	$-1\frac{3}{4}$	-3	$-3\frac{3}{4}$	-4	$-3\frac{3}{4}$	-3	$-1\frac{3}{4}$	0	$2\frac{1}{4}$	5

73

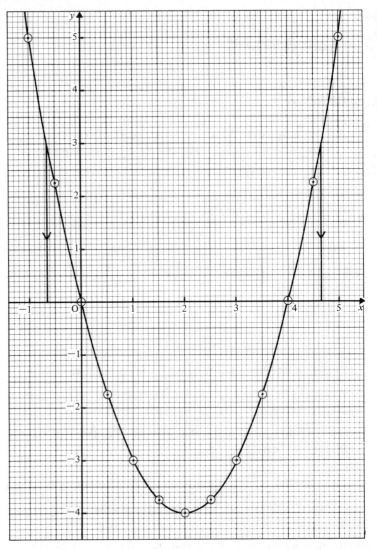

From the graph we see that the curve crosses the x-axis when $x = 0$ and when $x = 4$.

If we wish to find the value(s) of x that correspond to a given value of $x(x-4)$, i.e. a given value of y, we draw a line parallel to the x-axis for the given value of y, find where this intersects the curve, and read off the corresponding value(s) of x.

For example, if $x(x-4) = 3$, i.e. $y = 3$,
the corresponding values of x are -0.65 and 4.65.

EXERCISE 5a

1. Draw the graph of $y = 1 + 3x - x^2$ for values of x from -1 to 4 at intervals of 0.5. Use 2 cm as 1 unit on both axes.

   Use your graph to find

   a) the highest value of $1 + 3x - x^2$, and the corresponding value of x

   b) the values of x when $1 + 3x - x^2$ has a value of   i) 0   ii) 3

2. Draw the graph of $y = x^2 - 4x + 3$ for values of x from -1 to 5 at half-unit intervals. Use 4 cm to represent 1 unit on both axes.

   Use your graph to find

   a) the lowest value of $x^2 - 4x + 3$, and the corresponding value of x

   b) the values of x when $x^2 - 4x + 3$ has a value of   i) 2   ii) -1 iii) 4

3. Draw a graph of $y = x^2 - 4x - 9$ for values of x from -2 to $+6$ at unit intervals. Use 2 cm as 1 unit on the x-axis and 1 cm as 1 unit on the y-axis.

   Use your graph to find

   a) the values of x when $x^2 - 4x - 9$ has a value of -6

   b) the value of $x^2 - 4x - 9$ when x is 1.4

4. Draw the graph of $y = (x - 2)(x - 3)$ for values of x from 0 to 5 at half-unit intervals. Use 2 cm as the unit on both axes.

   Use your graph to find

   a) the values of x when $(x - 2)(x - 3) = 0$

   b) the lowest value of $(x - 2)(x - 3)$

   c) the values of x for which the value of $(x - 2)(x - 3)$ is 4

5. Draw the graph of $y = 4 + 2x - x^2$ for values of x from -2 to 4 at half-unit intervals. Use 2 cm to represent 1 unit on both axes.

   Use your graph to find

   a) the highest value of $4 + 2x - x^2$ and the corresponding value of x

   b) the value of $4 + 2x - x^2$ when x is 2.7

   c) the values of x for which the value of $4 + 2x - x^2$ is 3

6. Draw the graph of $y = (4 + x)(1 - x)$ for values of x from -5 to 2 at unit intervals. Use 2 cm to 1 unit on both axes.

   Use your graph to find

   a) the highest value of $(4 + x)(1 - x)$ and the corresponding value of x

   b) the values of x for which $(4 + x)(1 - x) = 2$

USING A GRAPH TO SOLVE QUADRATIC EQUATIONS

From a single graph it is often possible to solve several different quadratic equations.

EXERCISE 5b

Use the graph of $y = x^2 - 2x - 4$, which is given below, to solve the equations

a) $x^2 - 2x - 4 = 0$
b) $x^2 - 2x - 4 = 6$
c) $x^2 - 2x - 2 = 0$
d) $2x^2 - 4x + 1 = 0$
e) $1 + 2x - x^2 = 0$

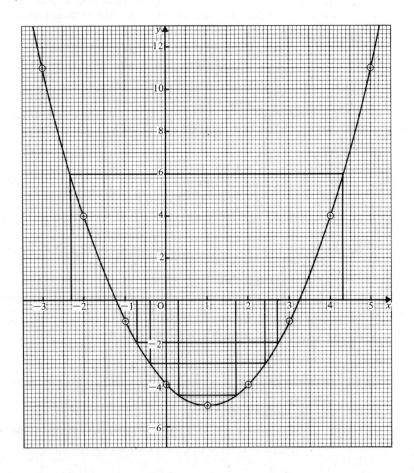

a) When this graph crosses the x-axis the value of y is 0, i.e. $x^2 - 2x - 4 = 0$. When $y = 0$ the corresponding values of x are -1.25 and 3.25. These values of x are therefore the solutions of the equation $x^2 - 2x - 4 = 0$

b) When $x^2 - 2x - 4 = 6$, $y = 6$
The values of x that correspond to a y value of 6 are -2.3 and 4.3

Therefore the solutions of the equation $x^2 - 2x - 4 = 6$ are $x = -2.3$ and $x = 4.3$

c) To use this graph to solve the equation $x^2 - 2x - 2 = 0$ we must convert the left-hand side to $x^2 - 2x - 4$
Subtract 2 from both sides: $\quad x^2 - 2x - 4 = -2 \quad$ i.e. $\quad y = -2$

From the graph, when $y = -2$ the values of x are -0.7 and 2.7

The solutions of the equation $x^2 - 2x - 2 = 0$ are therefore $x = -0.7$ and $x = 2.7$

(Note that the equation $x^2 - 2x - 2 = 0$ cannot be solved by factorising. The graphical solution of equations of this type is the only method available to us at the moment.)

d) To use the graph to solve $2x^2 - 4x + 1 = 0$ we must convert the LHS to $x^2 - 2x - 4$.
Divide both sides by 2 $\qquad x^2 - 2x + \frac{1}{2} = 0$
Subtract $4\frac{1}{2}$ from both sides $\qquad x^2 - 2x - 4 = -4\frac{1}{2}$
i.e. $\qquad\qquad\qquad\qquad\qquad y = -4\frac{1}{2}$
When $y = -4\frac{1}{2}$, $x = 0.3$ and 1.7
The solutions of the equation $2x^2 - 4x + 1 = 0$ are therefore $x = 0.4$ and $x = 1.7$

e) $1 + 2x - x^2 = 0$
(First convert the LHS to $x^2 + 2x - 4$)
Multiply both sides by -1 $\qquad -1 - 2x + x^2 = 0$
i.e. $\qquad\qquad\qquad x^2 - 2x - 1 = 0$
Subtract 3 from both sides $\qquad x^2 - 2x - 4 = -3$

From the graph, when $y = -3$, $x = 2.4$ and -0.4

The solutions of the equation $1 + 2x - x^2 = 0$ are therefore $x = 2.4$ and $x = -0.4$

1. Use the graph of $y = x^2 - 3x - 3$, which is given below, to solve the equations

a) $x^2 - 3x - 3 = 0$

b) $x^2 - 3x - 3 = 5$

c) $x^2 - 3x - 7 = 0$

d) $x^2 - 3x + 1 = 0$

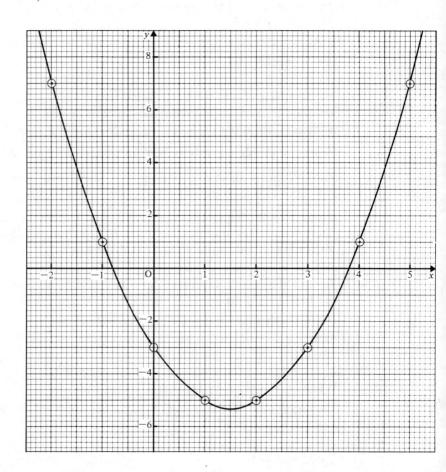

2. The graph of $y = 4 + 4x - x^2$, in the range $-1 \leqslant x \leqslant 5$, is given opposite. Use this graph to solve the equations

a) $4 + 4x - x^2 = 0$

b) $4 + 4x - x^2 = 5$

c) $4 + 4x - x^2 = 1$

d) $1 + 4x - x^2 = 0$

e) $-2 + 4x - x^2 = 0$

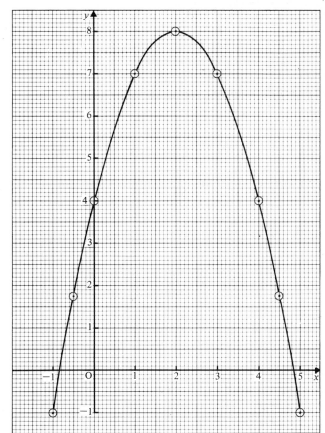

3. Use the graph of $y = x^2 - 4x + 3$, drawn for question 2 of Exercise 5a, to solve the equations

a) $x^2 - 4x + 3 = 0$

b) $x^2 - 4x + 1 = 0$

c) $x^2 - 4x - 1 = 0$

4. Use the graph of $y = 1 + 3x - x^2$, drawn for question 1 of Exercise 5a, to solve the equations

a) $1 + 3x - x^2 = 0$

b) $2 + 3x - x^2 = 0$

Is it possible to use this graph to solve the equation $x^2 - 3x + 4 = 0$?
If it is possible, give the solutions. If it is not possible, explain why.

5. Draw the graph of $y = x^2 - 6x + 3$ for whole number values of x from 0 to 7 calculating the values at unit intervals. Take 2 cm as 1 unit on the x-axis and 1 cm as 1 unit on the y-axis.

Use your graph

a) to find the values of x when the graph crosses the x-axis and the equation that has these x values as solutions

b) to solve the equation $x^2 - 6x + 7 = 0$.

6. Copy and complete the following table which gives values of $(2-x)(x+1)$ for values of x from -3 to 4.

x	-3	$-2\frac{1}{2}$	-2	-1	$-\frac{1}{2}$	0	$\frac{1}{2}$	1	$1\frac{1}{2}$	2	3	$3\frac{1}{2}$	4
$(2-x)$	5	$4\frac{1}{2}$		3	$2\frac{1}{2}$		$1\frac{1}{2}$	1		0	-1	$-1\frac{1}{2}$	-2
$(x+1)$	-2	$-1\frac{1}{2}$		0	$\frac{1}{2}$		$1\frac{1}{2}$	2		3	4	$4\frac{1}{2}$	5
$(2-x)(x+1)$	-10	$-6\frac{3}{4}$		0	$1\frac{1}{4}$		$2\frac{1}{4}$	2		0	-4	$-6\frac{3}{4}$	-10

Hence draw the graph of $y = (2-x)(x+1)$ for values of x from -3 to 4. Take 2 cm as 1 unit for x and 1 cm as 1 unit for y.

Use your graph to solve the equations

a) $x^2 - x - 2 = 0$

b) $x^2 - x - 5 = 0$

7. The table gives values of y for certain values of x on the curve given by the equation $y = 2x^2 - 7x + 8$.

x	0	$\frac{1}{2}$	1	$1\frac{1}{2}$	2	$2\frac{1}{2}$	3	$3\frac{1}{2}$	4
y	8	5		2	2	3		8	12

Complete this table.

[Remember that $2x^2$ means square x first and then double it.

e.g., if $x = 2\frac{1}{2}$, $y = 2 \times \frac{25}{4} - 7 \times \frac{5}{2} + 8$

$= 12\frac{1}{2} - 17\frac{1}{2} + 8 = 3$]

Use the table to draw the graph of $y = 2x^2 - 7x + 8$ for values of x from 0 to 4. Take 4 cm as 1 unit for x and 2 cm as 1 unit for y.

Use your graph

a) to find the lowest value of $2x^2 - 7x + 8$

b) to solve the equation $2x^2 - 7x + 4 = 0$.

8. Complete the following table which shows values of $7 - 6x - 2x^2$ for values of x from -4 to 1.

x	-4	$-\frac{7}{2}$	-3	$-\frac{5}{2}$	-2	$-\frac{3}{2}$	-1	$-\frac{1}{2}$	0	$\frac{1}{2}$	1
7	7	7		7	7	7		7	7	7	
$-6x$	24	21		15	12	9		3	0	-3	
$-2x^2$	-32	$-24\frac{1}{2}$		$-12\frac{1}{2}$	-8	$-4\frac{1}{2}$		$-\frac{1}{2}$	0	$-\frac{1}{2}$	
$7 - 6x - 2x^2$	-1	$3\frac{1}{2}$		$9\frac{1}{2}$	11	$11\frac{1}{2}$		$9\frac{1}{2}$	7	$3\frac{1}{2}$	

Hence draw the graph of $y = 7 - 6x - 2x^2$ for values of x from -4 to 1. Take $4\,\text{cm}$ as 1 unit on the x-axis and $1\,\text{cm}$ as 1 unit on the y-axis. (If necessary turn your graph paper sideways.)

a) Use your graph to solve the equation $7 - 6x - 2x^2 = 0$.

b) Draw the line $y = 5$ so that it intersects your graph. Write down the x values of the points where the line $y = 5$ meets the curve $y = 7 - 6x - 2x^2$. Find, in as simple a form as possible, the equation for which these x values are the roots.

9. Complete the following table which gives values of $3x^2 - x + 2$ for values of x from -2 to $+2$.

x	-2	-1.5	-1	-0.5	0	0.5	1	1.5	2
$3x^2$	12	6.75	3		0	0.75		6.75	
$-x$	2	1.5	1		0	-0.5		-1.5	
$+2$	2	2	2		2	2		2	
$3x^2 - x + 2$	16		6		2	2.25		7.25	

Hence draw the graph of $y = 3x^2 - x + 2$ for values of x from -2 to $+2$. Take $4\,\text{cm}$ as 1 unit for x and $8\,\text{cm}$ as 5 units for y.

Use your graph to solve the equations

a) $3x^2 - x + 2 = 0$

b) $3x^2 - x - 7 = 0$

c) $3x^2 - x - 1 = 0$

10. Draw a graph to solve the equation $x^2 + 2x - 4 = 0$. Take values of x from -5 to 2, and use $2\,\text{cm}$ to represent one unit on the x-axis and $1\,\text{cm}$ to represent one unit on the y-axis.

Hint: To solve the equation $x^2 + 2x - 4 = 0$, we need to draw the graph of $y = x^2 + 2x - 4$ and then find the values of x when $y = 0$.

11. Draw a graph to solve the equation $3 - 5x - x^2 = 0$. Take values of x from -6 to 2. Use $2\,\text{cm}$ to represent 1 unit on the x-axis and choose your own scale for the y-axis.

12. Draw a graph to show that the equation $x^2 + 6x + 10 = 0$ cannot be solved. Take values of x from -6 to 0. Choose your own scale on each axis.

INTERSECTING GRAPHS INVOLVING QUADRATICS

In the previous exercises we have solved a quadratic equation by drawing the graph of a quadratic and finding either where the graph crossed the x-axis or where it had a particular value of y.

Sometimes it is easier to draw the simplest quadratic graph, i.e. $y = x^2$, together with a suitable straight line graph.

Suppose that we draw the graphs of $y = x^2$ and $y = 2x + 3$ on the same axes. At the points where these graphs intersect, their y values are the same. Hence the value of y on the curve (which is x^2) is equal to the value of y on the line (which is $2x + 3$) i.e., at the points of intersection of the graphs

$$x^2 = 2x + 3$$

i.e.

$$x^2 - 2x - 3 = 0$$

The values of x at the points of intersection must therefore be the values of x that satisfy the equation $x^2 - 2x - 3 = 0$.

This method can be used to solve a given quadratic equation. For example, to solve $x^2 - 3x - 7 = 0$ we rearrange the equation as $x^2 = 3x + 7$. Then we draw, on the same axes, the graphs of $y = x^2$ and $y = 3x + 7$.
At the points where these graphs intersect, the y values are equal,
i.e. $x^2 = 3x + 7$.

Therefore the x values at the points of intersection are the solutions of the equation $x^2 - 3x - 7 = 0$.

EXERCISE 5c

What equation can we solve by finding where the graph of $y = 5x - 2$ intersects the graph of $y = x^2$?

When the graphs intersect their y values are equal

i.e. $\qquad\qquad\qquad x^2 = 5x - 2$

or $\qquad\qquad\qquad x^2 - 5x + 2 = 0$

The values of x at the points of intersection must therefore be the solutions of the equation $x^2 - 5x + 2 = 0$.

1. What equations can be solved by finding where the graph of $y = x^2$ intersects the graphs of the straight lines with the following equations?

a) $y = x + 7$

b) $y = 2x + 5$

c) $y = 6x - 4$

d) $y = 5 - 3x$

2. What straight line graphs should be drawn to intersect the graph of $y = x^2$ in order to solve the following quadratic equations?

a) $x^2 - 2x - 1 = 0$

b) $x^2 - 7x + 2 = 0$

c) $x^2 + 6x + 4 = 0$

d) $2x^2 + 7x + 2 = 0$

3. *Sketch* on the same axes the graphs of $y = x^2$ and $y = x + 4$ for values of x in the range -4 to 4.
Estimate the values of x at the points of intersection of the two graphs. What equation has these values of x as roots?

4. *Sketch* the graphs of $y = x^2$ and $y = 5x + 20$ for values of x in the range -6 to 9.
Estimate the values of x at the points where the two graphs intersect. What equation, in its simplest form, is satisfied at these points?

Draw the graph of $y = x^2 + 5x + 4$ for whole number values of x from -6 to 1.

Use your graph to find the lowest value of $x^2 + 5x + 4$, and the corresponding value of x.

Draw, on the same axes, the graph of $y = x + 6$. Write down the values of x at the points of intersection of the two graphs. Use your graph to find the range of values of x for which $x^2 + 5x + 4$ is less than $x + 6$. Find, in its simplest form, the equation for which the values of x at the points of intersection of the two graphs are the roots.

x	-6	-5	-4	-3	-2	-1	0	1
x^2	36	25	16	9	4	1	0	1
$5x$	-30	-25	-20	-15	-10	-5	0	5
4	4	4	4	4	4	4	4	4
$y = x^2 + 5x + 4$	10	4	0	-2	-2	0	4	10

From the graph the lowest value of $x^2 + 5x + 4$ is -2.2 which occurs when x is -2.5.

(The graph of $y = x + 6$ is a straight line so we take only three values of x and find the corresponding values of y.)

x	-6	-2	0
$y = x + 6$	0	4	6

The graphs intersect when $x = -4.45$ and 0.45.

From $x = -4.45$ to $x = 0.45$ the curve, which has equation $y = x^2 + 5x + 4$, is below the straight line, which has equation $y = x + 6$.

Therefore $x^2 + 5x + 4 < x + 6$ for all values of x greater than -4.45 but less than 0.45.

At $x = -4.45$ and $x = 0.45$ the values of y for the curve and for the straight line are equal

i.e. $$x^2 + 5x + 4 = x + 6$$

i.e. $$x^2 + 4x - 2 = 0$$

The equation $x^2 + 4x - 2 = 0$ therefore has as roots the values of x at the points of intersection of the two graphs.

$y = x + 6$

5. Complete the following table which gives values of $12 - x^2$ for values of x in the range -4 to 4.

x	-4	-3	-2	-1	0	1	2	3	4
$12 - x^2$	-4	3		11	12		8	3	-4

Using $2\,cm$ as 1 unit for x and $1\,cm$ as 1 unit for y, draw the graph of $y = 12 - x^2$.
Use your graph to solve the equation $12 - x^2 = 0$.
On the same axes draw the graph of $y = 2x + 7$.
What equation is satisfied by the values of x at the points of intersection of the two graphs?
Write down the values of x that satisfy this equation.

6. Copy and complete the following table which gives values of $x^2 + 2x - 2$ for values of x in the range -4 to 2.

x	-4	-3.5	-3	-2	-1	0	1	1.5	2
$x^2 + 2x - 2$	6	3.25	1	-2	-3	-2			6

Using $2\,cm$ as unit on both axes draw the graph of $y = x^2 + 2x - 2$.
On the same axes draw the graph of $y = 2 - \frac{2}{3}x$ and write down the values of x at the points where the graphs intersect.
For what range of values of x is $x^2 + 2x - 2$ less than $2 - \frac{2}{3}x$?
Find, in its simplest form, the equation for which the values of x at the intersection of the graphs, are the roots.

7. Copy and complete the following table which gives values of $9x - x^2$ for values of x in the range -2 to 10.

x	-2	-1	0	1	2	3	4	5	6	7	8	9	10
$9x - x^2$	-22		0	8	14	18	20		18	14			-10

Using $1\,cm$ as 1 unit for x and $2\,cm$ as 5 units for y, draw the graph of $y = 9x - x^2$.
On the same axes draw the graph of $y = 5x - 10$.
Write down the range of values of x for which $9x - x^2$ is greater than $5x - 10$.
Write down the values of x at the points of intersection of the graphs and the equation for which these values of x are the roots.

8. Write down the three values missing from the following table, which gives values of $2x^2 - 7x - 3$ for values of x in the range -1 to 5.

x	-1	-0.5	0	1	1.5	2	3	4	4.5	5
$2x^2 - 7x - 3$	6		-3	-8		-9	-6	1		12

Using 2 cm as 1 unit on the x-axis and 4 cm as 5 units on the y-axis, draw the graph of $y = 2x^2 - 7x - 3$.
Use your graph to solve the equation $2x^2 - 7x - 3 = 0$.
On the same axes draw the graph of $5x - 4y + 4 = 0$.
For what values of x is $2x^2 - 7x - 3$ less than $\frac{1}{4}(5x + 4)$?
Write down the values of x at the points of intersection of the two graphs and the equation for which these values are the roots.

9. What graph should be used, together with the graph of $y = x^2$, to solve the equation $2x^2 - x - 12 = 0$?
Sketch the two graphs for values of x in the range -4 to 4.
Use your sketch to estimate the solutions of the equation $2x^2 - x - 12 = 0$.

10. What graph should be used, together with the graph of $y = x^2$, to solve the equation $2 - 5x - x^2 = 0$?
Sketch the two graphs for values of x in the range -6 to 2.
Use your sketch to estimate the solutions of the equation $2 - 5x - x^2 = 0$.

11. Write down the three values missing from the following table, which gives values of $4x^2 - 16x + 15$ for values of x in the range 0 to 4.

x	0	0.5	1	1.5	2	2.5	3	3.5	4
$4x^2 - 16x + 15$		8	3	0	-1			8	15

Using 4 cm as 1 unit on the x-axis and 1 cm as 1 unit on the y-axis, draw the graph of $y = 4x^2 - 16x + 15$.
Use your graph to find the values of x when $y = 6$. What equation is satisfied by these values of x?
On the same axes draw the graph of $2x + y - 10 = 0$.
For what values of x is $4x^2 - 16x + 15$ less than $10 - 2x$?
Write down the values of x at the points of intersection of the two graphs and the equation for which these values are the roots.

USING GRAPHS TO SOLVE QUADRATIC INEQUALITIES

Suppose that we want to find the range of values of x for which $x^2 \leqslant 9$. If we draw the graphs of $y = x^2$ and $y = 9$, then we can read off the range of values of x for which the curve $y = x^2$ is below the line $y = 9$. However, with the help of some algebra, we can get the information we need by *sketching* the graphs.

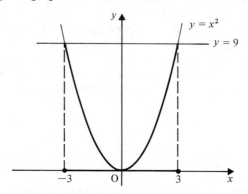

From the sketch we can see that the curve is below the line (i.e. $x^2 < 9$) for the range of values of x between the points where the line and curve intersect.

Now the curve and line intersect where $x^2 = 9$ and this is a quadratic equation which can be solved algebraically, i.e.

$$x^2 = 9$$
$$x^2 - 9 = 0$$
$$(x - 3)(x + 3) = 0$$

Therefore $x = 3$ or $x = -3$.

Hence $x^2 \leqslant 9$ when $-3 \leqslant x \leqslant 3$.

If we wanted the values for which $x^2 > 9$, then we can see from the sketch that the curve is above the line when $x < -3$ and when $x > 3$,

i.e. $x^2 > 9$ when $x < -3$ and $x > 3$

Note that these two inequalities cannot be combined into one statement because in this case the values of x do not lie between two numbers.

It is also interesting to note that a linear equation has one solution and the solution of a linear inequality is a range of values with one boundary value, whereas a quadratic equation usually has two solutions and the range(s) of values that satisfy a quadratic inequality have two boundary values; this realisation should prevent incorrect statements such as '$x^2 < 9$ therefore $x < 3$' being made.

EXERCISE 5d

1. Find the range(s) of values of x for which
   a) $x^2 < 4$ b) $x^2 > 25$ c) $x^2 \leqslant 1$ d) $x^2 \geqslant 36$

Find the values of x for which $x^2 > 2x$

(First we sketch the graphs of $y = x^2$ and $y = 2x$)

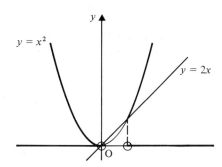

The graphs intersect where $x^2 = 2x$

i.e. where
$$x^2 - 2x = 0$$
$$x(x - 2) = 0$$
$$x = 0 \quad \text{and} \quad x = 2$$

Therefore $x^2 > 2x$ for $x < 0$ and $x > 2$.

(Note that the inequality could be given in the form $x^2 - 2x > 0$.)

---

2. Find the range(s) of values of x for which
   a) $x^2 < 3x$ b) $x^2 \geqslant 4x$ c) $x^2 < -2x$ d) $x^2 \leqslant -x$

3. a) Factorise $x^2 - 3x + 2$.
   b) Sketch the graphs of $y = x^2$ and $y = 3x - 2$.
   c) Write down the equation whose roots are the values of x where the graphs in (b) intersect.
   d) Find the range of values of x for which $x^2 - 3x + 2 \leqslant 0$.

4. Find the range of values of x for which $x^2 - 6x + 8 \leqslant 0$.

USING ALGEBRA TO SOLVE QUADRATIC INEQUALITIES

Instead of drawing a sketch graph to solve an inequalit, we can use a table.

Consider the inequality $x^2 < 7x$.

First we rearrange the inequality to give zero on the RHS,

i.e. $$x^2 - 7x < 0$$

(Remember that adding or subtracting the same quantity on each side of an inequality does not alter the truth of the inequality.)

Then we find the values of x where $x^2 - 7x = 0$, i.e. where $x(x - 7) = 0$. These are $x = 0$ and $x = 7$.
Hence we need to find whether $x^2 - 7x$ is greater than or less than zero (i.e. positive or negative) for the ranges $x < 0$, $0 < x < 7$ and $x > 7$. This is best done in tabular form.

	$x < 0$	$0 < x < 7$	$x > 7$
$x^2 - 7x$	$+$	$-$	$+$

(To find the sign of $x^2 - 7x$ for a range of values of x in the table, substitute any value of x in that range; e.g. for $x < 0$, try $x = -1$.)

Now we can see that $x - 7x < 0$ when $0 < x < 7$.

EXERCISE 5e

Find the range of values of x for which

1. $x^2 < 6x$

2. $x^2 + 5x < 0$

3. $x^2 < 49$

4. $x^2 - 5x + 4 > 0$

5. $x^2 > 9x$

6. $x^2 < 6x + 7$

CUBIC GRAPHS

When an x^3 term appears in addition to the types of terms we have already considered, we obtain what is known as a cubic graph.

Examples are:

$$y = x^3 + x, \quad y = 2x^3 - 5, \quad y = x^3 - 2x^2 + 3, \quad \text{and} \quad y = 3x^3 + x^2 - 5x + 2$$

The following table gives values of x^3 for values of x in the range -4 to 4.

x	-4	-3.5	-3	-2.5	-2	-1.5	-1	-0.5	0	0.5	1	1.5	2	2.5	3	3.5	4
x^3	-64	-43	-27	-16	-8	-3.4	-1	-0.1	0	0.1	1	3.4	8	16	27	43	64

These values are plotted on a graph and joined by a smooth continuous curve to give the graph shown opposite.

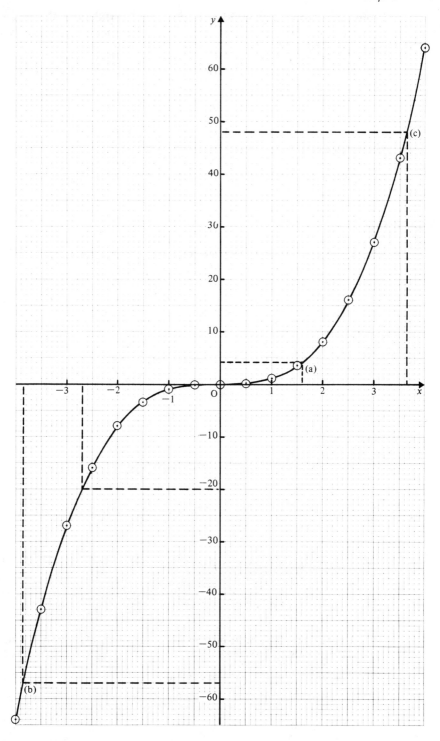

From the graph on page 91 it is possible to find the cube of any number between -4 and $+4$ and to find the cube root of any number between -64 and $+64$.

For example, from the graph
a) $1.6^3 = 4.1$ (i.e. when $x = 1.6$, $y = 4.1$)
b) $-3.85^3 = -57$ (i.e. when $x = -3.85$, $y = -57$)
c) $\sqrt[3]{48} = 3.65$ (i.e. when $y = 48$, $x = 3.65$)
d) $\sqrt[3]{-20} = -2.7$ (i.e. when $y = -20$, $x = -2.7$)

EXERCISE 5f

1. Copy and complete the following table which gives values of $\frac{1}{5}x^3$, correct to one decimal place, for values of x from -3 to $+3$.

x	-3	-2.5	-2	-1.5	-1	-0.5	0	0.5	1	1.5	2	2.5	3
x^3	-27	-15.6	-8	-3.4		-0.13		0.13	1				27
$\frac{1}{5}x^3$	-5.4	-3.1	-1.6	-0.7		-0.03		0.03	0.2				5.4

Hence draw the graph of $y = \frac{1}{5}x^3$ for values of x from -3 to $+3$. Take 2 cm as unit on each axis.

Use your graph to solve the equations

a) $\frac{1}{5}x^3 = 4$

b) $x^3 = -15$

2. Copy and complete the following table which gives values of $\frac{1}{10}x^3$ for values of x from -4 to $+4$.

x	-4	-3.5	-3	-2.5	-2	-1	0	1	2	2.5	3	3.5	4
x^3	-64	-42.9	-27	-15.6		-1	0	1	8			42.9	64
$\frac{1}{10}x^3$	-6.4	-4.3	-2.7	-1.6		-0.1	0	0.1	0.8			4.3	6.4

Hence draw the graph of $y = \frac{1}{10}x^3$ for values of x from -4 to $+4$ taking 2 cm as unit on both axes.

Use your graph to solve the equations

a) $\frac{1}{10}x^3 = 5$

b) $x^3 = -40$

Complete the following table which gives the values of
$(x+1)(x-1)(x-3)$ for values of x between -2 and $+4$.

x	-2	-1.5	-1	-0.5	0	0.5	1
$(x+1)(x-1)(x-3)$	-15	-5.6	0	2.6	3	1.9	

x	1.5	2	2.5	3	3.5	4
$(x+1)(x-1)(x-3)$	-1.9	-3			5.6	15

Hence draw the graph of $y = (x+1)(x-1)(x-3)$ for values of x
between -2 and $+4$.

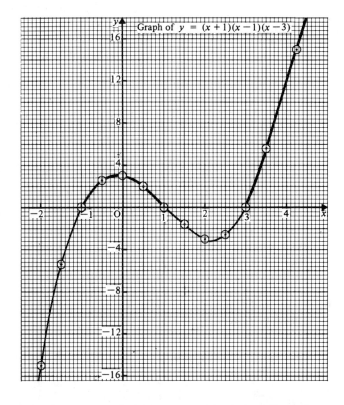

Use your graph to find

a) the value(s) of x when   i) $y = 1$ ii) $y = -8$

b) the range of values of x for which $(x+1)(x-1)(x-3)$ is
    positive.

(The missing values are found by substituting in the expression $(x+1)(x-1)(x-3)$.)

x	1	2.5	3
$x+1$	2	3.5	4
$x-1$	0	1.5	2
$x-3$	-2	-0.5	0
$(x+1)(x-1)(x-3)$	0	-2.625	0

a) From the graph   i) if $y=1$, $x=-0.9$, 0.75 3.1
                    ii) if $y=-8$, $x=-1.6$

b) If $(x+1)(x-1)(x-3)$ is positive, then y is positive. The part of the graph for which $y>0$ lies above the x-axis and, for these sections, x either lies between -1 and $+1$, or is greater than 3.

These sections are shown on the graph with a heavy line.

3. Copy and complete the table which gives the values of y when $y=x(x-2)(x-4)$ for values of x from 0 to 4.

x	0	0.5	1	1.5	2	2.5	3	3.5	4
$x-2$		-1.5						1.5	
$x-4$		-3.5						-0.5	
y		2.625						-2.625	

Hence draw the graph of $y=x(x-2)(x-4)$, using 4 cm for 1 unit on each axis.

Use your graph to find   a) the lowest value   b) the highest value of $x(x-2)(x-4)$ within the given range of values for x.

4. Copy and complete the table which gives the value of $\frac{1}{3}x^3-2x+3$ for values of x from -2 to 2.

x	-2	-1.5	-1	-0.5	0	0.5	1	1.5	2
$\frac{1}{3}x^3$	-2.67	-1.13	-0.33		0		0.33	1.13	
$-2x$	4	3	2		0		-2	-3	
$+3$	3	3	3		3		3	3	
$\frac{1}{3}x^3-2x+3$	4.33	4.87	4.67		3		1.33	1.13	

Hence draw the graph of $y=\frac{1}{3}x^3-2x+3$ using 4 cm for 1 unit on each axis.

Estimate the value(s) of x where the graph crosses the x-axis.

5. Copy and complete the table which gives the value of $1-x+2x^2-x^3$ for values of x from -1 to 3.

x	-1	-0.5	0	0.5	1	1.5	2	3
$1-x$	2	1.5		0.5		-0.5		-2
$2x^2$	2	0.5		0.5		4.5		18
$-x^3$	1	0.125		-1.125		-3.375		-27
$1-x+2x^2-x^3$	5	2.125				0.625		-11

Hence draw the graph of $y = 1-x+2x^2-x^3$ using 1 cm for 1 unit on the y-axis and 2 cm for 1 unit on the x-axis.
Write down the value(s) of x where the graph crosses the x-axis.

6. *Sketch* the graph of $y = x^3$ for values of x from -2 to 2.
   a) What line would you have to draw to use the graph to solve the equation $x^3 = x$?
   b) Use your sketch to estimate the solution(s) of $x^3 = x$.

THE GRAPH OF $y = \dfrac{a}{x}$ WHERE a IS A CONSTANT

EXERCISE 5g

1. Draw a graph of $y = \dfrac{2}{x}$ for values of x from -4 to $-\frac{1}{2}$ and from $\frac{1}{2}$ to 4. Use 2 cm as unit on both axes.
How many lines of symmetry does this curve have? Show any lines of symmetry on your diagram. Why is there no point on the graph when $x = 0$?
Use your graph to find
   a) the value of y when x is 2.6
   b) the value of x when y is -3.2

2. Draw the graph of $y = \dfrac{12}{x}$ for values of x from 1 to 12. Use 1 cm as unit on both axes.
Use your graph to find
   a) the value of x when y is 4.6
   b) the range of x values for which y is smaller than 5.6
   c) the lowest value of y within the given range and the value of x for which it occurs.

3. Draw the graph of $y = \dfrac{16}{x}$, taking unit intervals for x in the range 1 to 16. Take 1 cm as unit on both axes. Draw on the same axes the graph of $x + y = 12$.

a) Write down the value(s) of x at the point(s) where the graphs intersect.

b) What equation has these x values as its roots?

c) Write down the range of values of x for which $12 - x \geqslant \dfrac{16}{x}$

4. Draw the graph of $y = \dfrac{8}{x}$ for values of x in the range -8 to -1 at unit intervals. Take 2 cm as unit on both axes. Draw on the same axes the graph of $y = x + 2$

a) Write down the value of x at the point where these graphs intersect.

b) What equation has this value as *one* of its roots? How many roots would you expect this equation to have? Explain how you could obtain the other root.

5. *Sketch* the graph of $y = \dfrac{1}{x}$ for values of x from -10 to $-\frac{1}{10}$ and $\frac{1}{10}$ to 10.

a) What happens to values of y as the value of x increases beyond $x = 10$?

b) Is there a value of y for which $x = 0$?

c) Is there a value of x for which $y = 0$?

6. Write down the three values missing from the following table, which gives values of $\dfrac{4}{x} + 1$, correct to two decimal places, for values of x in the range 0.5 to 8.

x	0.5	0.8	1	1.5	2	2.5	3	3.5	4	5	6	7	8
$\dfrac{4}{x} + 1$			6		3.67	3	2.6	2.33	2.14	2	1.8		1.57	1.5

Using the same axes, draw the graphs of $y = \dfrac{4}{x} + 1$ and $y = 4(2 - \dfrac{x}{3})$, for values of x from 0.5 to 8 taking 2 cm as 1 unit on both axes.

Use your graphs to write down the range of values of x for which $\dfrac{4}{x} + 1$ is less than $8 - \dfrac{4x}{3}$.

Write down, and simplify, the equation which is satisfied by the values of x at the points of intersection of the two graphs.

7. Sketch the graph of $y = \dfrac{10}{x}$ for values of x from 1 to 100.

a) What line has to be sketched to solve the equation $\dfrac{10}{x} = x + 1$?

b) Sketch the line on the same set of axes.

c) Does the value of x at the intersection of the graphs give *all* the solutions of $\dfrac{10}{x} = x + 1$?

EXERCISE 5h

In this exercise several possible answers are given. Write down the letter that corresponds to the correct answer.

1.

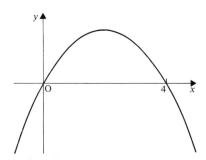

The equation of this curve could be

A $y = x^2$ **B** $y = x^3$ **C** $y = \dfrac{1}{x}$ **D** $y = 4x - x^2$

2.

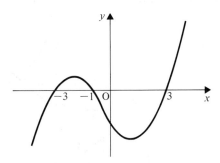

The equation of this curve could be

A $y = x^2 + x - 9$ **B** $y = (x - 3)(x + 3)(x + 1)$

C $y = \dfrac{9}{x}$ **D** $y = x^3$

3.

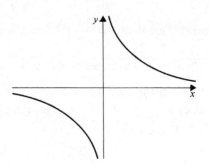

The equation of this curve could be

A $y = \dfrac{12}{x}$ **B** $y = x^2 - 9$ **C** $y = 9 - x^2$ **D** $y = x^3$

4.

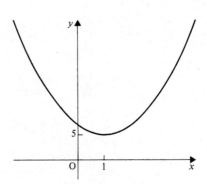

The equation of this curve could be

A $y = x^2$ **B** $y = 4 - x^2$

C $y = x^2 - 2x + 6$ **D** $y = x^3 - 4x^2 + 3$

5.

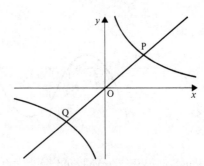

The values of x at P and Q could be the solutions of the equation.

A $x = x^2$ **B** $x = \dfrac{1}{x}$ **C** $x^2 = \dfrac{1}{x}$ **D** $x^3 = x$

6.

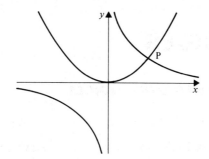

The value of x at P could be the solution of the equation

A $x^2 = \dfrac{1}{x}$ **B** $x^2 = \dfrac{1}{x^2}$ **C** $\dfrac{1}{x} = 1 + x$ **D** $x^3 = \dfrac{1}{x}$

7.

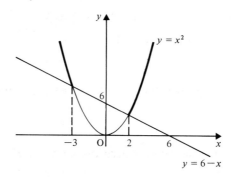

$x^2 + x - 6 < 0$ when

A $2 < x < 6$ **B** $x < -3$

C $-3 < x < 2$ **D** $x < -3$ and $x > 2$

6 INDICES

POSITIVE AND NEGATIVE INDICES

In the term a^4, 4 is called the index or power and a^4 means $a \times a \times a \times a$

We can multiply one number to a power by the *same* number to another power by adding its powers. We can divide one number to a power by the same number to another power by subtracting the powers,

e.g. $a^3 \times a^2 = a^{3+2} = a^5$ and $a^3 \div a^2 = a^{3-2} = a^1 = a$

Using the rule for division gives meaning to negative powers,

e.g. $a^3 \div a^5 = a^{-2}$ but $a^3 \div a^5 = \dfrac{a \times a \times a}{a \times a \times a \times a \times a} = \dfrac{1}{a^2}$

i.e. a^{-2} means $\dfrac{1}{a^2}$

Hence a negative sign in front of the index means 'the reciprocal of',

i.e. $a^{-b} = \dfrac{1}{a^b}$

Also, using the rule for division we have $a^2 \div a^2 = a^0$
but $a^2 \div a^2 = 1$

i.e. (any number)$^0 = 1$

EXERCISE 6a

Simplify a) $2^2 \times 2^3$ b) $3^5 \div 3^7$ c) $(0.5)^{-3}$

a) $2^2 \times 2^3 = 2^5$

$= 32$

b) $3^5 \div 3^7 = 3^{-2}$

$= \dfrac{1}{3^2}$

$= \dfrac{1}{9}$

c) $(0.5)^{-3} = \left(\frac{1}{2}\right)^{-3}$

$= \left(\frac{2}{1}\right)^{3}$

$= 8$

Find the value of:

1. $3^2 \times 3^2$	**9.** $(0.5)^{-2}$	**17.** $(0.04)^{-1}$
2. $(2^2)^2$	**10.** $(5)^0$	**18.** $\left(\frac{3}{4}\right)^2$
3. $2^4 \times 3^2$	**11.** $(1.6)^0$	**19.** $\left(\frac{2}{5}\right)^{-2}$
4. $8^5 \div 8^3$	**12.** $\left(\frac{3}{4}\right)^{-1}$	**20.** $\left(\frac{2}{3}\right)^3$
5. $12^4 \div 12^2$	**13.** $2^6 \div 4^2$	**21.** $\left(\frac{1}{6}\right)^0$
6. $7^2 \div 5^2$	**14.** $\left(\frac{1}{3}\right)^{-3}$	**22.** $\left(\frac{3}{5}\right)^3$
7. 2^{-1}	**15.** 2^5	**23.** $\left(\frac{2}{5}\right)^{-1}$
8. $\left(\frac{1}{6}\right)^{-1}$	**16.** 3^3	**24.** $(0.125)^{-2}$

Simplify   a) $a^2 \div a^5$ b) $\left(\frac{x}{y}\right)^{-2}$

a) $a^2 \div a^5 = a^{-3}$

$= \frac{1}{a^3}$

b) $\left(\frac{x}{y}\right)^{-2} = \left(\frac{y}{x}\right)^{2}$

$= \frac{y^2}{x^2}$

Simplify:

25. $b^2 \times b^3$

26. $c^7 \div c^5$

27. $\left(\dfrac{1}{c}\right)^{-2}$

28. $x^3 \div x^7$

29. $b^3 \times b^4$

30. $\left(\dfrac{a}{b}\right)^{-1}$

31. $b \times b^3$

32. $y^3 \div y$

33. $\left(\dfrac{1}{x}\right)^{-2}$

34. $\left(\dfrac{d}{2}\right)^{-2}$

35. $(x^3)^{-1}$

36. $(p^{-1})^2$

Simplify   a) $(2^3)^2$ b) $(x^3)^2$

a) $(2^3)^2 = 8^2$
           $= 64$

b) $(x^3)^2 = x^3 \times x^3$
            $= x^6$

Simplify:

37. $(3^2)^2$

38. $(2^2)^3$

39. $(5^2)^3$

40. $(x^2)^4$

41. $(a^5)^2$

42. $(x^2)^3$

43. $(2^3)^3$

44. $(3^2)^3$

45. $(4^2)^2$

46. $(x^3)^5$

47. $(y^2)^4$

48. $(x^3)^{-2}$

Simplify $15x^5 \div 3x^3$

$$15x^5 \div 3x^3 = \frac{15x^5}{3x^3}$$
$$= 5x^2$$

Simplify:

49. $8a^3 \times 2a^2$ **53.** $6x^2 \div 3x$ **57.** $24a^2 \div 6a^4$

50. $8p^3 \div 2p^2$ **54.** $5a^2 \div 10a^3$ **58.** $3x^3 \times 4x^2$

51. $4x \div 2x^3$ **55.** $12x^6 \div 3x^2$ **59.** $8y \times 3y^3$

52. $6x^2 \times 3x$ **56.** $5y \times 3y^2$ **60.** $30y^3 \div 6y^5$

STANDARD FORM (SCIENTIFIC NOTATION)

A number between 1 and 10 multiplied by the appropriate power of 10 is said to be in standard form,

e.g.   when 0.0043 is written in standard form it becomes 4.3×10^{-3}

EXERCISE 6b

Write in standard form   a) 3700   b) 0.052

a) $3700 = 3.7 \times 10^3$

b) $0.052 = 5.2 \times 10^{-2}$

Write the following numbers in standard form.

1. 280   **4.** 0.097   **7.** 0.8

2. 0.39   **5.** 2770   **8.** 8000

3. 707   **6.** 0.00008   **9.** 0.025

If $a = 1.2 \times 10^{-2}$ and $b = 6 \times 10^{-4}$ express in standard form

a) ab b) $\dfrac{a}{b}$ c) $a + b$

If $a = 1.2 \times 10^{-2}$ and $b = 6 \times 10^{-4}$ then

a) $ab = 1.2 \times 10^{-2} \times 6 \times 10^{-4}$

$= 7.2 \times 10^{-6}$

b) $\dfrac{a}{b} = \dfrac{1.2 \times 10^{-2}}{6 \times 10^{-4}}$

$= \dfrac{1.2}{6} \times 10^{-2-(-4)}$

$= 0.2 \times 10^{2}$

(This number must now be converted to standard form)

$= 2.0 \times 10^{-1} \times 10^{2}$

$= 2 \times 10^{1}$

c) $a + b = 1.2 \times 10^{-2} + 6 \times 10^{-4}$

(Multiplication must be done before addition, so each number must be written in full.)

$a + b = 0.012 + 0.0006$

$= 0.0126$

$= 1.26 \times 10^{-2}$

Write down the value of ab in standard form if

10. $a = 2.1 \times 10^{2}, \ b = 4 \times 10^{3}$

11. $a = 5.4 \times 10^{4}, \ b = 2 \times 10^{5}$

12. $a = 7 \times 10^{-2}, \ b = 2.2 \times 10^{-3}$

13. $a = 5 \times 10^{-4}, \ b = 2.3 \times 10^{-2}$

14. $a = 1.6 \times 10^{-2}, \ b = 2 \times 10^{4}$

15. $a = 6 \times 10^{5}, \ b = 1.3 \times 10^{-7}$

Write down the value of $\dfrac{p}{q}$ in standard form if

16. $p = 6 \times 10^5$, $q = 3 \times 10^2$

17. $p = 1.4 \times 10^8$, $q = 2 \times 10^3$

18. $p = 9 \times 10^3$, $q = 3 \times 10^5$

19. $p = 7 \times 10^{-3}$, $q = 5 \times 10^2$

20. $p = 1.8 \times 10^{-3}$, $q = 6 \times 10^{-4}$

21. $p = 2.5 \times 10^4$, $q = 2 \times 10^{-4}$

Write down the value of $x + y$ in standard form if

22. $x = 2 \times 10^2$, $y = 3 \times 10^3$

23. $x = 3 \times 10^{-2}$, $y = 2 \times 10^{-3}$

24. $x = 2.1 \times 10^4$, $y = 3.1 \times 10^5$

25. $x = 1.3 \times 10^{-4}$, $y = 4 \times 10^{-3}$

26. $x = 1.9 \times 10^{-3}$, $y = 2.4 \times 10^{-2}$

27. $x = 3 \times 10^5$, $y = 2.5 \times 10^6$

28. If $x = 1.2 \times 10^5$ and $y = 5 \times 10^{-2}$ find, in standard form, the value of

a) xy b) $x \div y$ c) $x + 1000y$

29. If $m = 7.2 \times 10^{-7}$ and $n = 1.2 \times 10^{-5}$ find, in standard form, the value of

a) mn b) $m \div n$ c) $n - m$

30. If $u = 2.6 \times 10^5$ and $v = 5 \times 10^{-3}$ find, in standard form, the value of

a) uv b) $u \div v$ c) $\dfrac{u}{100} + 100v$ d) $\dfrac{u}{10} - 1000v$

FRACTIONAL INDICES

Consider $a^{1/2}$.

To give a meaning to $a^{1/2}$ we use the fact that

$$a^{1/2} \times a^{1/2} = a^{1/2 + 1/2} = a^1$$

Now when one number is multiplied by itself, the result is called the square of this number,

i.e. a is the *square* of $a^{1/2}$.

Taking $a^{1/2}$ as a positive number, this means that

$a^{1/2}$ is the *positive square root* of a

Hence $4^{1/2}$ means 'the positive square root of 4'

i.e. $$4^{1/2} = \sqrt{4} = 2$$

Similarly, $a^{1/3} \times a^{1/3} \times a^{1/3} = a^{1/3+1/3+1/3} = a^1$ so that $a^{1/3}$ is the *cube root* of a

Hence $27^{1/3}$ means 'the cube root of 27',

i.e. $$27^{1/3} = \sqrt[3]{27} = 3$$

In the same way $a^{1/4}$ means 'the positive fourth root of a' so that

$$16^{1/4} = \sqrt[4]{16} = 2$$

(since $2 \times 2 \times 2 \times 2 = 16$)

In general $a^{1/n}$ means 'the n th root of a',
i.e. $a^{1/n}$ is the number which, when n of them are multiplied together, gives a.

When a number can have both a positive and a negative root, $a^{1/n}$ means the positive root only,
e.g. both 2 and -2 are square roots of 4
    but $4^{1/2} = 2$

EXERCISE 6c

Simplify:

1. $9^{1/2}$

2. $16^{1/2}$

3. $36^{1/2}$

4. $8^{1/3}$

5. $125^{1/3}$

6. $64^{1/3}$

7. $\left(\frac{1}{4}\right)^{1/2}$

8. $(0.04)^{1/2}$

9. $\left(\frac{1}{8}\right)^{1/3}$

10. $\left(\frac{4}{9}\right)^{1/2}$

11. $(0.25)^{1/2}$

12. $\left(\frac{8}{27}\right)^{1/3}$

Consider $8^{2/3}$

$$8^{2/3} = 8^{1/3} \times 8^{1/3} = (8^{1/3})^2$$

Therefore $8^{2/3}$ can be read as 'the square of the cube root of 8', i.e. $(\sqrt[3]{8})^2$

Alternatively, since $8^{2/3} \times 8^{2/3} \times 8^{2/3} = 8^2$, $8^{2/3}$ can be read as 'the cube root of 8 squared', i.e. $\sqrt[3]{(8^2)}$

Therefore $8^{2/3}$ can be evaluated by

either   1) finding the cube root of 8 and squaring the result
        i.e. $8^{2/3} = (8^{1/3})^2 = 2^2 = 4$
or   2) squaring 8 and finding the cube root of the result
        i.e. $8^{2/3} = (8^2)^{1/3} = 64^{1/3} = 4$

Finding the required root first (method 1) keeps the size of the numbers down, so this should be used whenever possible.

EXERCISE 6d

Simplify   a) $4^{3/2}$ b) $\left(\frac{1}{4}\right)^{-1/2}$

    a) $4^{3/2} = (\sqrt{4})^3 = 2^3 = 8$

    b) $\left(\frac{1}{4}\right)^{-1/2} = (4)^{1/2} = 2$

Simplify:

1. $(27)^{2/3}$	**5.** $(0.008)^{2/3}$	**9.** $32^{2/5}$
2. $\left(\frac{1}{8}\right)^{2/3}$	**6.** $(144)^{3/2}$	**10.** $(1000)^{2/3}$
3. $(16)^{3/4}$	**7.** $(0.36)^{3/2}$	**11.** $(0.0001)^{3/4}$
4. $(125)^{2/3}$	**8.** $81^{3/4}$	**12.** $(100\,000)^{2/5}$

13. $\left(\frac{1}{9}\right)^{-1/2}$	**17.** $8^{-2/3}$	**21.** $(1000)^{-2/3}$
14. $\left(\frac{4}{49}\right)^{-1/2}$	**18.** $(32)^{-3/5}$	**22.** $\left(\frac{1}{9}\right)^{-3/2}$
15. $(0.04)^{-1/2}$	**19.** $(16)^{-1/4}$	**23.** $(0.027)^{-2/3}$
16. $\left(\frac{8}{27}\right)^{-1/3}$	**20.** $(0.01)^{-3/2}$	**24.** $(6.25)^{-1/2}$

25. $(x^2)^{1/4}$	**27.** $(y^4)^{1/2}$	**29.** $(x^8)^{3/4}$
26. $(x^{1/3})^6$	**28.** $(a^6)^{1/3}$	**30.** $(x^{2/3})^6$

USING A CALCULATOR

To find the cube root of 12 using a calculator, first write $\sqrt[3]{12}$ as $12^{1/3}$ then

a)   if your calculator has a key $\boxed{y^{1/x}}$, use the following sequence:

    $\boxed{1}$ $\boxed{2}$ $\boxed{y^{1/x}}$ $\boxed{3}$ $\boxed{=}$

b)   if your calculator has a key $\boxed{y^x}$ but not $\boxed{y^{1/x}}$, change the fractional index to a decimal, i.e.

    $\boxed{1}$ $\boxed{2}$ $\boxed{y^x}$ $\boxed{.}$ $\boxed{3}$ $\boxed{3}$ $\boxed{3}$ $\boxed{3}$ $\boxed{=}$

Any root can be found in a similar manner,

e.g. $\sqrt[4]{20} = 20^{1/4} = 20^{0.25}$ and $(0.27)^{2/3} = (0.27)^{0.667}$

EXERCISE 6e

Use your calculator to evaluate the following roots, giving your answers correct to 3 s.f.

1. $\sqrt[3]{24}$

2. $(24)^{1/2}$

3. $\sqrt[4]{100}$

4. $\sqrt[5]{216}$

5. $\sqrt[3]{0.01}$

6. $(1.8)^{2/3}$

7. $\sqrt[3]{502}$

8. $\sqrt[4]{36}$

9. $(0.2)^{3/5}$

10. $(1.5)^{1/5}$

11. $\sqrt[6]{0.1}$

12. $\sqrt[4]{24.2}$

MIXED EXERCISES

EXERCISE 6f

In this exercise each question is followed by several alternative answers. Write down the letter that corresponds to the correct answer.

1. The value of $\left(\frac{1}{10}\right)^{-3}$ is

   A $\frac{1}{30}$ **B** $\frac{1}{1000}$ **C** 1000   **D** 30

2. The value of $(1.6)^0$ is

   A 0   **B** 1   **C** 1.6   **D** $\frac{1}{16}$

3. When $a = 2 \times 10^2$ and $b = 3 \times 10^4$, the value of $a \times b$ is

   A 5×10^6 **B** 6×10^8 **C** -1×10^{-2} **D** 6×10^6

4. The value of $\left(\frac{27}{8}\right)^{-1/3}$ is

   A $1\frac{1}{2}$ **B** $\frac{2}{3}$ **C** $-\frac{8}{81}$ **D** $-\frac{27}{24}$

5. If $x = 4 \times 10^{-3}$ and $y = 2 \times 10^{-2}$ then the value of $x + y$ is

   A 6×10^{-5} **B** 4.2×10^{-3} **C** 8×10^{-5} **D** 2.4×10^{-2}

6. $2p^2 \times 3p^3$ can be written as

   A $5p^5$ **B** $6p^6$ **C** $6p^5$ **D** $5p^6$

7. $\left(\frac{x}{y}\right)^{-2}$ can be written as

   A $\frac{y^2}{x^2}$ **B** xy^2 **C** $\sqrt{\left(\frac{x}{y}\right)}$ **D** $x^2 y^2$

EXERCISE 6g

1. Simplify:

a) $\left(\frac{1}{2}\right)^{-2}$ b) $49^{-1/2}$ c) $8^{4/3}$ d) $25^{3/2}$

2. If $x = 16$ and $y = 27$ find

a) $x^{-1/2}$ b) $y^{1/3}$ c) $(xy)^0$ d) $\left(\dfrac{x}{y}\right)^{-1}$

3. If $a = \frac{1}{4}$ and $b = \frac{1}{25}$ find

a) a^2 b) b^0 c) $\left(\dfrac{b}{a}\right)^{1/2}$ d) $a^{1/2}b^{-1}$

4. If $u = 2.7 \times 10^4$ and $v = 3 \times 10^2$ find, in standard form, the value of

a) uv b) $u + v$ c) $u \div v$

5. Simplify:

a) $x^2 \times x^{-3}$ b) $4a^5 \div 2a^7$ c) $\left(\dfrac{x^2}{y}\right)^{-1}$

6. Find the value of x when   a) $x^3 = 8$ b) $2^x = 16$

EXERCISE 6h

1. Simplify:

a) $\left(\frac{3}{4}\right)^2$ b) $\left(\frac{3}{5}\right)^{-1}$ c) $8^{1/3}$ d) $\left(\frac{1}{3}\right)^0$

2. If $x = 1.8 \times 10^{-3}$ and $y = 2.4 \times 10^{-2}$ find, in standard form the value of

a) xy b) $\dfrac{x}{y}$ c) $x + y$ d) $y - x$

3. If $p = 25$ and $q = 6$ find

a) $p^{1/2}$ b) q^{-2} c) $p^{-3/2}$ d) $\left(\dfrac{p}{q}\right)^{-1}$

4. If $a = \frac{2}{3}$ and $b = \frac{3}{5}$ find

a) a^{-2} b) b^2 c) $(ab)^{-1}$ d) $\left(\dfrac{a}{b}\right)^2$

5. Simplify:

a) $p^{-2} \times p^4$ b) $4x^2 \div 8x^3$ c) $(x^3)^4$

6. Find the value of x when

a) $x^4 = 81$ b) $4^x = 64$

EXERCISE 6i

1. Find:

   a) $\left(\frac{2}{3}\right)^4$
   b) $\left(\frac{4}{9}\right)^{1/2}$
   c) $\left(\frac{3}{7}\right)^{-2}$
   d) $4^{3/2}$

2. Find:

   a) $(2^2)^3$
   b) $(125)^{2/3}$
   c) $32^{2/5}$
   d) $\left(\frac{1}{2}\right)^{-3}$

3. Simplify:

   a) $x^5 \div x^3$
   b) $12y^2 \div 8y^5$
   c) $(y^2)^4$

4. If $a = 3.2 \times 10^5$ and $b = 2 \times 10^4$ find in standard form the value of

   a) ab
   b) $a \div b$
   c) $b \div a$
   d) $a - b$

5. Simplify:

   a) $(p^2)^5$
   b) $(x^{1/2})^3$
   c) $8y^3 \div 20y^4$

6. Find the value of x when

   a) $x^2 = \frac{4}{9}$
   b) $8^x = 2$

7 CYLINDERS, CONES AND SPHERES

AREA AND CIRCUMFERENCE

In Book 2A we found that the circumference, C, of a circle of radius r is given by the formula

$$C = 2\pi r$$

where π is the symbol for a number which has no exact numerical value and for which we use the approximations 3.14 or 3.142 or the value given in your calculator or occasionally $\frac{22}{7}$.

The area, A, of a circle is given by the formula

$$A = \pi r^2$$

For all calculations in this chapter use the value of π given by your calculator unless otherwise instructed. For estimations (i.e. checks on answers) take $\pi \approx 3$.

EXERCISE 7a

Find the circumference and area of a circle of radius 6.2 m.

$$r = 6.2$$

Using $C = 2\pi r$

the circumference $= 2 \times \pi \times 6.2 \, \text{cm}$

$$= 38.95 \, \text{cm}$$

(Check: circumference $\approx 2 \times 3 \times 6 \, \text{cm} = 36 \, \text{cm}$)

Using $A = \pi r^2$

the area $= \pi \times (6.2)^2 \, \text{cm}^2$

$$= 120.7 \, \text{cm}^2$$

(Check: area $\approx 3 \times 6^2 \approx 3 \times 40 = 120 \, \text{cm}^2$)

The circumference is 39.0 cm and the area is 121 cm² correct to 3 s.f.

Find the circumference and area of the circle whose radius is given.

1.	9 cm	**4.**	23 mm	**7.**	1.06 cm
2.	3.2 cm	**5.**	13 cm	**8.**	14.2 mm
3.	24 m	**6.**	2 m	**9.**	2.9 cm

10.	7.3 cm	**13.**	8.8 cm	**16.**	19 cm
11.	0.9 m	**14.**	103 mm	**17.**	40.7 cm
12.	19.1 mm	**15.**	1.2 m	**18.**	93 mm

Find the area of a circle of radius 4 cm, giving your answer as a multiple of π.

$$r = 4$$

Using $A = \pi r^2$

the area $= \pi \times (4)^2 \, \text{cm}^2$

$= 16\pi \, \text{cm}^2$

In each question from 19 to 24, find the circumference and area of the circle whose radius is given. Give your answer as a multiple of π.

19.	3 cm	**21.**	80 cm	**23.**	4.5 m
20.	12 cm	**22.**	1 m	**24.**	11 mm

25. Find the circumference of a bicycle wheel of diameter 66 cm.

26. Find the area of a dartboard of diameter 44 cm.

27. A circle of radius 4 cm is cut from a square piece of paper of side 10 cm. Find the area of the remaining paper.

28. Find the perimeter and area of a semicircle of radius 18 cm.

29.

The shaded ring (sometimes called an *annulus*) is bounded by two concentric circles (i.e. circles with the same centre) of radii 10 cm and 6 cm. Find the shaded area.

30.

20 m   30 m

75 m

The diagram shows a running track in which the curved boundaries are semicircles.

Find   a) the outer perimeter of the track
        b) the inner perimeter of the track
        c) the shaded area.

31. Find the area of the annulus which is bounded by circles of radii 9 cm and 5 cm. Give your answer as a multiple of π.

In questions 32 and 33 several alternative answers are given. Write down the letter that corresponds to the correct answer.

32. The area of a circle of radius 6 cm is

   A $6\pi^2 \, \text{cm}^2$ **B** $72\pi \, \text{cm}^2$ **C** $12\pi \, \text{cm}^2$ **D** $36\pi \, \text{cm}^2$

33. The circumference of a circle of radius 21 cm is approximately

   A 66 cm   **B** 1400 cm   **C** 130 cm   **D** 1300 cm

INVERSE PROBLEMS

EXERCISE 7b

The circumference of a circle is 40 cm. Find its radius.

$$C = 40$$

$$C = 2\pi r$$

$$\therefore \qquad 40 = 2\pi r$$

$$\frac{40}{2\pi} = r$$

$$r = 6.366$$

$$\left(\text{Check: } r \approx \frac{40}{2 \times 3} \approx 6 \right)$$

The radius is 6.37 cm correct to 3 s.f.

In each question from 1 to 18 find the radius of the circle whose circumference is given.

1.	18.2 cm	**4.**	2.6 cm	**7.**	4.2 m
2.	6.8 cm	**5.**	30 m	**8.**	108 cm
3.	14 cm	**6.**	192 m	**9.**	13 mm

10.	148 mm	**13.**	3.4 m	**16.**	236 mm
11.	99 cm	**14.**	63 mm	**17.**	6.9 m
12.	14π cm	**15.**	76π mm	**18.**	90π cm

The area of a circle is $28\,\text{cm}^2$. Find its radius.

$$A = 28$$
$$A = \pi r^2$$
$$\therefore \qquad 28 = \pi r^2$$
$$\therefore \qquad \frac{28}{\pi} = r^2$$
$$\therefore \qquad r = \sqrt{\frac{28}{\pi}}$$
$$= 2.985$$

$$\left(\text{Check: } r^2 \approx \frac{28}{3} \approx 9, r \approx 3\right)$$

The radius is 2.99 cm correct to 3 s.f.

In each question from 19 to 27 find the radius of the circle whose area is given.

19. $42\,\text{cm}^2$ **22.** $4\,\text{m}^2$ **25.** $9\,\text{cm}^2$

20. $119\,\text{m}^2$ **23.** $124\,\text{cm}^2$ **26.** $1200\,\text{mm}^2$

21. $26\,\text{mm}^2$ **24.** $56\,\text{cm}^2$ **27.** $13\,\text{m}^2$

28. Find the radius of a circle whose circumference is 220 mm. What is the area of the circle?

29. Find the radius and area of a circle whose circumference is 100 cm.

30. Liquid spilt on a floor forms a circular patch of area $30.6\,\text{cm}^2$. What is the radius of the patch?

31. Find the radius and circumference of a circle whose area is $62\,\text{cm}^2$.

32. Find the radius of a semicircle whose area is $15\,\text{cm}^2$.

ARC AND SECTOR ─────────────────────────────

Part of the circumference of a circle is called an *arc* of a circle.

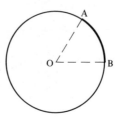

Its shape is defined by the radius of the circle and the angle it subtends at the centre, i.e. $\widehat{AOB}$.

A *sector* is a slice of a circle, defined by the radius and the angle at the centre.

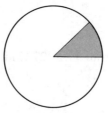

Do not confuse a sector with a *segment,* which is cut from a circle by a chord.

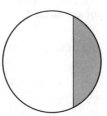

A chord divides a circle into two segments, a minor segment (shaded) and a major segment (unshaded).

EXERCISE 7c

a) Find the length of an arc that subtends an angle of 30°
at the centre of a circle of radius 8 cm.

Arc length is $\dfrac{30}{360}$ of circumference

$$= \dfrac{\overset{1}{\cancel{30}}}{\underset{12}{\cancel{360}}} \times 2\pi r$$

$$= \dfrac{1}{12} \times 2 \times \pi \times 8 \, \text{cm}$$

$$= 4.189 \, \text{cm}$$

∴ the length of the arc is 4.19 cm correct to 3 s.f.

b) Find the area of the sector described in (a).

Area of sector is $\dfrac{30}{360}$ of area of circle

$$= \dfrac{\overset{1}{\cancel{30}}}{\underset{12}{\cancel{360}}} \times \pi r^2$$

$$= \dfrac{1}{12} \times \pi \times (8)^2 \, \text{cm}^2$$

$$= 16.75 \, \text{cm}^2$$

∴ the area of the sector is 16.8 cm² correct to 3 s.f.

In each question from 1 to 6 find

a) the length of the arc   b) the area of the sector.

1.

2.

3.

5.

4.

6.

7. Find the perimeter and area of a quadrant of a circle of radius 10 cm.

8.

A figure is formed from a square of side 12 cm and two quadrants. Find its perimeter and area.

9.

A sector of a circle of radius 4.2 cm contains an angle of 60°.

Find a) the perimeter of the sector

       b) the area of the sector.

Find the angle at the centre of a circle of radius 10 cm subtended by an arc of length 5 cm.

$$\frac{\text{Arc length}}{\text{Circumference}} = \frac{\theta^{\circ}}{360^{\circ}}$$

$$\frac{5}{2\pi r} = \frac{\theta}{360}$$

$$\frac{\overset{18\ \ 36}{\cancel{360} \times 5}}{\cancel{2} \times \pi \times \underset{\scriptscriptstyle 1}{\cancel{10}}} = \theta$$

$$\theta = 28.64^{\circ}$$

The angle at the centre is 28.6°.

In each question from 10 to 12 find the angle subtended at the centre of the circle.

10. Arc length 7 cm, radius of circle 6 cm.

11. Arc length 60 cm, radius of circle 80 cm.

12. Arc length 3.2 cm, radius of circle 12 cm.

In each question from 13 to 15 find the radius of the circle.

13. Arc length 3 cm, angle at the centre 20°.

14. Arc length 7 cm, angle at the centre 45°.

15. Arc length 9 m, angle at the centre 150°.

16. Use $\pi = 3.142$ for this question, *not* the value of π given by a calculator.

The length of the arc AB is 3.142 cm and the radius of the circle is 5 cm.

a) Find $A\widehat{O}B$.

b) Find the area of the shaded sector.

17. A cone made of cardboard has a base of radius 2 cm and slant height 6 cm.

a) Find the circumference of the base circle.

b) The curved surface of the cone is flattened out into a sector of a circle. Draw a diagram and mark in its measurements.

c) Find the angle of the sector.

d) Find the area of the sector.

e) Find the total surface area of the cone.

18.

Using the data given in the diagram, find

a) the area of △ABC

b) the area of the shaded segment.

19.

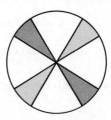

A pattern is formed by painting a white circle of radius 15 cm with four sectors of angle 27° each. Two are painted red and two blue. Find the total area of

a) the white parts

b) the red parts.

ANOTHER APPROXIMATE VALUE FOR π

If the radius of the circle is a multiple of 7, then $\frac{22}{7}$ may be used as an approximate value of π. The result is not as accurate as the one given by using the value of π from a calculator but the arithmetic may be so easy that a calculator is not needed.

EXERCISE 7d

In this exercise use $\frac{22}{7}$ for π. Do not use a calculator.

Find the circumference of a circle of radius $3\frac{1}{2}$ cm.

$$r = 3\tfrac{1}{2}, \quad \pi = \tfrac{22}{7}$$

Using $C = 2\pi r$

the circumference $= {}^1\!\!\not{2} \times \dfrac{22}{\not{7}} \times \dfrac{\not{7}}{\not{2}_1}$ cm

$= 22$ cm

In each question from 1 to 6 find the circumference and area of the circle whose radius is given.

1. 7 cm   **3.** $17\frac{1}{2}$ cm   **5.** $\frac{7}{10}$ cm

2. $1\frac{3}{4}$ cm   **4.** 70 m   **6.** $2\frac{1}{3}$ m

7. Find the perimeter of a semicircle of radius $3\frac{1}{2}$ cm.

8. Find the area of a quadrant of a circle of radius 7 cm.

9. Find the length of an arc subtending an angle of 45° at the centre of a circle of radius 28 m.

10. Find the area of a sector of a circle of radius 21 cm if the angle at the centre is 40°.

Find the radius of a circle of area $9\frac{5}{8}$ cm².

$$A = 9\frac{5}{8},\ \pi = \frac{22}{7}$$

Using $A = \pi r^2$

$$\frac{77}{8} = \frac{22}{7} \times r^2$$

Multiply both sides by $\frac{7}{22}$

$$\frac{7}{{}_2\cancel{22}} \times \frac{\cancel{77}^7}{8} = \frac{\cancel{7}^1}{{}_1\cancel{22}} \times \frac{\cancel{22}^1}{\cancel{7}_1} \times r^2$$

$$\therefore \quad r^2 = \frac{49}{16}$$

$$r = \frac{7}{4}$$

$$= 1\frac{3}{4}$$

The radius is $1\frac{3}{4}$ cm.

In each question from 11 to 16, find the radius of the circle whose area or circumference is given.

11. Circumference 44 cm

12. Circumference 176 cm

13. Area $9\frac{5}{8}$ cm²

14. Circumference 33 cm

15. Area $6\frac{4}{25}$ m²

16. Area 15 400 cm²

CYLINDERS

THE CURVED SURFACE AREA OF A CYLINDER

If we have a cylindrical tin with a paper label covering its curved surface, we can take off the label and flatten it out to give a rectangle whose length is equal to the circumference of the tin.

Therefore the area A of the curved surface is given by $2\pi r \times h$

i.e. $$A = 2\pi rh$$

EXERCISE 7e

In each question from 1 to 8, find the curved surface area of the cylinder whose measurements are given.

1. Radius 4 cm, height 6 cm

2. Radius 30 cm, height 2 cm

3. Radius 6.2 cm, height 5.8 cm

4. Radius 2 m, height 82 cm

5. Radius 0.06 m, height 32 cm

6. Radius 5.2 cm, height 7.8 cm

7. Radius 72.6 cm, height 30 cm

8. Radius 4.2 m, height 9.8 m.

9. A closed cylinder has radius 6 cm and height 10 cm.
Find   a) the area of its curved surface
        b) the area of its base
        c) the total surface area.

10. A closed cylinder has radius 3.2 cm and height 4.8 cm.
Find   a) the area of its curved surface
        b) the total surface area.

11. Find the area of the paper label covering the side of a cylindrical soup tin of height 9.6 cm and radius 3.3 cm. The label has an overlap of 1 cm.

12. What area of card is needed to make a cylindrical tube of length 42 cm and radius 3.2 cm? The card overlaps by 2 cm.

13. A garden roller is in the form of a cylinder of radius 0.25 m and width 0.7 m. In four revolutions of the roller what area of lawn does it roll?

VOLUME OF A CYLINDER

We can think of a cylinder as a solid of uniform circular cross-section. Its volume, V, is therefore found by multiplying the area of the cross-section by the length, so $V = \pi r^2 \times h$

i.e. $$V = \pi r^2 h$$

EXERCISE 7f

a) Find the volume inside a hollow cylinder of radius 9.8 cm and height 6.7 cm.
b) What is its capacity in litres ?

a) $r = 9.8$ $h = 6.7$

$V = \pi r^2 h$

$= \pi \times (9.8)^2 \times 6.7$

$= 2021$

(Check: $V \approx 3 \times 100 \times 7 = 2100$)

The volume is 2020 cm³ correct to 3 s.f.

b)   the capacity of the cylinder $= 2021 \div 1000$ litres

$= 2.021$ litres

$= 2.02$ litres correct to 3 s.f.

In each question from 1 to 8, find the volume of the cylinder whose measurements are given. First make sure that the units are consistent.

1. Radius 6 cm, height 3.8 cm   **5.** Radius 7.6 cm, height 7.3 cm

2. Radius 3.2 cm, height 8 cm   **6.** Radius 28 cm, height 14 cm

3. Radius 150 cm, height 3 m   **7.** Radius 58 cm, height 0.07 m

4. Radius 0.6 cm, height 9 mm   **8.** Radius 1.2 m, height 68 cm.

9. A cylindrical water tank is of radius 36 cm. How much water is there in the tank when the depth of water is 15 cm? Give your answer in
    a) cm^3 b) litres.

10. A solid cylinder of gold has a radius of 2.5 cm and a height of 2.2 cm. One cubic centimetre of gold has a mass of 19.3 g.
    Find   a) the volume of the cylinder
           b) the mass of the gold.

11. Cement is used to fill cylindrical holes of diameter 20 cm and depth 32 cm.
    a) Find the volume of one hole.
    b) If the amount of cement available is 201 100 cm^3, how many holes will it fill?

Find the radius of a cylinder of volume 72 cm^3 and height 9 cm.

$$V = 72 \qquad h = 9$$

$$V = \pi r^2 h$$

$$72 = \pi \times r^2 \times 9$$

$$\frac{72}{\pi \times 9} = r^2$$

$$r^2 = 2.546$$

$$r = 1.595$$

The radius is 1.60 cm correct to 3 s.f.

$$\left(\text{Check: } r^2 \approx \frac{72}{3 \times 9} = \frac{28}{3}, \text{ i.e. } r \approx \frac{5}{3} = 1.\dot{6} \right)$$

In each question from 12 to 17, find the missing measurement of the cylinder.

	Radius	Height	Volume
12.	3.1 cm		72 cm³
13.	11 cm		1024 cm³
14.		1.6 m	15 m³
15.		0.7 m	9.83 m³
16.	3.8 cm		760 cm³
17.		0.12 cm	0.56 cm³

---

50 litres of water are poured into a cylindrical tank of radius 0.3 m. Find the depth of water in the tank in centimetres.

$$\text{Volume} = 50 \text{ litres}$$
$$= 50\,000 \text{ cm}^3$$
$$V = 50\,000, \quad r = 0.3 \times 100 = 30$$
$$V = \pi r^2 h$$
$$50\,000 = \pi \times 30^2 \times h$$
$$\frac{50\,000}{\pi \times 30^2} = h$$
$$h = 17.68$$

The depth of water is 17.7 cm correct to 3 s.f.

---

18. 1 m³ of water fills a cylindrical drum of radius 50 cm. Find the height of the drum.

19. Water from a full rectangular tank measuring 1 m by 2 m by 0.5 m is emptied into a cylindrical tank and fills it to a depth of 1.2 m.

Find   a) the volume of water involved

b) the diameter of the cylindrical tank.

20. A cylindrical metal rod of radius 1 cm and length 80 cm is melted down and recast into a cylindrical rod of radius 2 cm. How long is the new rod?

21. A cylindrical water butt has a diameter of 80 cm and a height of 1 m. It is half full of water. If a further 20 100 cm³ of water are poured in, find the new depth of water.

22. Water pours out of a cylindrical pipe at the rate of 1 m/s. The diameter of the pipe is 3 cm. How much water comes out in 1 minute?

CONES

VOLUME OF A CONE

We already know that the volume of a pyramid is given by

$\frac{1}{3}$ × area of base × perpendicular height

where a pyramid is a solid with a flat base and which comes up to a point called the vertex.

This definition applies to a cone so the volume of a cone is given by

$V = \frac{1}{3}$ × area of circular base × perpendicular height

i.e. $V = \frac{1}{3}\pi r^2 h$

A cone whose vertex is directly above the centre of the base is called a *right* circular cone; this is the only type of cone that we deal with in this book.

EXERCISE 7g

Find the volume of a cone of base radius 3.2 cm and of height 7.2 cm.

$$r = 3.2 \qquad h = 7.2$$

$$V = \tfrac{1}{3}\pi r^2 h$$

$$= \frac{\pi \times (3.2)^2 \times 7.2}{3}$$

$$= 77.20$$

$$\left(\text{Check: } V \approx \frac{3 \times 10 \times 7}{3} = 70 \right)$$

The volume is 77.2 cm³ correct to 3 s.f.

In each question from 1 to 6 find the volume of the cone whose dimensions are given.

1. Base radius 9 cm, height 20 cm

2. Base radius 2.2 cm, height 5.8 cm

3. Base radius 26.8 cm, height 104 cm

4. Base radius 0.6 cm, height 1.4 cm

5. Base diameter 4.2 cm, height 5.9 cm

6. Base diameter 0.62 m and height 106 cm. Give the volume in cubic metres.

7.

A tower of a toy fort is formed by placing a cone on top of a cylinder. The total height of the tower is 20 cm, the common radius is 5 cm and the height of the cone is 8 cm. Find the volume of the tower.

8.

A *frustum* of a cone is formed by cutting the top off a cone.

The original cone has base radius 6 cm and height 10 cm. The part cut off has base radius 3 cm and height 5 cm. Find the volume of the frustum.

9.

A cylindrical piece of wood of radius 3.6 cm and height 8.4 cm has a conical hole cut in it. The cone has the same radius and the same height as the cylinder. Find the volume of the remaining solid.

10.

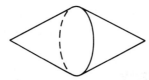

A solid is formed of two equal cones whose diameters are equal to their heights. The distance from the vertex of one cone to the vertex of the other is 12 cm. Find the volume of the solid.

SURFACE AREA OF A CONE

The curved surface area of a cone is given by

$$A = \pi r l$$

where l is the *slant* height.

EXERCISE 7h

In each question from 1 to 4 find the area of the curved surface of the cone whose measurements are given.

1. Radius 4 cm, slant height 10 cm

2. Radius 9.2 cm, slant height 15 cm

3. Radius 0.6 m, slant height 2.2 m

4. Radius 67 mm, slant height 72 mm

5. Find the total surface area of a cone of base radius 4 cm and with slant height 9 cm.

6. The radius of a cone is 6 cm and its perpendicular height is 8 cm. Find
a) the volume of the cone
b) its slant height
c) its curved surface area.

SPHERES

VOLUME OF A SPHERE

The volume of a sphere is given by the formula

$$V = \tfrac{4}{3}\pi r^3$$

EXERCISE 7i

In each question from 1 to 6 find the volume of the sphere whose radius is given.

1. 3 cm   **3.** 38 cm   **5.** 1.8 m

2. 7.2 cm   **4.** 0.62 cm   **6.** 13 mm

7. Find the volume of a hemisphere of radius 5 cm.

8. Twenty lead spheres of radius 1.2 cm are melted down and recast into a cuboid of length 8 cm and width 4 cm.
a) Find the volume of lead involved.
b) How high is the cuboid?

9. Find, in terms of π, the volume of a sphere of radius $1\frac{1}{2}$ cm. (Do not use a calculator.)

SURFACE AREA OF A SPHERE

The surface area, A, of a sphere of radius r is given by the formula

$$A = 4\pi r^2$$

EXERCISE 7j

In each question from 1 to 4 find the surface area of the sphere whose radius is given.

1. 9 cm   **3.** 41 cm

2. 4.5 cm   **4.** 0.9 cm

5. Find the curved surface area of a hemisphere of radius 23 cm.

6. 240 spheres of radius 0.22 m are to be painted. Each pot of paint contains enough to cover 26 m². How many pots of paint are needed?

PROBLEMS ON VOLUMES OF CONES AND SPHERES

EXERCISE 7k

1. The radius of a ball-bearing is 0.2 cm. How many ball-bearings can be made from 20 cm³ of metal?

2.

A toy is formed from a cone and a hemisphere. The radius of the hemisphere is 5.2 cm and the total height of the toy is 15 cm. Find the total volume.

3. A hollow metal sphere has an outer radius of 16 cm and its walls are 1 cm thick. Find

a) the inner radius

b) the volume of metal.

4.

A concrete bollard is in the shape of a cylinder surmounted by a hemisphere. The radius of the hemisphere and of the cylinder is 25 cm and the total height is 130 cm. Find the volume of the bollard.

5. Which has the greater volume, a cone of radius 3.5 cm and a perpendicular height of 12 cm or a sphere of radius 3.5 cm? What is the difference in volume?

6.

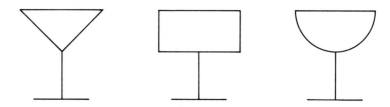

Three glasses are in the shape of a cone, a cylinder and a hemisphere respectively. The radius of each is 4 cm and the depth of the cone and of the cylinder is also 4 cm.

Find, in terms of π, the capacity of   a) the cone shaped glass
                                              b) the cylindrical glass
                                              c) the hemispherical glass.

7. Find in terms of π, the volume of

a) a sphere of radius 2 cm

b) a sphere of radius 8 cm.

The larger sphere is made of metal. It is melted down and made into spheres of radius 2 cm.

c) How many of the smaller spheres can be made from the larger sphere?

PROBLEMS ON SURFACE AREAS OF CONES AND SPHERES

EXERCISE 7I

1. Which has the greater surface area, a cone of radius 3.5 cm and slant height 9 cm or a sphere of radius 3.5 cm? What is the difference between the areas?

2. Find the total surface area of a hemisphere of radius 7 cm. ($\frac{22}{7}$ may be used for π.)

3.

A solid is formed from a cone joined to a hemisphere as shown in the diagram. Find

a) the slant height of the cone

b) the total surface area of the solid.

4. A sphere of radius 1.2 m and a cone of radius 1.2 m and slant height 2.6 m are being painted for a funfair. The tin of paint available contains enough paint to cover 30 m². Is there enough paint for the purpose ?
Give details of the extra amount needed or the amount of paint left over.

5.

A container is made of sheet metal in the form of an open cone joined to an open-ended cylinder. The radius of the cylinder and of the base of the cone is 8.6 cm, the depth of the cylinder is 4 cm and the slant height of the cone is 10.9 cm. Find the area of sheet metal used.

MIXED EXERCISE

EXERCISE 7m

In each question several alternative answers are given. Write down the letter that corresponds to the correct answer. Do not use your calculator, but remember that using $\pi \approx 3$ gives a quick estimate.

1. The circumference of a circle of radius 10 cm is
   A 18.8 cm   **B** 31.4 cm   **C** 62.8 cm   **D** 314 cm

2. The circumference of a circle is 15 cm. Its diameter is
   A 50.3 cm   **B** 4.77 cm   **C** 2.38 cm   **D** 9.54 cm

3. The area of a circle is 60 cm². Its radius is
   A 4.37 cm   **B** 9.55 cm   **C** 19.1 cm   **D** 3.09 cm

4. A sector of a circle of radius 8 cm contains an angle of 45°. Its area is
   A 25.1 m²   **B** 12.6 cm²   **C** 50.3 cm²   **D** 25.1 cm²

5. An arc of a circle of radius 4 cm subtends an angle of 36° at the centre of the circle. The length of the arc is
   A 50.3 cm   **B** 1.25 cm   **C** 5.03 cm   **D** 2.51 cm

6. A cylinder has radius 2 cm and height 5 cm. The area of its curved surface is
   A 62.8 cm²   **B** 31.4 cm²   **C** 126 cm²   **D** 98.7 cm²

7. A cylinder has radius 2 cm and height 9 cm. Its volume is
   A 509 cm³   **B** 113 cm³   **C** 56.5 cm³   **D** 226 cm³

8. A cylinder has radius 10 cm and height 10 cm. The area of its curved surface is
   A 100π cm³   **B** 1000π cm³   **C** 400π cm³   **D** 200π cm³

9. 400 cm³ of water fills a cylindrical container of radius 4 cm. The height of the container is
   A 63.7 cm   **B** 31.8 cm   **C** 7.96 cm   **D** 15.9 cm

10. A cylinder has radius 3 cm and height 5 cm. Its volume is
   A 30π cm³   **B** 45π cm³   **C** 30π cm²   **D** 48π cm³

8 SIMILAR SHAPES

SIMILAR FIGURES

Similar figures have exactly the same shape, i.e. one figure is an enlargement of the other.

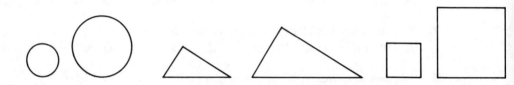

Enlarging a figure does not alter the angles. It does change the lengths of lines, but all the lengths change in the same ratio, i.e. if one line is doubled in length, *all* lines are doubled in length. These facts are particularly useful when we are dealing with similar triangles.

SIMILAR TRIANGLES

When we have a pair of similar triangles, corresponding angles are equal and corresponding sides are in the same ratio.

i.e. $\widehat{A} = \widehat{P}, \quad \widehat{B} = \widehat{Q}, \quad \widehat{C} = \widehat{R}$

and $\dfrac{AB}{PQ} = \dfrac{BC}{QR} = \dfrac{AC}{PR}$

$\left(\text{or } \dfrac{PQ}{AB} = \dfrac{QR}{BC} = \dfrac{PR}{AC} \right)$

136

It follows that any other pair of corresponding lines has the same ratio as the corresponding sides,

e.g.

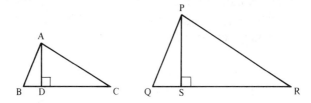

$$\frac{AD}{PS} = \frac{AB}{PQ} \quad \text{and} \quad \frac{\text{perimeter of } \triangle ABC}{\text{perimeter of } \triangle PQR} = \frac{AB}{PQ}$$

To check that two triangles are similar, we need to show that

either   a) the angles of one triangle are equal to the angles of the other triangle

or   b) the three pairs of corresponding sides are in the same ratio

or   c) there is one pair of equal angles and the sides containing these equal angles are in the same ratio.

EXERCISE 8a

In triangles PQR and XYZ, $P\widehat{Q}R = 16°$, $R\widehat{P}Q = 42°$, $X\widehat{Y}Z = 16°$ and $X\widehat{Z}Y = 122°$. State whether these triangles are similar.

In $\triangle$PQR $\widehat{R} = 122°$ (angles of a triangle)

In $\triangle$XYZ $\widehat{Y} = 42°$ (angles of a triangle)

$\therefore$ $\widehat{Q} = \widehat{X}$, $\widehat{P} = \widehat{Y}$ and $\widehat{R} = \widehat{Z}$

$\therefore$ $\triangle$s $\dfrac{PQR}{XYZ}$ are similar

(We line up the corresponding vertices.)

In questions 1 to 8 state whether the two triangles are similar, giving brief reasons:

1.

2.

3.

4.

5.

6.

7.

8.

9.

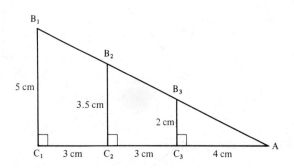

a) Show that $\triangle AB_1C_1$, $\triangle AB_2C_2$ and $\triangle AB_3C_3$ are all similar.

b) Find the values of $\dfrac{B_1C_1}{AC_1}$, $\dfrac{B_2C_2}{AC_2}$ and $\dfrac{B_3C_3}{AC_3}$

10.

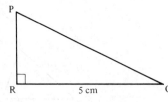

$\widehat{Q}$ is equal to $\widehat{A}$ in question 9.
Is $\triangle PQR$ similar to the triangles in question 9?

If it is, write down the value of $\dfrac{PR}{QR}$

and find PR.

11.

$\widehat{X}$ is equal to $\widehat{A}$ in question 9.
Write down the value of $\dfrac{ZY}{ZX}$ and find ZY.

ABE and DCE are two triangles drawn such that BEC and AED are straight lines and AB is parallel to CD. Show that △ABE is similar to △DEC.

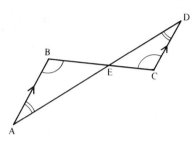

$$\widehat{B} = \widehat{C} \qquad (\text{alt. } \angle s)$$

$$\widehat{A} = \widehat{D} \qquad (\text{alt. } \angle s)$$

$$B\widehat{E}A = D\widehat{E}C \qquad (\text{vert. opp. } \angle s)$$

$\therefore \triangle s \dfrac{BEA}{CED}$ are similar.

12.

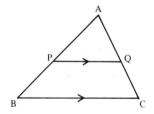

If PQ is parallel to BC, show that △APQ is similar to △ABC.

13.

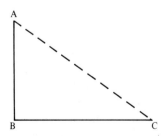

BC is the shadow cast by a flagpole AB. QR is the shadow cast by a stick PQ. Are △ABC and △PQR similar?

14.

LM is a ladder leaning against a vertical wall with its foot on level ground. PQ is a vertical stick placed so that one end Q is on the ground and the other end P is on the ladder. Show that △LMN and △PMQ are similar.

15.

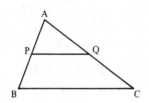

In △ABC, P is the midpoint of AB and Q is the midpoint of AC. Show that △APQ and △ABC are similar.

16.

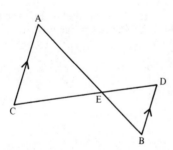

AB and CD are two straight lines that intersect at E in such a way that AC is parallel to DB. Show that △ACE is similar to △BDE.

17.

XS and YT are both perpendicular to WZ. Show that △XSZ and △YTZ are similar.

USING SIMILAR TRIANGLES ────────────────────────

If we can find a pair of similar triangles we can then use their properties to find angles or lengths of sides.

EXERCISE 8b

In △ABC, X is a point on AB and Y is a point on AC such that AX = 3 cm, XB = 2 cm, AY = 4.5 cm and YC = 3 cm. Show that XY is parallel to BC.

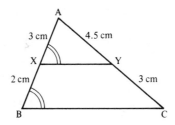

$\left(\text{We will first show that } \triangle\text{s } \dfrac{\text{AXY}}{\text{ABC}} \text{ are similar.}\right)$

AB = 5 cm and AX = 3 cm

$\therefore \qquad \dfrac{\text{AX}}{\text{AB}} = \dfrac{3}{5}$

AC = 7.5 cm and AY = 4.5 cm

$\therefore \qquad \dfrac{\text{AY}}{\text{AC}} = \dfrac{4.5}{7.5} = \dfrac{45}{75} = \dfrac{3}{5}$

$\widehat{\text{A}}$ is common to △AXY and △ABC

$\therefore \quad \triangle\text{s } \dfrac{\text{AXY}}{\text{ABC}} \text{ are similar}$

$\therefore \quad \text{A}\widehat{\text{X}}\text{Y} = \text{A}\widehat{\text{B}}\text{C}$

With respect to XY and BC these are corresponding angles.

$\therefore \quad$ XY is parallel to BC.

1.

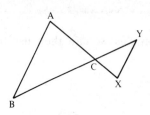

The straight lines AX and BY intersect at C. AC = 4 cm, BC = 6 cm, CY = 3 cm and CX = 2 cm. Show that △ACB and △XCY are similar and hence prove that AB is parallel to XY.

2.

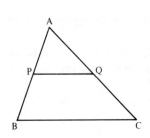

In △ABC, AB = 6 cm and AC = 8 cm. P is the midpoint of AB and Q is the midpoint of AC. Show that △APQ and △ABC are similar. Hence prove that PQ is parallel to BC.

3.

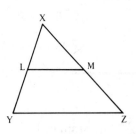

In △XYZ, L is the midpoint of XY and M is the midpoint of XZ. Write down the values of $\dfrac{XL}{XY}$ and $\dfrac{XM}{XZ}$. Are △XLM and △XYZ similar? Is LM parallel to YZ?

4.

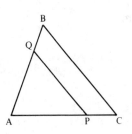

In △ABC, P is a point on AC and Q is a point on AB such that
$$\frac{AQ}{AB} = \frac{2}{3} \quad \text{and} \quad \frac{AP}{AC} = \frac{2}{3}$$
Show that △APQ is similar to △ACB.
If $\widehat{A} = 70°$ and $\widehat{APQ} = 50°$, find $\widehat{ABC}$.

5.

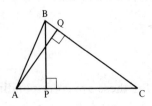

In △ABC, AQ is perpendicular to BC and BP is perpendicular to AC. Show that △BPC and △AQC are similar. Hence show that
$$\frac{CP}{CQ} = \frac{BC}{AC}$$

6. Use the diagram and the results from question 5 to show that, if PQ is joined, △CPQ is similar to △CBA. Is PQ parallel to AB?

In △ABC, P is a point on AB and Q is a point on AC such that PQ is parallel to BC. AP = 5 cm, PB = 2 cm and AQ = 7 cm. Find AC.

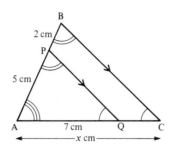

$$\widehat{ABC} = \widehat{APQ} \quad (\text{corresponding} \angle s)$$

$$\widehat{ACB} = \widehat{AQP} \quad (\text{corresponding} \angle s)$$

$\widehat{A}$ is common to △ABC and △APQ

∴ $\triangle s \dfrac{ABC}{APQ}$ are similar.

∴ $\dfrac{AC}{AQ} = \dfrac{AB}{AP}$

∴ $\dfrac{x}{7} = \dfrac{7}{5}$

$$x = \frac{7}{5} \times 7$$

$$= \frac{49}{5}$$

$$= 9.8$$

∴ AC = 9.8 cm

7.

 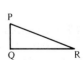

The shadow cast by a tree AB is BC, where BC = 20 m. The shadow cast by a stick PQ is QR, where QR = 4 m. If PQ = 1 m, find the height of the tree.

8. Try using the method described in question 7 to find the height of a tree, lamp post or building near you. You will need a one metre rule, a long tape measure (or use the rule and a piece of chalk) and a sunny day!

9.

LM is a ladder leaning against a vertical wall LN with its foot, M, on level ground such that NM = 1.5 m. PQ is a straight stick placed so that it is vertical, with one end P on the ladder and the other end Q resting on the ground. If QM = 0.5 m and PM = 2 m, find the length of the ladder.

10. Here is a way to find (roughly) the width of a river without crossing it. Place a stake B on one bank opposite a landmark A (such as a tree) on the other bank. Walk a distance of 5 m along the bank at right angles to AB and place another stake C. Walk another 1 m in the same direction and place another stake D. Now walk at right angles to BD until A and C are in line, then place a stake E. The width of the river is five times the distance between D and E. Draw a diagram showing this and explain why it works.

11. In △ABC, P is a point on AC and Q is a point on BC such that PQ is parallel to AB.

a) Show that △ABC and △PQC are similar.

b) If AC = 8 cm, BC = 6 cm and PC = 5 cm find QC.

c) Find BQ.

d) Write down the values of AP : PC and BQ : QC.

12.

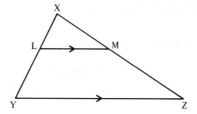

L and M are points on the sides XY and XZ respectvely of a triangle XYZ such that LM is parallel to YZ.

a) Show that △XLM and △XYZ are similar.

b) If XY = 6 cm, XZ = 10 cm and XM = 4 cm, find XL.

c) Find MZ.

d) Write down the values of XL : LY and XM : MZ.

13.

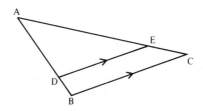

In △ABC, D is a point on AB and E is a point on AC such that DE is parallel to BC.

a) Show that △ADE and △ABC are similar.

b) If AE = 8 cm, AC = 10 cm and AB = 5 cm, find AD.

c) Write down the values of AD : DB and AE : EC.

14. In △ABC, X is a point on AB and Y is a point on AC such that XY is parallel to BC.

a) Show that △AXY and △ABC are similar.

b) If AB = 24 cm, AC = 30 cm and AX = 8 cm, find AY.

c) Write down the values of AX : XB and AY : YC.

THE INTERCEPT THEOREM

From the last exercise we can see that

> if a line is drawn parallel to one side of a triangle it divides the other two sides in the same ratio.

This is known as the intercept theorem, and can now be used.

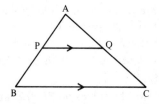

For example, in $\triangle ABC$, PQ is parallel to BC.

$\therefore \qquad \dfrac{AP}{PB} = \dfrac{AQ}{QC} \quad$ (intercept theorem)

EXERCISE 8c

In $\triangle LMN$, XY is drawn parallel to MN such that $LX = 8\,cm$, $LY = 12\,cm$ and $XM = 3\,cm$. Find YN.

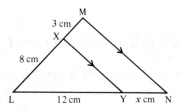

Let YN be x cm

$$\frac{x}{12} = \frac{3}{8} \quad \text{(intercept theorem)}$$

$${}^1\!\cancel{12} \times \frac{x}{\cancel{12}_1} = {}^1\!\cancel{12} \times \frac{3}{\cancel{8}_2}$$

$$x = 4.5$$

$\therefore \qquad\qquad YN = 4.5\,cm$

In each question from 1 to 8, find the length of the line marked x. All measurements are in centimetres.

1.

5.

2.

6.

3.

7.

4.

8.

9.

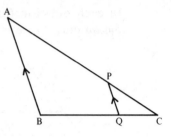

In △ABC, PQ is drawn parallel to AB
such that AC = 18 cm and PC = 6 cm.
If BC = 12 cm, find BQ.

10.

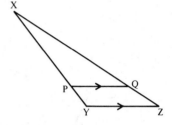

In △XYZ, PQ is drawn parallel to YZ.
If XQ = 12 cm, QZ = 3 cm and
XY = 10 cm, find PY.

DIVIDING A LINE INTO A GIVEN NUMBER OF EQUAL PARTS

Suppose that we want to divide the line drawn below into three equal
parts.

We can do it with a ruler, i.e. measure AB, calculate one third of its length
and then measure this distance from A and from B.

Using the intercept theorem, however, we can divide AB into three equal
parts without any measuring.

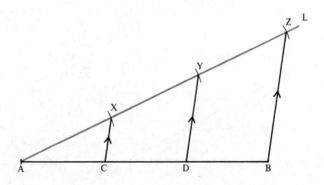

1. Draw a line AL at an angle to AB. (Any angle will do but one of about 30° is convenient.)

2. Open your compasses to any radius. (Roughly 3 cm is a convenient radius to work with in this case.)

3. With the point on A draw an arc to cut AL at X.

4. Without changing the radius, move the point to X and draw an arc to cut AL at Y.

5. Without changing the radius, move the point to Y and draw an arc to cut AL at Z.

6. Join ZB.

7. Draw lines parallel to ZB through X and Y to cut AB at C and D.

Now C and D divide AB into three equal lengths.

To divide AB into five equal parts, we cut five equal lengths off AL.

EXERCISE 8d

1. Describe some advantages and disadvantages of the two methods given for dividing a line into a number of equal parts.

2. Draw a line 10 cm long. Divide it into three equal parts by
a) calculation and measurement   b) construction.

3. Draw a line 9 cm long. Divide it into five equal parts by
a) calculation and measurement   b) construction.
Which of these two methods looks more accurate?

4. Draw a line AB that is 11 cm long. Divide AB into five equal parts, by construction.

5. In the diagram, P, Q, R and S divide the line AB into five equal parts.

a) If the length of AP is x cm, write down, in terms of x, the lengths of AQ, AR, AS and AB.

b) Write down the values of the ratios AP : PB,   AQ : QB,   AR : RB, AS : SB.

6. Draw a line AB that is 12 cm long.
a) Divide AB into three equal parts by calculation and measurement.
b) Mark the point P on AB such that AP : PB = 2 : 1.
(The point P is said to divide AB in the ratio 2 : 1.)

7. Draw a line AB that is 15 cm long.

a) Divide AB into five equal parts by calculation and measurement.

b) Mark the point P on AB such that AP : PB = 2 : 3.
(The point P is said to divide AB in the ratio 2 : 3.)

8. Draw a line AB that is 13 cm long.

a) Divide AB into three equal parts by construction.

b) Mark the point P on AB such that AP : PB = 1 : 2.

c) Is it necessary to draw all three parallel lines in order to find P ?

9.

P is a point on the line XY such that XP : PY = 3 : 4. To find the point P, into how many equal parts must the line XY be divided ?

a) Draw a line XY that is 14 cm long. Find P by measurement.

b) Draw a line XY that is 16 cm long. Find P by construction, but draw only those parallel lines that are necessary.

AREAS OF SIMILAR FIGURES

These four squares are similar.

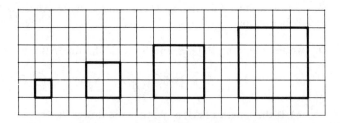

The ratio of the lengths of their sides is 1 : 2 : 3 : 4. Counting squares gives the ratio of their areas as 1 : 4 : 9 : 16.

But $1 : 4 : 9 : 16 = 1^2 : 2^2 : 3^2 : 4^2$

i.e. the ratio of the areas is equal to the ratio of the squares of corresponding lengths.

EXERCISE 8e

1. These four rectangles are similar.

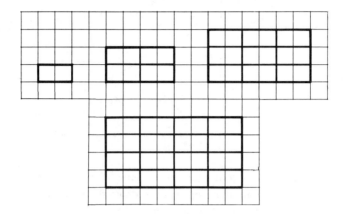

    a) Write down the ratio of the lengths of their bases.

    b) By counting rectangles, write down the ratio of their areas.

    Is there a relationship between these two ratios?

2. These four parallelograms are similar.

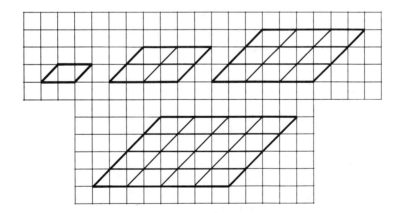

    a) Write down the ratio of the lengths of their bases.

    b) By counting parallelograms, write down the ratio of their areas.

    Is there a relationship between these two ratios?

3. These four triangles are similar.

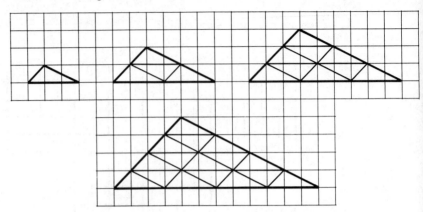

a) Write down the ratio of the lengths of their bases.

b) By counting triangles, write down the ratio of their areas.

What is the relationship between these two ratios ?

4.

 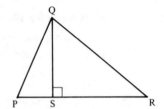

Triangles ABC and PQR are similar and the scale factor for enlarging △ABC to △PQR is 2, i.e. AB : PQ = 1 : 2.

a) If AC = 10 cm, find PR.

b) If BD = 6 cm, find QS.

c) Find the area of each triangle.

d) Find the ratio of the areas of these triangles.

In questions 5 to 8, the pairs of figures are similar. First find the length required and then find the area of each figure.

5. Find XW.

6. Find LN.

7. Find BC.

8. Find LP.

9. Using your answers to questions 5 to 8, complete the following table.

Similar figures	Ratio of sides	Ratio of areas
Triangles in question 5		
Triangles in question 6		
Rectangles in question 7		
Parallelograms in question 8		

What is the relationship between the ratio of the areas and the ratio of corresponding sides for each of these pairs of similar figures ?

THE RELATIONSHIP BETWEEN THE AREAS OF SIMILAR FIGURES

For similar figures, the ratio of their areas is equal to the ratio of the squares of corresponding lengths.

EXERCISE 8f

Parallelograms ABCD and PQRS are similar.
If $CD = 8\,cm$ and $RS = 12\,cm$, what is the value of the ratio of area ABCD to area PQRS?

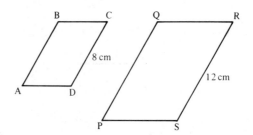

CD and RS are corresponding sides and

$$\frac{CD}{RS} = \frac{\overset{2}{\cancel{8}}}{\underset{3}{\cancel{12}}}$$

$$= \frac{2}{3}$$

$\therefore \qquad \dfrac{\text{area ABCD}}{\text{area PQRS}} = \dfrac{2^2}{3^2}$

$$= \frac{4}{9}$$

For each pair of similar figures in questions 1 to 6, write down the ratio of their areas:

1.

2.

3.

4.

5.

6.

In questions 7 to 9 the pictures are from catalogues, but the dimensions given are those of the actual object.

7.

700 mm

The width of the picture of the door is 20 mm. Find the ratio of the area of the picture of the door to the area of the actual door.

8.

60 cm

The width of the drawing of the chest is 3 cm. Find the ratio of the area of the front of the chest in the picture to the area of the front of the actual chest of drawers.

9.

15 cm

The dimension marked 15 cm in the picture of the tin is $2\frac{1}{2}$ cm. Find the ratio of the area of the catalogue picture to the area of the real tin.

Triangles ABC and XYZ are similar and $\widehat{C} = \widehat{Z}$. If the area of $\triangle ABC$ is 3.2 cm^2 and the area of $\triangle XYZ$ is 1.8 cm^2, find the value of AB : XY.

3.2 cm^2

1.8 cm^2

$$\frac{\text{area ABC}}{\text{area XYZ}} = \frac{3.2}{1.8}$$

$$= \frac{32^{16}}{18^{9}}$$

$$= \frac{16}{9}$$

but

$$\frac{\text{area ABC}}{\text{area XYZ}} = \frac{AB^2}{XY^2}$$

$$\therefore \quad \frac{AB^2}{XY^2} = \frac{16}{9}$$

$$\therefore \quad \frac{AB}{XY} = \frac{4}{3}$$

Find the value of AB : XY for each of the following pairs of similar figures.

10.

25 cm²

9 cm²

11.

18 cm²

8 cm²

12.

8 cm²

2 cm²

<u>**13.**</u>

2.5 cm²

1.6 cm²

14.

15.

Triangles ABC and PQR are similar, with $\widehat{A} = \widehat{P}$ and $\widehat{C} = \widehat{R}$. If AC = 4 cm, PR = 3 cm and area $\triangle PQR = 4.5$ cm², find area $\triangle ABC$.

AC and PR are corresponding sides and $\dfrac{AC}{PR} = \dfrac{4}{3}$

$\therefore$ $\dfrac{\text{area } \triangle ABC}{\text{area } \triangle PQR} = \dfrac{16}{9}$

i.e. $\dfrac{x}{4.5} = \dfrac{16}{9}$

i.e. $4.5 \times \dfrac{x}{4.5} = \dfrac{16}{9} \times 4.5$

$x = 8$

$\therefore$ area $\triangle ABC = 8$ cm²

16.

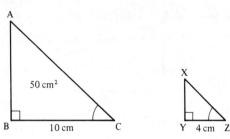

Triangles ABC and XYZ are similar. From the information given in the diagram, find the area of △XYZ.

17.

ABCD and PQRS are squares and AB : PQ = 3 : 2. If the area of ABCD is 36 cm², find the area of PQRS.

18. Rectangles ABCD and WXYZ are similar. If BD = 4 cm, XZ = 5 cm and area ABCD = 4.8 cm², find the area of WXYZ.

19.

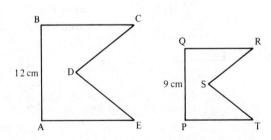

ABCDE and PQRST are similar shapes. If AB = 12 cm, PQ = 9 cm and area PQRST = 36 cm², find the area of ABCDE.

20. Triangles ABC and XYZ are both equilateral triangles.
If area △ABC : area △XYZ = 36 : 25, find the value of AB : XY.

21. Rectangles ABCD and PQRS are similar. If area ABCD = 2.5 cm², area PQRS = 4.9 cm² and AB = 1.5 cm, find PQ.

22.

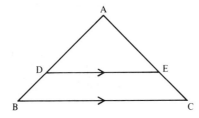

DE is parallel to BC. If AE = 10 cm, EC = 4 cm and the area of △ABC is 98 cm², find the area of △ADE.

HARDER EXAMPLES

EXERCISE 8g

In this exercise, it may be necessary first to show that the triangles are similar.

1.

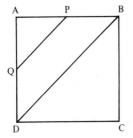

ABCD is a square of area 12 cm². P is the midpoint of AB and Q is the midpoint of AD. Find the area of △APQ.

2. Triangles ABC and PQR are similar. If the area of △ABC is four times that of △PQR and AB and PQ are corresponding sides, what is the value of AB : PQ?

3. The scale of a map is 1 : 1000. On the map, the area representing a mansion is 2 cm². What is the actual area in m² occupied by the mansion?

4.

The area of the larger circle is sixteen times that of the smaller circle. What is the ratio of the radii of the two circles ?

5. ABC is a triangle with X a point on AB and Y a point on AC such that XY is parallel to BC. If $AY = 3\,cm$, $YC = 4\,cm$ and $XB = 3\,cm$, find

a) AX   b) $\dfrac{\text{area } \triangle AXY}{\text{area } \triangle ABC}$ c) $\dfrac{\text{area } \triangle AXY}{\text{area trapezium XYCB}}$.

6.

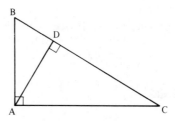

Triangle ABC has a right angle at A and AD is perpendicular to BC. The area of $\triangle ABD$ is $4\,cm^2$ and the area of $\triangle ADC$ is $5\,cm^2$. Find the ratio of the area of $\triangle ABD$ to the area of $\triangle ABC$ and hence the value of $AB : BC$.

7.

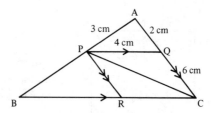

In the diagram, PQ is parallel to BC and PR is parallel to AC.
$AQ = 2\,cm$, $QC = 6\,cm$, $AP = 3\,cm$ and $PQ = 4\,cm$

a) Calculate   i) PB   ii) BR   iii) $\dfrac{\text{area } \triangle APQ}{\text{area } \triangle ABC}$ iv) $\dfrac{\text{area } \triangle BPR}{\text{area } \triangle ABC}$

b) If the area of triangle APQ is $a\,cm^2$, express in terms of a
   i) area $\triangle ABC$ ii) area $\triangle CPQ$

8. Construct a triangle ABC such that $BC = 10\,cm$, $AC = 9\,cm$ and $AB = 6\,cm$. Find a point D on AB and a point E on AC, such that DE is parallel to BC and the area of $\triangle ADE$ is one ninth of the area of $\triangle ABC$.

VOLUMES OF SIMILAR SHAPES

These four cubes are similar.

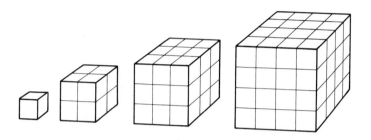

The ratios of the lengths of their sides is $1:2:3:4$. By counting cubes, the ratio of their volumes is $1:8:27:64$

$$\text{But } 1:8:27:64 = 1^3:2^3:3^3:4^3$$

i.e. the ratio of the volumes is equal to the ratio of the cubes of corresponding lengths.

EXERCISE 8h

1. These three solids are similar.

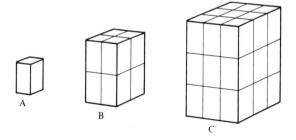

a) Write down the ratio of the lengths of the bases.

b) Write down the ratio of the lengths of the heights.

c) By counting cuboids equal in shape and size to the cuboid given in A, write down the ratio of the volumes.

Is there a relationship between your answers to (a), (b) and (c)?

2.

These are two similar rectangular blocks.

a) Write down the ratio of their
   i) longest edges   ii) depths   iii) heights.

b) By counting cubes of side 1 cm write down the ratio of their volumes.

Is there any relationship between the ratios in (a) and (b)?

3.

These three solids are spheres.

a) Write down the ratio of the radii of the three spheres.

b) If the volume of a sphere of radius r is given by the formula $V = \frac{4}{3}\pi r^3$ express the volume of each sphere as a multiple of π. Hence write down the ratio of their volumes.

Is there a relationship between the ratio found in (a) and the ratio found in (b)?

4. These three cans are similar cylinders.

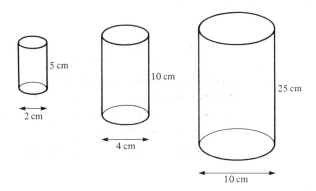

a) Write down the ratio of
   i) their heights   ii) their base radii

b) If the volume of a cylinder of height h and base radius r is given by
   the formula $V = \pi r^2 h$, express the capacity of each can in terms of π.
   Hence find the ratio of their capacities.

Is there a relationship between these ratios ?

THE RELATIONSHIP BETWEEN THE VOLUMES OF SIMILAR SHAPES

> For similar solids, the ratio of their volumes is equal to the
> ratio of the cubes of corresponding linear dimensions.

In the same way, the ratio of the capacities of similar containers is equal
to the ratio of the cubes of corresponding linear dimensions.

In problems where ratios are used to find an unknown quantity it is wise
to write down the ratio so that the unknown quantity is in the numerator
rather than in the denominator.

EXERCISE 8i

A sculptor is commissioned to create a bronze statue 2 m high. He begins by making a clay model 30 cm high.

a) Express, in its simplest form, the ratio of the height of the completed bronze statue to the height of the clay model.

b) If the total surface area of the model is 360 cm², find the total surface area of the statue.

c) If the volume of the model is 1000 cm³ find the volume of the statue.

a) $\dfrac{\text{height of bronze statue}}{\text{height of clay model}} = \dfrac{200}{30} = \dfrac{20}{3}$

b) $\dfrac{\text{surface area of statue}}{\text{surface area of model}} = \dfrac{20^2}{3^2}$

i.e. $\dfrac{\text{surface area of statue}}{360} = \dfrac{400}{9}$

∴ $\text{surface area of statue} = \dfrac{400}{9_1} \times \overset{40}{360} \text{cm}^2$

$= 16\,000 \text{ cm}^2$

$= 1.6 \text{ m}^2$

c) $\dfrac{\text{volume of statue}}{\text{volume of model}} = \dfrac{20^3}{3^3}$

i.e. $\dfrac{\text{volume of statue}}{1000} = \dfrac{8000}{27}$

∴ $\text{volume of statue} = \dfrac{8000}{27} \times 1000 \text{ cm}^3$

$= \dfrac{8000 \times 1000}{27 \times 1\,000\,000} \text{ m}^2$

$= \dfrac{8}{27} \text{ m}^3$

In this exercise objects referred to in the same question are mathematically similar.

1. The sides of two cubes are in the ratio $2:1$. What is the ratio of their volumes?

2. The radii of two spheres are in the ratio $3:4$. What is the ratio of their volumes?

3. Two regular tetrahedrons have volumes in the ratio $8:27$. What is the ratio of their sides?

4. Two right cones have volumes in the ratio $64:27$. What is the ratio of
   a) their heights   b) their base radii?

5. Two similar bottles are such that one is twice as high as the other. What is the ratio of   a) their surface areas   b) their capacities?

6. Each linear dimension of a model car is $\frac{1}{10}$ of the corresponding car dimension. Find the ratio of
   a) the areas of their windscreens   b) the capacities of their boots
   c) the widths of the cars   d) the number of wheels they have.

7. Three similar jugs have heights $8\,cm$, $12\,cm$ and $16\,cm$. If the smallest jug holds $\frac{1}{2}$ pint, find the capacities of the other two.

8. A cylindrical cola can $10\,cm$ high costs $2\,p$ to make. What is the cost of a can standing $15\,cm$ high?

9. Three similar drinking glasses have heights $7.5\,cm$, $9\,cm$ and $10.5\,cm$. If the tallest glass holds 343 centilitres find the capacities of the other two.

10. The capacities of three similar jugs are $486\,cl$, $1152\,cl$ and $2250\,cl$.
   a) If the jug with the largest capacity is $15\,cm$ high, find the heights of the other two.   b) If the base area of the smallest jug is $36\,cm^2$ find the base areas of the other two.

11. A toy manufacturer produces model cars which are similar in every way to the actual cars. If the ratio of the door area of the model to the door area of the car is $1:2500$ find
   a) the ratio of their lengths
   b) the ratio of the capacities of their petrol tanks
   c) the width of the model, if the actual car is $150\,cm$ wide
   d) the area of the rear window of the actual car if the area of the rear window of the model is $3\,cm^2$.

12. The ratio of the areas of two similar labels on two similar jars of coffee is $144:169$. Find the ratio of   a) the heights of the two jars   b) their capacities.

13. A wax model has a mass of $1\,kg$. Find the mass of a similar model which is twice as tall and made from metal eight times as heavy as wax.

The radius of a spherical soap bubble increases by 5%. Find, correct to the nearest whole number, the percentage increase in
a) its surface area   b) its volume.

If the original radius is r the increased radius is $\dfrac{105}{100} \times r$ i.e. $1.05r$

Therefore
$$\frac{\text{new radius}}{\text{old radius}} = \frac{1.05r}{r}$$

$$= \frac{1.05}{1}$$

a) $\dfrac{\text{new surface area}}{\text{original surface area}} = \dfrac{(1.05)^2}{1^2}$

$$= 1.1025$$

i.e. new surface area $= 1.1025$ of the original surface area

i.e. new surface area $= 1.1025 \times 100\%$ of original surface area

$$= 110.25\% \text{ of the original surface area.}$$

The surface area has therefore increased by 10%.

b) $\dfrac{\text{new volume}}{\text{original volume}} = \dfrac{(1.05)^3}{1^3}$

$$= \frac{1.158}{1}$$

$$= 1.158$$

i.e. new volume $= 1.158$ of the original volume

$$= 115.8\% \text{ of the original volume}$$

The volume has therefore increased by 16%.

14. The radius of one sphere is 10% more than the radius of another. Find, correct to the nearest whole number, the percentage difference in
a) their surface areas   b) their volumes.

15. The radius of a spherical snowball increases by 80%. Find, correct to the nearest whole number, the percentage increase in   a) its surface area   b) its volume.

16. The side of one cube is 20% greater than the side of another. Find, correct to the nearest whole number, the percentage difference in   a) their surface areas   b) their volumes.

17. The volume of a cone increases by 100%. Find the percentage increase in

a) its height   b) its base radius   c) its surface area.

Give your answers correct to the nearest whole number.

18. A spherical grapefruit has a diameter of 10 cm. If its peel is 1 cm thick, find, correct to the nearest whole number, the percentage of the volume of the grapefruit that is thrown away as peel.

MIXED EXERCISES

EXERCISE 8j

1. In $\triangle ABC$, P is a point on AB and Q is a point on AC such that AP $= 5$ cm, PB $= 10$ cm,   AQ $= 4$ cm   and   QC $= 8$ cm.   Show that PQ is parallel to BC.

2. The ratio of the areas of two similar triangles is $49 : 25$. What is the ratio of corresponding sides ?

3. In $\triangle XYZ$, P is a point on XY and Q is a point on XZ such that PQ is parallel to YZ.

a) Show that $\triangle XPQ$ and $\triangle XYZ$ are similar

b) If XY $= 36$ cm, XZ $= 30$ cm and XP $= 24$ cm,
    find   i) XQ   ii) QZ

c) Write down the values of XP : PY and PQ : YZ.

4. Draw a line 9.7 cm long. Use a constructional method to divide it into four equal parts.

5.

Triangles ABC and DEF are similar. If the area of $\triangle ABC$ is 12.5 cm², the area of $\triangle DEF$ is 4.5 cm², and AB $= 5$ cm find

a) DE   b) the value of AC : DF   c) the value of EF : BC.

EXERCISE 8k

1. Two similar rectangles have areas in the ratio $49 : 81$. What is the ratio of
a) their longer sides   b) their shorter sides?

2.

Triangles ABC and DEF are similar. From the information given in the diagrams, find
a) the area of $\triangle ABC$ b) the length of FE   c) ratio $AC : FD$.

3.

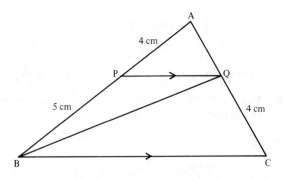

Use the information given in the diagram to find
a) AQ

b) $PQ : BC$

c) $\dfrac{\text{area } \triangle APQ}{\text{area } \triangle ABC}$

d) $\dfrac{\text{area } \triangle APQ}{\text{trapezium PQCB}}$

e) $\dfrac{\text{area } \triangle APQ}{\text{area } \triangle BPQ}$

f) $\dfrac{\text{area } \triangle BPQ}{\text{area } \triangle BCQ}$

4.

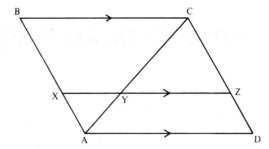

AC is the diagonal of a rhombus ABCD. The line XYZ is parallel to AD, AX = 3 cm and AB = 9 cm. Find

a) $\dfrac{XY}{BC}$ b) $\dfrac{AY}{AC}$ c) $\dfrac{CY}{AC}$ d) $\dfrac{YZ}{AD}$

e) $\dfrac{\text{area } \triangle AXY}{\text{area } \triangle ABC}$ f) $\dfrac{\text{area } \triangle CYZ}{\text{area } \triangle ACD}$

5. An inverted hollow cone is filled with water to half its depth. What fraction of the available capacity is filled?

9 INFORMATION MATRICES

MATRICES AS STORES OF INFORMATION

In Book 3A we have seen how matrices can be used for solving simultaneous equations. The advantage of this method for computer solutions is that it does not require decisions to be made. The fact that it is generally the longest method does not matter when computers do the solution because computers work fast!

Another widespread application of matrices in computer work is to store information.

For example, a hotel supplies three types of packed meal, A, B, and C. On Saturday, 5 meals of type A, 10 meals of type B and 7 meals of type C are ordered. On Sunday, 12 meals of type A, 6 meals of type B and 9 meals of type C are ordered. This information can be displayed in a matrix, $\mathbf{M}$, where

$$\mathbf{M} = \begin{array}{c} \\ \text{Sat} \\ \text{Sun} \end{array} \begin{array}{c} \text{A} \quad \text{B} \quad \text{C} \\ \begin{pmatrix} 5 & 10 & 7 \\ 12 & 6 & ⑨ \end{pmatrix} \end{array}$$

The columns represent the different meals and the rows represent the different days. The ringed entry indicates that 9 type C meals were ordered on Sunday.

We chose to use a 2×3 matrix, but we could equally well represent the information in a 3×2 matrix, $\mathbf{N}$, where

$$\mathbf{N} = \begin{array}{c} \\ \text{A} \\ \text{B} \\ \text{C} \end{array} \begin{array}{c} \text{Sat} \quad \text{Sun} \\ \begin{pmatrix} 5 & 12 \\ 10 & 6 \\ 7 & 9 \end{pmatrix} \end{array}$$

EXERCISE 9a

1. The matrix A shows the number of acres of land used for different purposes on two farms, A and B.

$$A = \begin{array}{c} \\ \text{Farm A} \\ \text{Farm B} \end{array} \begin{array}{ccc} \text{Wheat} & \text{Grazing} & \text{Other crops} \\ \begin{pmatrix} 100 & 300 & 50 \\ 200 & 0 & 300 \end{pmatrix} \end{array}$$

Copy this matrix and

a) ring the entry that gives the number of acres on Farm A used for other crops

b) put a square round the entry that gives the number of acres used for wheat on Farm B

c) find the total number of acres used for growing wheat on both farms.

2. The matrix T shows the number of packets of different brands of coffee sold in one week in three supermarkets A, B and C.

$$T = \begin{array}{c} \\ A \\ B \\ C \end{array} \begin{array}{ccc} \text{Brand X} & \text{Brand Y} & \text{Brand Z} \\ \begin{pmatrix} 50 & 25 & 37 \\ 100 & 150 & 89 \\ 92 & 250 & 340 \end{pmatrix} \end{array}$$

Copy this matrix and

a) ring the entry that gives the number of packets of Brand Y sold in Supermarket C

b) put a square round the entry that gives the number of packets of Brand X sold in Supermarket A

c) find the total number of packets sold in Supermarket B.

3. A carpet manufacturer makes three grades of carpet. The matrix shows the number of metres of each grade ordered in each of four consecutive weeks.

$$\begin{array}{c} \\ \text{Week 1} \\ \text{Week 2} \\ \text{Week 3} \\ \text{Week 4} \end{array} \begin{array}{ccc} \text{Grade I} & \text{Grade II} & \text{Grade III} \\ \begin{pmatrix} 200 & 150 & 120 \\ 350 & 200 & 70 \\ 190 & 250 & 100 \\ 280 & 210 & 110 \end{pmatrix} \end{array}$$

Copy this matrix and give its size.

a) Ring the entry that gives the number of metres of Grade II carpet ordered in week 3.

b) Underline the entry that gives the number of metres of Grade III carpet ordered in week 2.

c) How many metres of grade III carpet were ordered over the four week period?

d) How many metres of carpet were ordered in week 2?

e) Show the same information in a 3×4 matrix, and underline the entry giving the number of metres of grade II carpet ordered in week 4.

4. In shop A, potatoes cost 10p per lb, carrots cost 8p per lb and parsnips cost 12p per lb. In shop B, potatoes are 12p per lb, carrots are 9p per lb and parsnips are 10p per lb.

a) Show this information in a 2×3 matrix, **M**.

b) Ring the entry giving the cost of carrots in shop B.

c) Mr Smith buys 5lb of potatoes, 1lb of carrots and 2lb of parsnips. Show this information in a column matrix, **P**.

d) How much would Mr Smith's purchases cost in shop **A**?

e) Find the product **MP**.

f) What meaning can you give to the two entries in the product **MP**?

5. A school's supplier stocks chalk in three boxes of different sizes; Box A which contains 20 sticks of chalk, Box B which contains 50 sticks of chalk and Box C which contains 100 sticks of chalk. The matrix **M** shows the numbers of each box supplied in each of three months.

$$\mathbf{M} = \begin{array}{c} \\ A \\ B \\ C \end{array} \begin{array}{ccc} \text{Jan} & \text{Feb} & \text{Mar} \\ \left(\begin{array}{ccc} 200 & 100 & 200 \\ 50 & 10 & 20 \\ 150 & 70 & 100 \end{array} \right) \end{array}$$

a) How many sticks of chalk are supplied in January?

b) How many sticks of chalk are supplied in March?

c) Write down a 1×3 matrix, **N**, showing the number of sticks of chalk in each type of box.

d) Can you find a way of multiplying N and M together to give the information asked for in parts (a) and (b)?

6. A vending machine accepts ten-pence, twenty-pence, and fifty-pence coins only. The matrix **A** shows the numbers of each coin in the machine when emptied on two separate occasions.

$$\mathbf{A} = \begin{array}{c} \\ \text{1st emptying} \\ \text{2nd emptying} \end{array} \begin{array}{ccc} 10p & 20p & 50p \\ \left(\begin{array}{ccc} 50 & 10 & 20 \\ 70 & 30 & 80 \end{array} \right) \end{array}$$

a) How many coins were in the machine the first time it was emptied?

b) Evaluate $\mathbf{A} \begin{pmatrix} 1 \\ 1 \\ 1 \end{pmatrix}$ and give a meaning to the entries.

c) How much money was in the machine the first time it was emptied?

d) Write down a column matrix, **V**, giving the value of each coin.

e) Can you multiply **A** and **V** together so that the entries in the result give the amount of money in the machine on each occasion that it was emptied?

GETTING INFORMATION FROM MATRICES

Consider again the matrix **M**, showing the numbers of each type of packed meal ordered on each day of a weekend where

$$\mathbf{M} = \begin{array}{c} \\ \text{Sat} \\ \text{Sun} \end{array} \begin{array}{ccc} \text{A} & \text{B} & \text{C} \\ \left(\begin{array}{ccc} 5 & 10 & 7 \\ 12 & 6 & 9 \end{array} \right) \end{array}$$

The matrix **P** gives the cost of each type of meal, where

$$\mathbf{P} = \begin{array}{c} \\ \text{A} \\ \text{B} \\ \text{C} \end{array} \begin{array}{c} £ \\ \left(\begin{array}{c} 3 \\ 5 \\ 4 \end{array} \right) \end{array}$$

Now the total cost of meals ordered on Saturday is

$$£(5 \times 3 + 10 \times 5 + 7 \times 4) = £93$$

and the total cost of meals ordered on Sunday is

$$£(12 \times 3 + 6 \times 5 + 9 \times 4) = £102$$

But $\mathbf{MP} = \left(\begin{array}{ccc} 5 & 10 & 7 \\ 12 & 6 & 9 \end{array} \right) \left(\begin{array}{c} 3 \\ 5 \\ 4 \end{array} \right) = \left(\begin{array}{c} 5 \times 3 + 10 \times 5 + 7 \times 4 \\ 12 \times 3 + 6 \times 5 + 9 \times 4 \end{array} \right) = \left(\begin{array}{c} 93 \\ 102 \end{array} \right)$

Hence the information giving the cost of meals ordered on Saturday and the cost of meals ordered on Sunday can be obtained from a matrix product,

i.e.
$$\mathbf{MP} = \begin{array}{c} \\ \text{Sat} \\ \text{Sun} \end{array} \begin{array}{c} £ \\ \left(\begin{array}{c} 93 \\ 102 \end{array} \right) \end{array}$$

Now consider the product **DM** where $\mathbf{D} = (1 \quad 1)$,

i.e. $(1 \quad 1) \left(\begin{array}{ccc} 5 & 10 & 7 \\ 12 & 6 & 9 \end{array} \right) = (5+12 \quad 10+6 \quad 7+9) = (17 \quad 16 \quad 16)$

Hence premultiplying **M** by $(1 \quad 1)$ effectively adds together the two entries in each column of **M**. Reference to **M** shows that this gives the total numbers of each meal ordered over the two days,

i.e.
$$\begin{array}{ccc} \text{A} & \text{B} & \text{C} \end{array}$$
$$\mathbf{DM} = (17 \quad 16 \quad 16)$$

If we post multiply **M** by $\begin{pmatrix} 1 \\ 1 \\ 1 \end{pmatrix}$, this gives

$$\begin{pmatrix} 5 & 10 & 7 \\ 12 & 6 & 9 \end{pmatrix} \begin{pmatrix} 1 \\ 1 \\ 1 \end{pmatrix} = \begin{pmatrix} 22 \\ 27 \end{pmatrix}$$

This time it is the entries in each row of **M** that are added, so the result gives the total number of meals ordered on each of the two days,

i.e.

$$\begin{array}{c} \\ \text{Sat.} \\ \text{Sun.} \end{array} \begin{pmatrix} \text{No. of meals} \\ 22 \\ 27 \end{pmatrix}$$

EXERCISE 9b

1. A tennis club has three teams of players, team A, team B and team C. Each team plays in a league tournament and the results are displayed in the matrix **M** where

$$\mathbf{M} = \begin{array}{c} \\ \text{A} \\ \text{B} \\ \text{C} \end{array} \begin{pmatrix} \text{Won} & \text{Drawn} & \text{Lost} \\ 7 & 4 & 2 \\ 6 & 2 & 3 \\ 5 & 3 & 5 \end{pmatrix}$$

If **N** = (1 1 1) and $\mathbf{P} = \begin{pmatrix} 1 \\ 1 \\ 1 \end{pmatrix}$

evaluate NM and MP and interpret the results.

Given that 2 points are awarded for a win, 1 point for a draw and no points for a lost match, evaluate **M** $\begin{pmatrix} 2 \\ 1 \\ 0 \end{pmatrix}$ and interpret the result.

2. A furniture manufacturer makes three different types of table, A, B and C. The orders for each type of table for three separate months are displayed in the matrix **T** where

$$\mathbf{T} = \begin{array}{c} \\ \text{I} \\ \text{II} \\ \text{III} \end{array} \begin{pmatrix} \text{A} & \text{B} & \text{C} \\ 10 & 5 & 4 \\ 3 & 15 & 2 \\ 4 & 10 & 10 \end{pmatrix}$$

The cost of raw materials for each type of table is given in the matrix **C** where

$$C = \begin{matrix} A \\ B \\ C \end{matrix} \begin{pmatrix} £ \\ 10 \\ 15 \\ 12 \end{pmatrix}$$

and the time taken to make each type of table is given in the matrix **R** where

$$R = \begin{matrix} A \\ B \\ C \end{matrix} \begin{pmatrix} \text{Time (hrs)} \\ 5 \\ 4 \\ 5 \end{pmatrix}$$

Evaluate the following products and in each case interpret the result.

a) **TC**   b) **TR**

If the cost of labour in making any table is £10 per hour, evaluate **TC + 10TR** and interpret the result.

3. In one block of flats a milkman has three customers, A, B, and C. The matrix **M** shows the number of redtop, goldtop and silvertop bottles of milk ordered by each customer for one particular week. The matrix **C** shows the cost (in pence) of one bottle of each type of milk.

$$\text{If } M = \begin{matrix} A \\ B \\ C \end{matrix} \begin{pmatrix} r & g & s \\ 7 & 0 & 14 \\ 0 & 0 & 20 \\ 0 & 10 & 5 \end{pmatrix} \quad \text{and} \quad C = \begin{matrix} r \\ g \\ s \end{matrix} \begin{pmatrix} \text{pence} \\ 26 \\ 27 \\ 25 \end{pmatrix} \quad \text{evaluate}$$

a) $(1 \quad 1 \quad 1)M$ b) $M \begin{pmatrix} 1 \\ 1 \\ 1 \end{pmatrix}$ c) **MC**   d) $(1 \quad 1 \quad 1)MC$

and in each case interpret the result.

4. A company has three factories, A, B and C. The matrix **E** shows the numbers of full-time, half-time and trainee employees at each factory. The matrix **W** shows the weekly wage paid to each category of employee.

$$E = \begin{matrix} A \\ B \\ C \end{matrix} \begin{pmatrix} \text{Full-time} & \text{Part-time} & \text{Trainee} \\ 10 & 4 & 3 \\ 8 & 2 & 6 \\ 15 & 12 & 5 \end{pmatrix} \quad \text{and} \quad W = \begin{pmatrix} £ \\ 120 \\ 50 \\ 60 \end{pmatrix} \begin{matrix} \text{Full-time} \\ \text{Part-time} \\ \text{Trainee} \end{matrix}$$

Evaluate   a) $E \begin{pmatrix} 1 \\ 1 \\ 1 \end{pmatrix}$ b) $(1 \quad 1 \quad 1)E$ c) **EW**   d) $(1 \quad 1 \quad 1)EW$

and in each case interpret the result.

5. The matrix **P** shows the numbers of men, women and children under 12 living in a hostel. The matrix **C** shows the daily calories required by a man, a woman and a child where

$$\mathbf{P} = \begin{array}{c} \text{Men} \quad \text{Women} \quad \text{Children} \\ (\ 10 \quad\quad 30 \quad\quad 45\ ) \end{array} \quad \text{and} \quad \mathbf{C} = \begin{array}{c} \\ \text{Man} \\ \text{Woman} \\ \text{Child} \end{array} \begin{array}{c} \text{Calories} \\ \begin{pmatrix} 2000 \\ 1400 \\ 1000 \end{pmatrix} \end{array}$$

Find   a) **PC**   b) $\mathbf{P} \begin{pmatrix} 1 \\ 1 \\ 1 \end{pmatrix}$ and in each case interpret the result.

6. A garment manufacturer needs supplies of three items; machine yarn (y), zips (z), and buttons (b). These items are available from two sources, A and B. Matrix **Q** shows the quantities of each item needed for each of four yearly quarters. Matrix **C** shows the cost of each item from each of the two suppliers.

$$\text{If} \quad \mathbf{Q} = \begin{array}{c} y \\ z \\ b \end{array}\begin{array}{cccc} \ \text{I} & \text{II} & \text{III} & \text{IV} \\ \begin{pmatrix} 50 & 70 & 50 & 80 \\ 70 & 60 & 70 & 20 \\ 100 & 200 & 200 & 100 \end{pmatrix} \end{array} \quad \mathbf{C} = \begin{array}{c} A \\ B \end{array}\begin{array}{c} y \quad z \quad b \\ \begin{pmatrix} 10 & 20 & 2 \\ 12 & 15 & 3 \end{pmatrix}\end{array}$$

evaluate   a) **CQ**   b) $\mathbf{CQ}\begin{pmatrix} 1 \\ 1 \\ 1 \\ 1 \end{pmatrix}$

and interpret the results. Which supplier is cheaper if the cost is considered c) for the first quarter only   d) for the whole year?

7. A small firm employs three people, A, B and C. Matrix **W** shows the standard hourly rate (s.r.) and the overtime rate (o.r.) of each employee and matrix **T** shows the number of hours worked at the standard rate and the number of hours worked at the overtime rate for each employee for one week.

$$\text{If} \quad \mathbf{W} = \begin{array}{c} A \\ B \\ C \end{array}\begin{array}{c} \text{s.r.(£)} \quad \text{o.r.(£)} \\ \begin{pmatrix} 3 & 4 \\ 2.5 & 3 \\ 4 & 6 \end{pmatrix}\end{array} \quad \text{and} \quad \mathbf{T} = \begin{array}{c} \text{s.r.} \\ \text{o.r.} \end{array}\begin{array}{c} A \quad B \quad C \\ \begin{pmatrix} 36 & 30 & 10 \\ 5 & 4 & 1 \end{pmatrix}\end{array}$$

evaluate **WT** and state what the figures *x, y* and *z* in the leading diagonal of **WT**, represent.

If Z is the matrix $\begin{pmatrix} x & 0 & 0 \\ 0 & y & 0 \\ 0 & 0 & z \end{pmatrix}$ evaluate $(1\ \ 1\ \ 1)\mathbf{Z}\begin{pmatrix} 1 \\ 1 \\ 1 \end{pmatrix}$

and interpret the result.

8. The town Export has two mainline railway stations A and B. There are also four suburban railway stations C, D, E and F. Train services between A, B and C, D, E, F are provided, or not, as indicated by 1, or 0, in the matrix T, where

$$T = \begin{array}{c} \\ A \\ B \end{array} \begin{array}{c} C \quad D \quad E \quad F \\ \begin{pmatrix} 1 & 0 & 1 & 0 \\ 1 & 1 & 0 & 1 \end{pmatrix} \end{array}$$

Mainline services from stations A and B to the towns X, Y and Z, exist or not as indicated by 1 or 0 in the matrix S where

$$S = \begin{array}{c} \\ X \\ Y \\ Z \end{array} \begin{array}{c} A \quad B \\ \begin{pmatrix} 1 & 0 \\ 0 & 1 \\ 1 & 1 \end{pmatrix} \end{array}$$

Find the product **ST** and interpret the result.

FINDING THE APPROPRIATE MATRIX

We have seen that premultiplying a matrix by an appropriate row of 1's, adds the entries in the columns of the matrix.

Similarly postmultiplying a matrix by an appropriate column of 1's, adds the entries in the rows of the matrix.

Consider again the matrices **M** and **P** listing the orders for different meals and the price of the meals, as introduced earlier in this chapter.

On page 177 we found the product MP where

$$MP = \begin{array}{c} \\ Sat \\ Sun \end{array} \begin{array}{c} £ \\ \begin{pmatrix} 93 \\ 102 \end{pmatrix} \end{array}$$

i.e. **MP** lists the cost of meals ordered on Saturday and the cost of meals ordered on Sunday.

The total cost of the meals over the weekend is obtained by adding the entries in **MP**. To find a matrix operation which does this, we need an operation which adds the entries in the column. This can be achieved by premultiplying **MP** by a row of 1's. As there are two entries in the column of **MP**, we need two entries in the row of 1's.

i.e. premultiplying by (1   1) will achieve the required result:

$$(1 \quad 1)\begin{pmatrix} 93 \\ 102 \end{pmatrix} = (195)$$

Now suppose that we want to find a matrix operation that will tell us the total number of meals ordered over the weekend.

Starting with $\mathbf{M} = \begin{pmatrix} 5 & 10 & 7 \\ 12 & 6 & 9 \end{pmatrix}$, we need an operation which will add the entries in the columns and then the entries in the rows (or vice-versa).

Premultiplying $\mathbf{M}$ by $(1 \quad 1)$ adds the entries in the columns,

i.e. $(1 \quad 1)\begin{pmatrix} 5 & 10 & 7 \\ 12 & 6 & 9 \end{pmatrix} = (17 \quad 16 \quad 16)$

then postmultiplying by a column of 1's (we need three 1's) will add the entries in $(17 \quad 16 \quad 16)$,

$$(17 \quad 16 \quad 16)\begin{pmatrix} 1 \\ 1 \\ 1 \end{pmatrix} = (49)$$

This example illustrates how matrices can be used to extract information from separate lists. We have chosen a very simple example to illustrate the methods, but its extension to an organisation handling many more items over a much longer time span is obvious, and in this case using a computer to handle the information has clear advantages.

EXERCISE 9c

1. Over the three terms of the school year a school needs incidental supplies of boxes of chalk, pads of file paper and pads of graph paper. If these items cost respectively £5, £1, and £1.50 each and if the columns of $\mathbf{R}$ represent the requirements of these items for each of the three terms, find a suitable row or column matrix which when multiplied by $\mathbf{R}$ will give the total cost of these items for each term.

$$\mathbf{R} = \begin{pmatrix} 1 & 2 & 1 \\ 0 & 5 & 2 \\ 2 & 10 & 5 \end{pmatrix} \begin{matrix} \text{Chalk} \\ \text{File paper} \\ \text{Graph paper} \end{matrix}$$

What matrix product needs to be evaluated to give the total cost for all these items for the year?

2. A shop stocks three brands of tea, X, Y and Z. The numbers of packets of each of these three brands that are sold in each of four consecutive weeks are shown in the matrix $\mathbf{S}$, where

$$\mathbf{S} = \begin{matrix} \text{X} \\ \text{Y} \\ \text{Z} \end{matrix} \begin{matrix} \text{Wk 1} & \text{Wk 2} & \text{Wk 3} & \text{Wk 4} \\ \begin{pmatrix} 10 & 9 & 12 & 6 \\ 15 & 5 & 4 & 20 \\ 17 & 10 & 16 & 8 \end{pmatrix} \end{matrix}$$

Find the matrix operation which will give the number of each brand sold over the four week period.

The shopkeeper buys his supplies from either wholesaler A or wholesaler B. From A, packets of X, Y and Z cost 40p, 30p and 25p each respectively. From B, packets of X, Y and Z cost 35p, 30p and 29p each respectively. The shopkeeper wishes to compare the cost to him of replacing his stock of tea each week from the two wholesalers. Find the matrix product which will give him this information.

3. There are three secondary schools, A, B and C in Dovemouth. For administrative purposes each school is divided into upper, middle and lower schools. The matrix **F** gives the number of forms in each section of each school.

$$
\mathbf{F} = \begin{array}{c} \\ A \\ B \\ C \end{array} \begin{array}{ccc} \text{Upper} & \text{Middle} & \text{Lower} \\ \begin{pmatrix} 12 & 9 & 6 \\ 10 & 7 & 5 \\ 12 & 8 & 6 \end{pmatrix} \end{array}
$$

In each school, there are 30 pupils in each lower school form, 28 pupils in each middle school form and 25 pupils in each upper school form.

Find the appropriate matrix products which will give the following information.

a) the number of forms in each school

b) the number of pupils in each school

c) the numbers of each of upper, middle and lower school forms in the town

d) the number of pupils in all three schools.

4. There is a nonstop train service between two towns, X and Y. There is one village, A, on the road between the two towns and country buses operate the following routes: a direct non-stop service between X and Y, a service from X, stopping at A, to Y and then directly back to X.

The numbers of public service connections between X, Y, and A are shown in the matrix **R** where

$$
\mathbf{R} = \begin{array}{c} \\ X \\ Y \\ A \end{array} \begin{array}{ccc} X & Y & A \\ \begin{pmatrix} 0 & 3 & 1 \\ 3 & 0 & 0 \\ 0 & 1 & 0 \end{pmatrix} \end{array}
$$

a) Explain the significance of the rows and the columns of this matrix.

b) Find $\mathbf{R}^2$ (i.e. $\mathbf{R} \times \mathbf{R}$) and interpret the entries that appear in the main diagonal of $\mathbf{R}^2$.

5. The country Alphaland has two international airports, A_1 and A_2, and three provincial airports L, M and N. Internal flights between A_1, A_2 and L, M, N are shown by '1' if they exist, and by '0' if they do not exist, in the matrix **A**, where

$$\mathbf{A} = \begin{array}{c} A_1 \\ A_2 \end{array} \begin{pmatrix} \overset{L}{1} & \overset{M}{1} & \overset{N}{0} \\ 0 & 1 & 1 \end{pmatrix}$$

The country Betaland has two international airports, B_1 and B_2. The existence or otherwise or flights between Alphaland and Betaland is shown by the matrix **F** where

$$\mathbf{F} = \begin{array}{c} B_1 \\ B_2 \end{array} \begin{pmatrix} \overset{A_1}{1} & \overset{A_2}{0} \\ 1 & 1 \end{pmatrix}$$

Betaland has three provincial airports X, Y and Z and the existence or otherwise of internal flights between B_2, B_2 and X, Y, Z is shown by the matrix **B** where

$$\mathbf{B} = \begin{array}{c} X \\ Y \\ Z \end{array} \begin{pmatrix} \overset{B_1}{1} & \overset{B_1}{0} \\ 0 & 1 \\ 1 & 1 \end{pmatrix}$$

By finding the appropriate matrix product give the matrix which indicates the existence or otherwise of air routes between

a) the provincial airports in Alphaland and the international airports in Betaland

b) the provincial airports in Betaland and the international airports in Alphaland

c) the provincial airports of Alphaland and Betaland, and interpret the numbers other than 1 and 0 which appear.

10 GEOMETRIC PROOF

This chapter gives an idea of how to prove geometric properties and revises some of the properties covered in earlier books.

DEMONSTRATION BY DRAWING AND MEASUREMENT

Geometry is the study of the properties of figures. Most of the properties that we have looked at so far have been demonstrated and verified by drawing and measurement. For example, when we investigated the sum of the angles in a triangle we drew some triangles, measured the angles and added them up. The results, from triangles of several different shapes and sizes, always came to around 180°. From these results we concluded that the sum of the angles in *any* triangle is 180°.

This method could be called 'jumping to conclusions' and it is not satisfactory for many reasons. It is impossible to draw a line; if we could, we would not be able to see it because a line has no thickness. It is impossible to measure angles with absolute accuracy; the protractors used in schools are probably capable of measuring to the nearest degree. The only conclusion that can reasonably be drawn from our results is 'it *seems likely* that the angle sum of any triangle is 180°'. (The true result could really be 179.5°.) 'Proof' by demonstration of particular cases also leaves open the possibility that somewhere, as yet unfound, there lurks an exception to the rule.

DEDUCTIVE PROOF

Learning geometrical properties from demonstrations gives the impression that each property is isolated. However geometry can be given a logical structure where one property can be deduced from other properties. This forms the basis of deductive proof; we quote known and accepted facts and then make logical deductions from them.

For example, if we accept that
a)   vertically opposite angles are equal
b)   corresponding angles are equal,
then, using just these two facts, we can prove that alternate angles are equal.

185

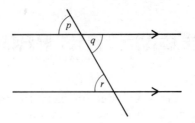

In the diagram $\widehat{p} = \widehat{q}$ (vertically opposite angles)

$\widehat{p} = \widehat{r}$ (corresponding angles)

$\Rightarrow \widehat{q} = \widehat{r}$

Therefore the alternate angles are equal.

The symbol $\Rightarrow$ means 'implies that' and indicates the logical deduction made from the two stated facts.

This proof does not involve angles of a particular size; p, q and r can be any size. Hence this proves that alternate angles are *always* equal whatever their size.

As a further example of deductive proof we will prove that, in *any* triangle, the sum of the interior angles *is* 180°.

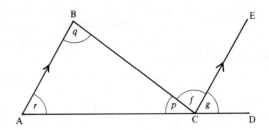

If $\triangle ABC$ is any triangle and if AC is extended to D and CE is parallel to AB then

$$\widehat{p} + \widehat{f} + \widehat{g} = 180°   \text{(angles on a st. line)} \qquad (1)$$

$$\widehat{f} = \widehat{q}   \text{(alt. } \angle\text{'s)} \qquad (2)$$

$$\widehat{g} = \widehat{r}   \text{(corr. } \angle\text{'s)} \qquad (3)$$

$$\Rightarrow \quad \widehat{p} + \widehat{q} + \widehat{r} = 180°$$

i.e. the sum of the interior angles of *any* triangle is 180°.

The statements above also lead to another useful fact about angles in triangles:

$$(2) \text{ and } (3) \quad \Rightarrow \quad \widehat{f} + \widehat{g} = \widehat{q} + \widehat{r}$$

i.e. an exterior angle of a triangle is equal to the sum of the two interior opposite angles.

Because this proof does not involve measuring angles in a particular triangle it applies to all possible triangles thus closing the loophole that there may exist a triangle whose angles do not add up to $180°$.

Notice how this proof uses the property proved in the first example, i.e. this proof follows the previous proof. The angle sum property of triangles can now be used to prove further properties.

Euclid was the first person to give a formal structure to Geometry. He started by making certain assumptions, such as 'there is only one straight line between two points'. Using only these assumptions (called axioms), he then proved some facts and used those facts to prove further facts and so on. Thus the proof of any one fact could be traced back to the axioms.

However when *you* are asked to give a geometric proof you do not have to worry about which property depends on which; you can use *any* facts that you know. One aspect of proof is that it is an argument used to convince other prople of the truth of any statement, so whatever facts you use must be clearly stated.

It is a good idea to marshal your ideas before starting to write out a proof. This is most easily done by marking right angles, equal angles and equal sides etc. on the diagram.

The exercises in this chapter give practice in writing out a proof.

For the next exercise the following facts are needed:

> vertically opposite angles are equal,
>
> corresponding angles are equal,
>
> alternate angles are equal,
>
> interior angles add up to $180°$,
>
> angle sum of a triangle is $180°$,
>
> an exterior angle of a triangle is equal to the sum of the interior opposite angles,
>
> an isosceles triangle has two sides of the same length and the angles at the base of those sides are equal,
>
> an equilateral triangle has three sides of the same length and each interior angle is $60°$.

EXERCISE 10a

1.

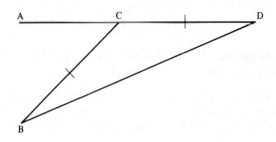

Prove that $\widehat{ACB} = 2\widehat{CDB}$.

2.

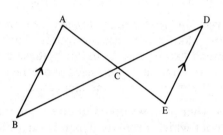

Prove that $\widehat{ACD} = \widehat{ABC} + \widehat{DEC}$.

3.

Prove that AD bisects BAC.

4.

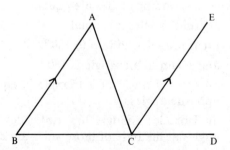

CE bisects $\widehat{ACD}$ and CE is parallel to BA. Prove that $\triangle ABC$ is isosceles.

5.

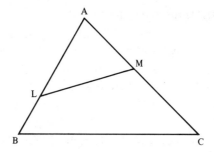

$A\widehat{M}L = A\widehat{B}C$. Prove that $A\widehat{L}M = A\widehat{C}B$.

6.

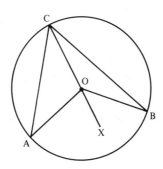

O is the centre of the circle.

a) Prove that $A\widehat{O}X = 2A\widehat{C}O$ b) Prove that $A\widehat{O}B = 2A\widehat{C}B$.

PARALLELOGRAMS, POLYGONS AND CONGRUENT TRIANGLES

The next exercise uses the following facts in addition to those already used.

In a parallelogram

> both pairs of opposite sides are parallel,
> both pairs of opposite sides are equal,
> both pairs of opposite angles are equal,
> the diagonals bisect each other.

To prove that a quadrilateral is a parallelogram we must show that it has *one* of the sets of properties listed.

Two triangles are congruent if

>   either the three sides of one triangle are equal to the three sides of the other triangle,

>   or two angles and one side of one triangle are equal to two angles and the corresponding side of the other triangle,

>   or two sides and the included angle of one triangle are equal to two sides and the included angle of the other triangle,

>   or if each triangle is right angled, the hypotenuse and one side of one triangle is equal to the hypotenuse and one side of the other triangle.

Only one of the above sets of properties need be established to prove the triangles congruent.

In a polygon

>   the sum of the exterior angles is 360°,

>   the sum of the interior angles is $(180n - 360)°$ where n is the number of sides.

If the polygon is regular, all the sides are equal and all the interior angles are equal.

EXERCISE 10b

ABC is an isosceles triangle in which AB = AC. A point D is inside the triangle and $D\widehat{B}C = D\widehat{C}B$. Prove that AD bisects $B\widehat{A}C$.

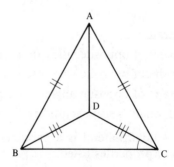

$$D\widehat{B}C = D\widehat{C}B \quad \text{(given)}$$

$\Rightarrow \qquad \triangle BCD$ is isosceles

$\Rightarrow \qquad BD = CD$

In $\triangle s \; \begin{matrix} ADB \\ ADC \end{matrix}$ $\qquad BD = CD \quad$ (proved)

$\qquad\qquad\qquad\qquad AB = AC \quad$ (given)

$\qquad\qquad\qquad\qquad AD$ is common

$\therefore \quad \triangle ADB$ and $\triangle ADC$ are congruent (SSS)

$\therefore \quad B\widehat{A}D = C\widehat{A}D$, i.e. AD bisects $B\widehat{A}C$.

1.

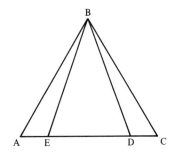

AEDC is a straight line. AB = BC and AE = DC.
Show that $\triangle AEB$ and $\triangle BDC$ are congruent. Hence prove that $\triangle BDE$ is isosceles.

2.

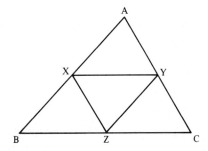

X, Y and Z are the midpoints of sides AB, AC and BC respectively.
Prove that $\triangle XYZ$ is congruent with $\triangle YZC$. Hence prove that BXYZ is a parallelogram.

3.

ABCD is a trapezium with BC parallel to AD and AB equal to CD. BE is parallel to CD and $C\hat{D}E = 60°$. Prove that $\triangle ABE$ is equilateral.

4. ABCDEF is a regular hexagon. Prove that ABDE is a rectangle.

5.

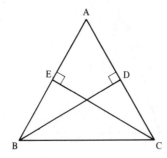

AB = AC,
BD is perpendicular to AC and CE is perpendicular to AB.
Prove that $\triangle BDC$ is congruent with $\triangle BEC$ and hence prove that $\triangle AED$ is isosceles.

6. ABCDEF is a hexagon in which AB is parallel and equal to ED and BC is parallel and equal to FE.

Join B to E and prove that $A\hat{B}C = F\hat{E}D$.
Hence prove that $\triangle ABC$ is congruent with $\triangle FED$.
Hence prove that ACDF is a parallelogram.

7.

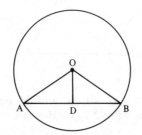

O is the centre of the circle and D is the midpoint of AB.
Prove that OD is perpendicular to AB.

8.

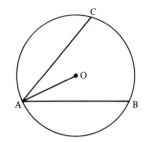

AB and AC are equal chords of a circle, centre O. Prove that AO bisects angle CAB.

CIRCLES

The next exercise introduces the use of the following facts.

The radius through the midpoint of a chord is perpendicular to the chord. (This was proved in question 7 of the last exercise.)

The angle subtended at the centre of a circle is equal to twice the angle subtended at the circumference by the same arc. (This is proved in question 6, Exercise 10a.)

All the angles subtended at the circumference by an arc of a circle are equal.

The angle in a semicircle is 90°.

The opposite angles of a cyclic quadrilateral add up to 180°.

The exterior angle of a cyclic quadrilateral is equal to the interior opposite angle.

EXERCISE 10c

1.

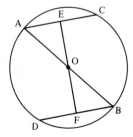

AB is a diameter and O is the centre of the circle. AC = BD and E, F are the midpoints of AC, BD. Prove that △AEO and △BFO are congruent. Hence prove that   a) EOF is a straight line   b) AC and DB are parallel.

2.

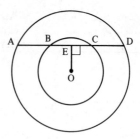

O is the centre of both circles (i.e. the circles are concentric). ABCD is a straight line and OE is perpendicular to ABCD. Prove that AB = CD.

3.

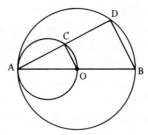

AB is a diameter and O is the centre of the larger circle. AO is a diameter of the smaller circle. ACD is a straight line. Prove that CO is parallel to DB.

4.

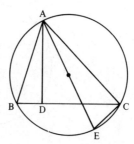

AE is a diameter of the circle and AD is perpendicular to BC. Prove that △AEC and △ABD are equiangular.

5.

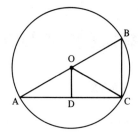

AOB is a diameter of the circle and OD bisects $A\widehat{O}C$. Prove that OD is parallel to BC.

6.

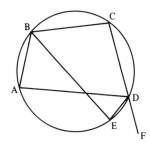

CDF is a straight line and BE bisects $A\widehat{B}C$. Prove that ED bisects $A\widehat{D}F$.

7.

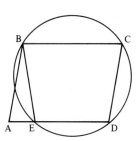

ABCD is a parallelogram. Prove that $B\widehat{A}E = B\widehat{E}A$.

11 CIRCLES AND TANGENTS

SECANTS AND TANGENTS

A straight line which cuts a circle in two distinct points is called a *secant*. The section of the line inside the circle is called a *chord*.

PQ is a secant and AB is a chord.

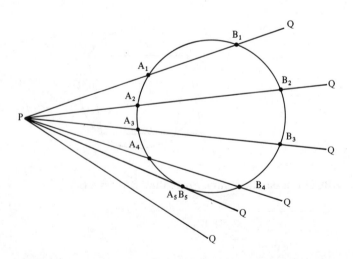

Imagine that the secant PQ is pivoted at P. As PQ rotates about P, we get successive positions of the points A and B, where the secant cuts the circle. As PQ moves towards the edge of the circle, the points A and B move closer together, until eventually they coincide.

When PQ is in this position it is called a *tangent* to the circle and we say that PQ touches the circle. (When PQ is rotated beyond this position it loses contact with the circle and is no longer either a secant or a tangent.)

We therefore define a tangent to a circle as a straight line which touches the circle.

The point at which the tangent touches the circle is called the point of contact.

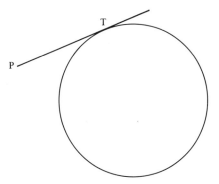

PT is a tangent to the circle.
T is the point of contact.

The *length of a tangent* from a point P outside the circle is the distance between that point and the point of contact. In the diagram the length of the tangent from P to the circle is the length PT.

EXERCISE 11a

1.

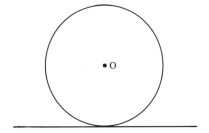

The diagram shows a disc, of radius 20 cm, rolling along horizontal ground. Describe the path along which O moves as the disc rolls. At any one instant,

a) how many points on the disc are in contact with the ground

b) how far is O from the ground

c) how would you describe the line joining O to the ground and what angle does it make with the ground?

2.

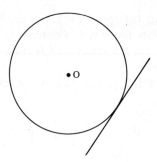

Copy the diagram and use a coloured or broken line to draw any line(s) of symmetry.

3.

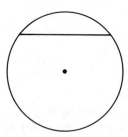

Copy the diagram and use a coloured or broken line to draw any line(s) of symmetry.

4.

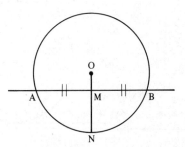

a) Show that the chord AB is perpendicular to the radius ON which bisects AB. (Join OA and OB.)

b) Now imagine that the chord AB slides down the radius ON. When the points A and B coincide with N, what has the line through A and B become ? What angle does this line make with ON ?

FIRST TANGENT PROPERTY

The investigational work in the last exercise suggests that

> a tangent to a circle is perpendicular to the radius drawn from the point of contact.

The general proof of this property is an interesting exercise in logic. We start by assuming that the property is *not* true and end up by contradicting ourselves.

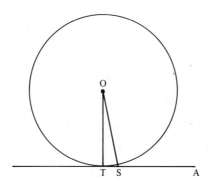

TA is a tangent to the circle and OT is the radius from the point of contact.

If we *assume* that $O\widehat{T}S$ is *not* 90° then it is possible to draw OS so that OS *is* perpendicular to the tangent, i.e. $O\widehat{S}T = 90°$.

Therefore △OST has a right angle at S.
Hence   OT is the hypotenuse of △OST
i.e.   OT > OS
∴   S is inside the circle, as OT is a radius.
∴   the line through T and S must cut the circle again.
But this is impossible, as the line through T and S is a tangent.
Hence the assumption that OTA ≠ 90° is wrong, i.e. $O\widehat{T}A$ *is* 90°.

EXERCISE 11b

Some of the questions in this exercise require the use of trigonometry.

The tangent from a point **P** to a circle of radius 4.2 cm is 7 cm long. Find the distance of P from the centre of the circle.

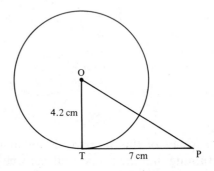

$$O\widehat{T}P = 90°$$ (tangent perpendicular to radius)

$$OP^2 = OT^2 + TP^2$$ (Pythagoras' theorem)

$$= (4.2)^2 + 7^2$$

$$= 17.64 + 49$$

$$= 66.64$$

∴ $$OP = 8.16 \text{ correct to 3 s.f.}$$

P is 8.16 cm from O.

In questions 1 to 8, O is the centre of the circle and AB is a tangent to the circle, touching it at A.

1.

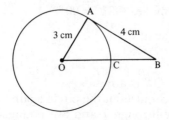

Find OB and CB.

2.

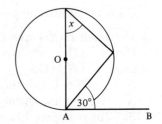

Find the angle marked x.

3.

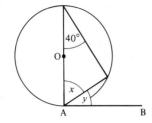

Find the angles marked *x* and *y*.

7.

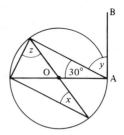

Find the size of the angles marked *x, y* and *z*.

4.

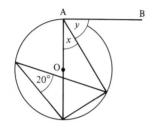

Find the angles marked *x* and *y*.

8.

Find AB̂O.

5.

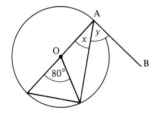

Find the angles marked *x* and *y*.

9.

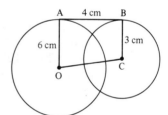

AB is a tangent to the circles with centres C and O, touching them at B and A respectively. Find OC.

6.

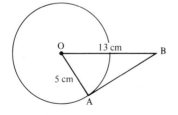

Find AB and OB̂A.

10.

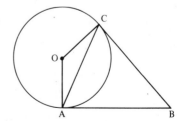

AB and BC are tangents to the circle touching it at A and C. Show that △ABC is isosceles.

11.

AB is a chord of the larger circle and a tangent to the smaller circle. If O is the centre of both circles, find the length of AB.

CONSTRUCTIONS

EXERCISE 11c

(Remember to draw a rough sketch before doing the construction.)

1. Draw a circle of radius 5 cm. Label the centre O and mark a point T on the circumference. Construct the tangent to the circle at T. (Use the fact that the radius OT is perpendicular to the tangent.)

2. Draw a circle of radius 4 cm. Label the centre of this circle C. Mark a point P distant 10 cm from C. Draw another circle on PC as diameter. Label the points where the two circles cut, A and B. What is the size of $C\widehat{A}P$? Describe the lines PA and PB in relation to the circle with centre C.

3. Draw a circle of radius 3 cm and mark a point P distant 6 cm from the centre of the circle. Use the method described in question 2 to construct the two tangents from P to the circle.

4.

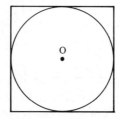

a) The diagram shows a circle, centre O, inscribed in a square (i.e. the sides of the square are tangents to the circle). The radius of the circle is 2 cm. Find the length of a side of the square.

b) Draw a square of side 8 cm. Construct the inscribed circle of the square.

PROOFS ──────────────────────────────

EXERCISE 11d

AD is the diameter of a circle and AB is a tangent to the circle at A. BD meets the circle again at E and DE = EB.
Prove that $\widehat{EAB} = 45°$.

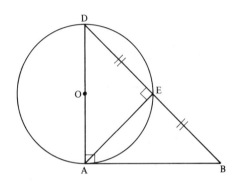

　　AD is a diameter

∴　　　$\widehat{DEA} = 90°$　　　　　(angle in semicircle)

In $\triangle AED$ and $\triangle AEB$

　　　　DE = EB　　　　　　　(given)

AE is common

　　　　$\widehat{DEA} = \widehat{AEB}$　　　　(both 90°)

∴　　$\triangle s \begin{matrix} AED \\ AEB \end{matrix}$ are congruent.　(S A S)

∴　$\widehat{DAE} = \widehat{EAB}$

But　$\widehat{DAB} = 90°$　　　　　(angle between tangent
　　　　　　　　　　　　　　　　　　　　and radius)

∴　　$\widehat{DAE} = 45°$

1. AB is the diameter of a circle and D is a point on the circumference of the circle. A circle is drawn on AD as diameter. Prove that BD is a tangent to this circle.

2. A circle centre A is drawn to cut a circle, centre B, at points C and D such that $\widehat{ACB} = 90°$. Prove that AC is a tangent to the circle centre B.

3. AOB is a diameter of a circle, centre O. AD is a tangent to the circle at A and DB meets the circle again at C. Prove that $D\widehat{A}C = ABC$.

4. P is a point outside a circle with centre O. Tangents from P to the circle touch the circle at R and S. Prove that $\triangle ROP$ is congruent with $\triangle SOP$. Hence show that the tangents from P to the circle are equal in length.

5. AOB is a diameter of a circle centre O. AP is a tangent to the circle at A. A chord AC is drawn so that C and P are on the same side of AB. Prove that $C\widehat{A}P = A\widehat{B}C$.

SECOND TANGENT PROPERTY

The property proved about tangents in question 4 of the last exercise can be quoted, i.e.

> the two tangents drawn from an external point to a circle are the same length.

EXERCISE 11e

1.

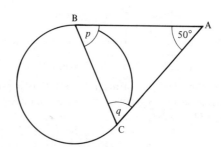

Find the sizes of the angles marked p and q.

2.

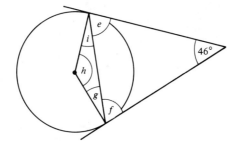

Find the sizes of the angles marked *e, f, g, h* and *i*.

3.

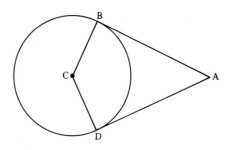

a) If $\widehat{BCD} = 130°$, find $\widehat{BAD}$.

b) What type of quadrilateral is ABCD ?

4.

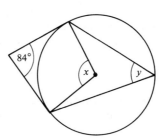

Find the sizes of the angles marked *x* and *y*.

5.

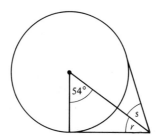

Find the sizes of the angles marked *r* and *s*.

6.

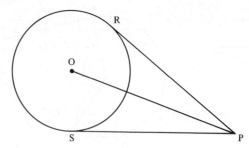

PR = 8 cm and OP = 10 cm. Calculate

a) the radius of the circle

b) the angle between the tangents.

7.

The diagram shows the cross-section through the centre of a ball placed in a hollow cone. The vertical angle of the cone is 60° and the diameter of the ball is 8 cm. Find the depth of the vertex of the cone below the centre of the ball.

8. A second ball is now placed in the cone described in question 7. If the diameter of the second ball is 20 cm, will it touch the first ball?

9.

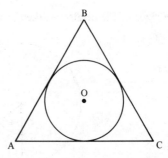

The circle, centre O, is inscribed in the equilateral triangle ABC. The sides of the triangle are each 20 cm long. Calculate the radius of the circle.

10. A circle of radius 4 cm is circumscribed by an equilateral triangle. Write down the angles between the sides of the triangle and the lengths of the lines joining the centre of the circle to the vertices of the triangle. Hence calculate the lengths of the sides of the triangle.

11. A circle of radius 4 cm is circumscribed by an isosceles right-angled triangle. Find the lengths of the sides of the triangle.

12. ABCD is a quadrilateral circumscribing a circle. If AC goes through the centre of the circle, prove that ABCD is a kite.

13. Construct a circle, centre O and radius 4 cm. Mark a point A on the circumference. Construct angle $O\hat{A}B = 90°$ and hence draw the tangent AB. Mark any two points D and C on the circumference. Join A to D and A to C.
Measure $C\hat{A}B$ and $A\hat{D}C$. How do they compare?

THIRD TANGENT PROPERTY ▬▬▬▬▬▬▬▬▬▬▬▬▬▬▬▬▬▬▬▬

Alternate segment theorem

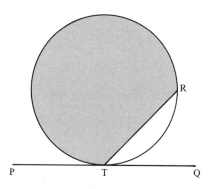

PQ is a tangent to the circle and TR is a chord. The major segment (which is shaded) is called the alternate segment with respect to the angle $R\hat{T}Q$. Similarly the minor (unshaded) segment is alternate to the angle $P\hat{T}R$.

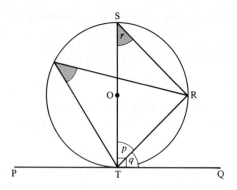

If TS is a diameter then

$$S\widehat{R}T = 90°$$ (angle in semi-circle)

$$S\widehat{T}Q = 90°$$ (angle between tangent and radius)

Now $\widehat{p} + \widehat{q} = 90°$

and $\widehat{p} + \widehat{r} = 90°$ (angles of $\triangle$)

$\Rightarrow$ $\widehat{q} = \widehat{r}$

But $\widehat{r}$ is equal to any angle subtended by the chord TR, i.e.

> the angle between a tangent and a chord drawn from the point of contact is equal to any angle in the alternate segment.

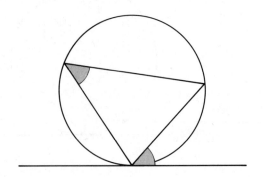

This result is known as the alternate segment theorem and can be quoted.

EXERCISE 11f

In questions 1 to 4, copy the diagram and shade the alternate segment with respect to the angle marked x.

1.

3.

2.

4.

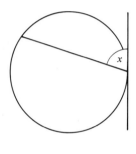

Find the size of the angles marked x and y in the diagram.

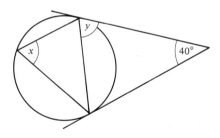

$y = 70°$ (base angle of isosceles triangle)

$x = y$ (alternate segment theorem)

$\therefore \quad x = 70°$

Find the sizes of the angles marked by the letters.

5.

9.

6.

10.

7.

11.

8.

12.

13.

17.

14.

18.

15.

19.

16.

20.

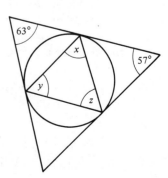

12 PROBABILITY

BASIC FACTS

Remember that

$$P(\text{an event occurs}) = \frac{\text{the number of outcomes resulting in the event}}{\text{the total number of possible outcomes}}$$

$P(\text{certainty}) = 1$

$P(\text{impossibility}) = 0$

In general, the probability that an event A occurs lies between 0 and 1,

i.e. $\qquad\qquad 0 \leqslant P(A) \leqslant 1$

The probability that A does not occur is denoted by $P(\overline{A})$, and

$$P(\overline{A}) = 1 - P(A)$$

TWO EVENTS – ADDING PROBABILITIES

If an ordinary dice is tossed, the possible scores are 1, 2, 3, 4, 5 or 6, so $P(2) = \frac{1}{6}$ and $P(\text{odd score}) = \frac{3}{6}$.

Now there is one way of scoring 2 and there are three ways of scoring an odd number. It is not possible to score *both* 2 *and* an odd number, so the two events are separate. Such events are called *mutually exclusive*. Hence there are four ways of scoring either 2 or an odd number, i.e.

$$P(2 \text{ or an odd number}) = \tfrac{4}{6} = P(2) + P(\text{odd score})$$

> $P(A \text{ or } B) = P(A) + P(B)$ provided that A and B are mutually exclusive, i.e. A and B cannot both occur.

Notice that $P(2 \text{ or an even score}) = \frac{3}{6}$.

This is *not* equal to $P(2) + P(\text{even score})$ because 2 is an even number, i.e. scoring 2 and getting an even score are *not* mutually exclusive.

TWO EVENTS - MULTIPLYING PROBABILITIES

If two dice are tossed, the score on the first dice has no bearing on what will be scored by the second dice. Now the probability of scoring 6 with the first dice, $P(6_1)$, is $\frac{1}{6}$, and the probability of scoring 6 with the second dice, $P(6_2)$, is $\frac{1}{6}$. There are 36 possible ways in which the two dice can land; scoring 6 on the first dice and 6 on the second dice is just one of these ways.

Therefore $P(6_1 \text{ and } 6_2) = \frac{1}{36} = P(6_1) \times P(6_2)$

$$P(A \text{ and } B) = P(A) \times P(B)$$

provided that event A has no effect on event B.

TREE DIAGRAMS

A probability tree is a useful way of sorting out probabilities concerning more than one event.

Suppose that I have two bags, each containing a red and a blue disc. One disc is removed at random from each bag. All the possible outcomes and their probabilities can be illustrated on this tree diagram.

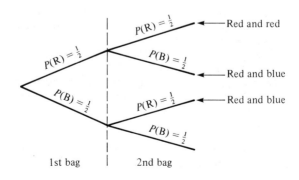

The probability of getting two red discs, $P(R_1$ and $R_2)$, is given by following a path along the branches of the tree. But $P(R_1$ and $R_2) = P(R_1) \times (R_2)$,

i.e.   we *multiply* probabilities when we follow a path along the branches of the tree.

The probability of getting a red disc and a blue disc is given by the following two paths along the branches because we can get a red disc first and a blue disc second, or vice-versa,

i.e. $P(R \text{ and } B) = P(R_1B_2 \text{ or } B_1R_2) = P(R_1B_2) + P(B_1R_2)$

We *add* the probabilities when following several paths.

EXERCISE 12a

1. If the two bags described above contain a red, a blue and a yellow disc, use a tree diagram to find the probability of
    a) taking out two yellow discs
    b) taking out a red disc and a yellow disc
    c) taking out a blue disc and a yellow disc.

2. Draw a probability tree to show the probabilities when three coins are tossed, one after the other.
    a) Find the probability of tossing three heads.
    b) What is the probability of tossing one head and two tails?
    c) What is the probability that the second coin tossed lands heads up?

3. An ordinary pack of playing cards has had all the hearts removed. It is then well shuffled and then cut to show a card. What is the probability that the card showing is black?
    The pack is then reshuffled and cut again. What is the probability that the card showing is not black?
    Draw a probability tree to show the probabilities of a black or a red card appearing when the pack is cut twice as described above. Use the tree to find the probability that
    a) just one black card is cut
    b) a red and a black card are cut
    c) both cards cut are black.

DEPENDENT EVENTS

In the previous exercise the second event (e.g. tossing a second coin) is not affected by what happened first. In the following exercise, however, the probability of the second event depends on what happened first.

EXERCISE 12b

> A card is drawn from a pack of 52 playing cards.
> a) What is the probability of drawing a red card?
> b) If the first card is red and is not replaced what is the probability that a second card drawn is red?
>
> a) There are 26 red cards out of 52,
>
> $$\text{therefore} \quad P(\text{red card}) = \tfrac{26}{52} = \tfrac{1}{2}$$
>
> b) There are now 25 red cards left out of 51 cards,
>
> $$\text{therefore} \quad P(\text{2nd red card}) = \tfrac{25}{51}$$

1. A bag contains 5 red beads and 3 blue beads.

a) What is the probability of drawing   i) a red bead   ii) a blue bead?

b) If a red bead is drawn first and is not replaced, what is now the probability of drawing a blue bead?

c) If a red bead is drawn first and not replaced, what is the probability of drawing a second red bead?

2. A card is drawn from a pack of 52 cards.

a) Give the probability of drawing
i) a nine   ii) a heart

b) If a heart is drawn and not replaced, what is now the probability of drawing a heart?

c) If a nine is drawn first and not replaced, what is now the probability of drawing a ten?

3. A hutch contains 4 white and 5 grey guinea pigs. When the door is opened they come out in random order.

a) Give the probability that the first out is white.

b) If the first out is white, what is the probability that the second out is
   i) white   ii) grey?

c) If the first out is grey, what is the probability that the second out is
   i) white   ii) grey?

USING TREE DIAGRAMS FOR DEPENDENT EVENTS

EXERCISE 12c

In this exercise, the first object drawn is not replaced before the second object is drawn.

A box contains ten counters; six are black and four are white. Two counters are drawn at random. Find the probability that
a) both are black   b) both are white.

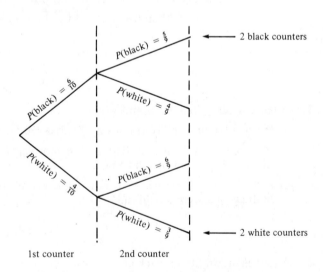

a) $P(2\,\text{black}) = \frac{6}{10} \times \frac{5}{9} = \frac{1}{3}$

b) $P(2\,\text{white}) = \frac{4}{10} \times \frac{3}{9} = \frac{2}{15}$

1. A bag contains four green beads and five yellow beads. Two beads are withdrawn at random.

a) Find the probability that the first bead is green.

b) If the first bead is yellow find the probability that the second bead is green.

Draw a probability tree to show the probabilities when two beads are withdrawn and find the probability that

c) both beads are green

d) the first bead is yellow and the second is green.

2. A hand of ten cards contains four hearts and six clubs. Two cards are drawn at random from the hand.

a) What is the probability that the first card is a heart?

b) If the first card is a heart what is the probability that the second card is a heart?

c) Draw a probability tree and find the probability that both cards are clubs.

3. Seven cards are numbered 1 to 7 and two cards are drawn at random. Draw a probability tree to show the probabilities of drawing odd or even cards. Find the probability that

a) the first card is even

b) both cards are even

c) both cards are odd

d) the first card is even and the second is odd

e) the first card is odd and the second is even

f) one card is odd and one even in any order. (Use the answers to (d) and (e) to answer (f).)

4. a) If a drawing pin is dropped, it is three times as likely to land point up as point down. What is the probability that it will land point up?

b) Two such drawing pins are dropped. What is the probability that both will land point up?

5. A birdcage contains six blue and three green budgerigars. When the door is opened the birds come out one at a time in random order.

a) What is the probability that the first bird is blue ?

b) If the first bird is blue, what is the probability that the second bird is blue ?

Find the probability that

c) one of the first two birds is blue and one green

d) the first three birds out are all blue.

SIMPLIFIED TREE DIAGRAMS

We do not always have to draw every possible branch of a tree diagram. If, for instance, in throwing a die three times, we are interested only in the number of 6s thrown, the tree diagram need have only two branches per throw. One branch is for 'throwing a 6', the other is for 'throwing a number other than 6'.

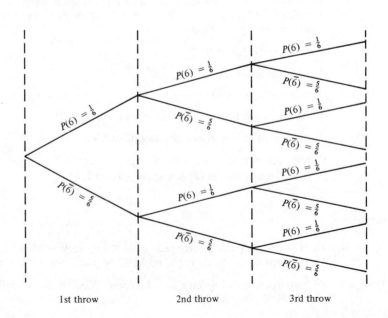

| 1st throw | 2nd throw | 3rd throw |

EXERCISE 12d

In this exercise, the first object drawn is not replaced before the second object is drawn.

Two dice are tossed. What is the probability of getting a prime number on one die and 1 on the other?

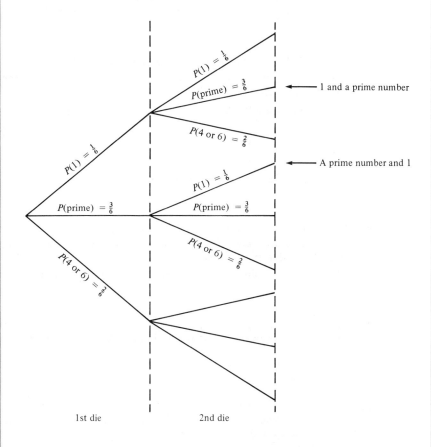

1st die   2nd die

$$P(\text{a prime number and 1 in any order}) = \left(\tfrac{1}{6} \times \tfrac{3}{6}\right) + \left(\tfrac{3}{6} \times \tfrac{1}{6}\right)$$
$$= \tfrac{1}{12} + \tfrac{1}{12}$$
$$= \tfrac{2}{12}$$
$$= \tfrac{1}{6}$$

1. A hand of cards contains eight cards of which five are hearts and three are spades. Two cards are drawn at random. Draw a tree diagram to show the probabilities and find the probability that

a) one card is a heart and one is a spade

b) the two cards belong to the same suit.

2. Simon has six grey socks and four white ones in a drawer. He takes out two socks in the dark.

What is the probability that they are of different colours?

3. The probability that the weather is fine on Monday is $\frac{1}{3}$. If it is fine, the probability that I can get on my bus is $\frac{3}{4}$. If it is not fine the probability that I can get on my bus is $\frac{1}{4}$.

Find the probability that I can get on my bus on Monday.

4. Three coins are tossed. Find the probability of getting

a) three heads   b) a head and two tails.

5. Two bags of hyacinth bulbs each contain four bulbs, a pink, a blue, a yellow and a white. If I take one bulb at random from each bag, find the probability that both bulbs are

a) pink   b) blue   c) yellow   d) white   e) the same colour.

6. A box contains eight hard-centred and nine soft-centred chocolates. Two are selected at random. What is the probability that one is hard-centred and one is soft-centred?

7. The probability that Mr Brown completes a crossword puzzle is $\frac{2}{3}$, that Mrs Black completes it is $\frac{1}{2}$ and that Mr White completes it is $\frac{1}{3}$.

Find the probability that

a) all three complete it

b) just two out of the three solve it.

8. The probability that Mr. Brodie, on his way to work, has to stop at the first set of traffic lights is $\frac{2}{5}$, and that he has to stop at the second set of traffic lights is $\frac{1}{3}$. Find the probability that he has to stop at just one of the sets of traffic lights.

PROBABILITY OF ANY TWO EVENTS

Thirty pupils are sitting examinations; 15 are taking history, 12 are taking geography and, of these, 6 are taking both history and geography. If, say, we want to find the probability that a pupil chosen at random is taking history but not geography, then we need to sort out the numbers of pupils taking the various options.

This is best done in diagrammatic form. We draw two circles to represent the pupils taking history and geography and overlap the circles to represent those taking both subjects. We can then draw a rectangle round the circles to enclose all the pupils. Finally we fill in the numbers taking each option.

Now we can see clearly what numbers are doing each option.

Hence $P(\text{H and not G}) = \frac{9}{30} = \frac{3}{10}$

Similarly, $P(\text{neither H nor G}) = \frac{9}{30} = \frac{3}{10}$

(Diagrams like the one opposite are called Venn diagrams.)

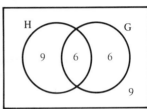

Check total = 30

EXERCISE 12e

The diagram shows the number of pupils in a class of 30 who have a computer (C) and the number who have a video recorder (V). Find the probability that a pupil chosen at random has

a) a computer and/or a video recorder
b) a computer but not a video recorder.

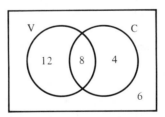

a) The number of pupils with at least one of the two is $12 + 8 + 4$, i.e. 24
   Therefore $P(\text{C or V or both}) = \frac{24}{30} = \frac{4}{5}$.

b) The number of pupils with just a computer is 4
   Therefore $P(\text{C only}) = \frac{4}{30} = \frac{2}{15}$.

1. The diagram shows the numbers of pupils in a class of 27 who are in the school soccer team (S) and who are in the school cricket team (C).

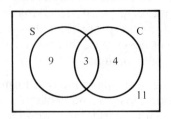

Find the probability that a pupil chosen at random is

a) in both teams   b) only in the cricket team   c) in just one team.

2. In a group of 24 children, each has a dog or a cat or both. If 18 keep a dog and 5 of these also keep a cat, show this information on a diagram. Hence find the probability that a child chosen at random has

a) a cat   b) only a dog   c) just one of these as a pet.

3. In a Youth Club 35 teenagers said that they went to football matches, discos or both. Of the 22 who said they went to football matches, 12 said they also went to discos. Show this information on a diagram. What is the probability that a person chosen at random went to football matches or discos, but not to both ?

4. The passengers on a coach were questioned about the newspapers they bought each day.

> 3 bought a morning and evening newspaper.
>
> 15 bought a morning newspaper.
>
> 8 bought an evening newspaper.
>
> 8 did not buy a newspaper at all.

Show this information on a diagram.

a) How many passengers were there on the coach ?

b) What is the probability that a passenger chosen at random bought a newspaper at some time in the day ?

5. During April, 36 cars were taken to a Testing Station for an MOT certificate. The results showed that 8 had defective brakes and lights, 10 had defective brakes, and 13 had defective lights. What is the probability that a car chosen at random

a) failed the test   b) passed the test   c) had exactly one defect ?

6. The 32 pupils in a class were asked whether they studied French or art or both. It was found that 8 studied both, 13 studied French and 5 did not study either subject. Find the probability that a pupil chosen at random studied

a) art but not French   b) French or art but not both ?

7. The diagram shows the methods of transport used by the staff of a London store where

A represents those using a taxi,
B represents those using a bus and
C represents those using a car.

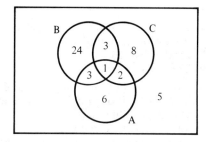

a) How many members of staff does the store employ ?

b) What is the probability that a member of staff chosen at random
  i) uses exactly one means of transport
  ii) uses more than one means of transport
  iii) does not use a bus ?

8. In a certain group of students some are in one or more of the school hockey, netball or swimming teams. The diagram shows these numbers where H are those in the hockey team, N are those in the netball team and S are those in the swimming team.

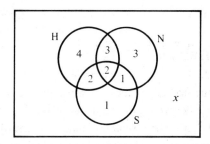

If there are 21 pupils in the group, what is the value of x ?

What is the probability that a pupil chosen at random is in

a) the hockey team only

b) at least two teams

c) exactly one team

d) the netball team.

HARDER PROBLEMS

EXERCISE 12f

1. In a test a group of one hundred pupils were given marks out of 60. The table shows the number achieving the various marks

Marks	1–10	11–20	21–30	31–40	41–50	51–60
Frequency	4	16	20	24	27	9

a) State the probability that a pupil chosen at random will have a mark
   i) from 41 to 50 inclusive
   ii) greater than 50
   iii) 20 or less.

b) A second group of one hundred pupils were tested and ten scored more than 50 marks. If one pupil is chosen at random from each of the groups, find the probability that
   i) both will have scored more than 50
   ii) just one will have scored more than 50.

2. Each of the following draws is from a set of four cards which are numbered 1, 3, 6, 8.

a) One card is drawn at random. Find the probability that the number on the card is a prime number.

b) Two cards are drawn at random. Find the probability that the numbers on both cards are multiples of 3.

c) Two cards are drawn at random. Find the probability that the sum of the two numbers is 9.

3. At a fête, thirty tickets numbered 1 to 30 are placed in a drum. A ticket drawn from the drum wins a prize if its number is a multiple of 5. A ticket, once drawn, is not replaced. Two tickets are drawn in succession. Find the probability that

a) the first ticket wins a prize

b) the first ticket does not win a prize but the second does.

Three tickets are drawn in succession.

c) What is the probability that no ticket wins a prize?

d) What is the probability that at least one ticket wins a prize?

4. A biased die is such that the probability of throwing a six is $\frac{1}{3}$, and the probability of scoring each of the other numbers is $\frac{2}{15}$.
I have two biased dice and two fair dice.
If I throw a) two biased dice b) one fair die and one biased die, calculate the probability of obtaining a total score of i) 12 ii) 11.

5. In a sideshow at a fête, a player is required to roll balls towards five channels marked with the scores 1 to 5.

1	3	5	4	2

The probabilities of achieving the various scores are

$$P(1) = \tfrac{1}{10}$$
$$P(3) = \tfrac{1}{5}$$
$$P(5) = \tfrac{2}{5}$$
$$P(4) = \tfrac{1}{5}$$
$$P(2) = \tfrac{1}{10}$$

With two balls, find the probability of achieving a total score of

a) 10   b) 3   c) 4

With three balls, find the probability of achieving a total score of

d) 15   e) 3

6. Alan and Bob play a game using a die. Alan tosses it and records the score. If he throws a one or a two he tosses it again. Alan wins if on either the first throw or the second he scores 5 or 6. If he does not, then Bob wins.

a) What is the probability that Alan wins?

b) Who is more likely to win, Alan or Bob?

7. Some tests were held in the fourth form in physics (P), chemistry (C) and biology (B). Forty-five pupils took part and the recorded passes were as follows: physics 24, chemistry 25, biology 30, physics and chemistry but not biology 3, physics and biology but not chemistry 6, biology and chemistry but not physics 7. If 10 pupils passed in all three and 2 pupils failed in all three draw a diagram to illustrate this information entering the correct number in each region.

Use your diagram to find the probability that a pupil chosen at random

a) passed in chemistry only

b) passed in more than one of these subjects

c) passed in exactly one of these subjects

d) did not pass in either biology or chemistry.

13 STATISTICS

SAMPLING

There are many situations where it is impossible or impractical to gather information on all the items in a survey.

For example, a car engine manufacturer will want information about the life of the engines. He cannot test them all to destruction because he would not then have any engines to sell! As another example, imagine trying to get information about the distribution of all the robins in the country; it is impossible to count them all.

In situations like these, we take just some of the items and measure them, i.e. we take a *sample*.

CHOOSING A SAMPLE

How the sample is chosen needs some thought because we want to be confident that the information gathered from a sample is likely to reflect the information that we would get if it were possible to use all the items. (Notice the use of the word 'likely' in the last sentence; however carefully a sample is chosen, we can never be certain that it gives the same information as would checking all the items.)

There are two factors to consider when choosing a sample:
how big should it be, and how do we select the items to be included in the sample.

Consider the size of the sample first. Commonsense would say 'as many as possible' but the engine manufacturer would say 'as few as possible'. We investigate this aspect of sampling in the next exercise. The items chosen for a sample should, as far as possible, be selected to be representative of known characteristics of all the items. For example if it is known that there are twice as many men as women employed in a factory, then a sample of employees should also contain twice as many men as women. If there are no known characteristics of the total, then the sample should be chosen so that any one item is as likely to be picked as any other. This is called a *random* sample.

EXERCISE 13a

Questions 1 to 3 refer to this problem.

Frank has to find out about the breakfast eating habits of pupils in his school. The school is co-educational and there are about 200 pupils in each year-group for the first five years. There are 150 pupils in the first year of the sixth form and 50 pupils in the second year of the sixth form. Frank decides that it is impractical to interview every pupil in the school, so he decides to gather the information from a sample of 100 to 200 pupils. Here are some ways in which he can choose his sample.

1. Frank can get to school early and use the first 100 pupils to arrive.

   a) Is any group of pupils likely to be under-represented?

   b) Are equal numbers of boys and girls likely to be included in this sample?

   c) Is each age group likely to be represented in the sample in the same proportion as they are in the school?

   d) Do you think whether a pupil arrives early has any relationship with breakfast?

   e) From experience of your own school, can you think of any reasons why this would not be a representative sample?

2. Frank can take one class from each year group as his sample.

   a) If the classes are banded (i.e. grouped according to ability), is this likely to affect their breakfast eating habits?

   b) Does the inclusion of a complete class from each of the sixth form year groups reflect the proportion of these pupils in the whole school?

   c) Are the age groups in the sample represented in the same proportion as they occur in the school?

   d) Can you suggest ways of improving the selection of the sample to make it as representative as possible?

This kind of sample (identifying groups with different characteristics and taking a sample of each group) is called a *stratified* sample.

3. Frank can draw his sample from the main school register. The pupils are listed in this register with the boys first in alphabetical order followed by the girls, also in alphabetical order.
Frank can take the first 50 boys and the first 50 girls as his sample. Alternatively, Frank can take every tenth pupil on the register as his sample. (This method of sampling is an attempt at random selection.)

   a) Can you suggest reasons why either method may not give a sample that represents the whole school population?

   b) Devise a way of selecting about 100 pupils from your own school so that they reflect, as nearly as possible, known characteristics of the whole set of pupils.

4. A common use of sampling is for opinion polls on voting intentions. Here is the story of one such poll that went very wrong!

During the USA presidential election campaign of 1936, a magazine gave questionnaires to a very large sample of people. The sample was drawn from readers of the magazine and people whose names were in the telephone directories. The results from the questionnaire indicated that Franklin D. Roosevelt would be defeated. In fact he achieved a landslide victory. Why do you think that the way in which the sample was chosen gave a misleading result?

5. For this question you will need an ordinary pack of playing cards. You will also find it helpful to work in groups of 3 or 4.

In an ordinary pack of 52 playing cards, there are 13 hearts.

a) If four cards are chosen at random, how many hearts should there be for these four cards to be representative of the proportion of hearts in the full pack?

b) Shuffle a full pack of playing cards thoroughly and then deal out the top four cards. This is a sample of size four. Write down the number of hearts.

c) Replace the cards dealt for the first sample and then repeat (b).

d) Repeat the process several more times. (You will need at least 30 samples.) Keep track of your results in a table like this one:

Sample number	1	2	3	4	5...
Number of hearts					

e) Use your table to copy and complete this frequency table.

Number of hearts	0	1	2	3	4
Frequency					

f) From your frequency table, find the relative frequency (i.e. the experimental probability) that a sample represents the proportion of hearts in the whole pack.

g) Now repeat parts (b) to (e) using a sample of 20 cards.

h) A sample of 20 cards should contain 5 hearts to represent exactly the proportion of hearts in the complete pack. If we allow 4, 5 or 6 hearts in a sample as 'good enough' to be representative, find the relative frequency of such samples.

RUNNING TOTALS

After a set of examinations, the results are usually given for one subject at a time. Most pupils, however, are interested in the total of the marks they have received at any stage, i.e. their 'running total'.

The following table shows the separate subject results achieved by a certain pupil, with the running total given in the fourth column.

Lesson	Subject	Mark	Running total
1	Physics	54	54
2	French	72	126
3	Biology	62	188
4	Chemistry	45	233
5	History	78	311
6	Mathematics	64	375
7	English	45	420
8	Geography	82	502

If a similar table gives the running totals only, and not the individual subject marks, we can extract the subject marks. For example, if the running total after four subjects is 233 and the running total after five subjects is 311 then the number of marks scored in the fifth subject is $311 - 233$, i.e. 78.

EXERCISE 13b

1. The table shows the running totals of pupils staying to school lunch each day during a certain school week. Complete the table to find out how many stayed on each day.

Weekday	Number of lunches served each day	Running total of lunches served
Monday		126
Tuesday		280
Wednesday		424
Thursday		599
Friday		717

2. The mileposts along the M4 motorway show the distances, in miles, between various places as follows:

Cardiff to Newport 10,   Newport to Severn Bridge 16,
Severn Bridge to Leigh Delamere 28,   Leigh Delamere to Swindon 18,
Swindon to Reading 39,   Reading to Heathrow Airport 28,
Heathrow to Central London 15.

Make a running total of the distances along the motorway from Cardiff to Central London.

3. During a weeks' holiday a family spent the following amounts

Day	Amount spent	Running total of expenditure
Monday	£ 12	
Tuesday	£ 26	
Wednesday	£ 5	
Thursday	£ 8	
Friday	£ 32	
Saturday	£ 27	
Sunday	£ 4	

Complete the table and check your answer by direct addition.

CUMULATIVE FREQUENCY

It is often useful to know how many pupils have scored *less than* a certain mark, or have *less than* a certain amount of pocket money.

For example, in a shooting competition, a competitor fired 50 shots at a target and obtained the following results.

Score	1	2	3	4	5
Number of shots	3	4	18	16	9

There are $3 + 4$, i.e. 7, shots with a score of 2 or less, and $7 + 18$, i.e. 25 shots with a score of 3 or less. A simple and effective way of giving this information is to make a *cumulative frequency table*. A cumulative frequency table is constructed by adding each frequency to the sum of all those that have gone before it. The cumulative frequency table for the data given above can be set out as follows:

Score	Frequency	Score	Cumulative frequency
1	3	$\leqslant 1$	3
2	4	$\leqslant 2$	$3 + 4 = 7$
3	18	$\leqslant 3$	$7 + 18 = 25$
4	16	$\leqslant 4$	$25 + 16 = 41$
5	9	$\leqslant 5$	$41 + 9 = 50$

Even if the second column is omitted, the frequency for any score from 1 to 5 can be found from the cumulative frequencies, e.g. the number of 3s scored is given by the cumulative frequency up to 3 minus the cumulative frequency up to 2, i.e. $25 - 7 = 18$.

Notice that the last number in the cumulative frequency column can be used as a check on accuracy. It confirms that the total number of shots fired was 50.

EXERCISE 13c

1. Complete the following table which shows the distribution of goals scored by the home sides in a football league one Saturday.

Score	Frequency	Score	Cumulative frequency
0	3	$\leqslant 0$	3
1	8	$\leqslant 1$	$3 + 8 = 11$
2	4	$\leqslant 2$	
3	3	$\leqslant 3$	
4	5	$\leqslant 4$	
5	2	$\leqslant 5$	
6	1	$\leqslant 6$	

2. Complete the following table which shows the distribution of the marks scored by the first year pupils in their English test.

Mark	Frequency (no. of pupils' scores within each range)	Mark	Cumulative frequency
1–10	7	$\leqslant 10$	
11–20	14	$\leqslant 20$	
21–30	18	$\leqslant 30$	
31–40	33	$\leqslant 40$	
41–50	36	$\leqslant 50$	
51–60	43	$\leqslant 60$	
61–70	21	$\leqslant 70$	
71–80	15	$\leqslant 80$	
81–90	8	$\leqslant 90$	
91–100	5	$\leqslant 100$	

a) How many first-year pupils are there ?

b) How many scored 50 or less ?

c) How many scored more than 60 ?

3. The table is based on a cricketer's scores in one season. Complete the table to show the cumulative frequencies.

Score	0–19	20–39	40–59	60–79	80–99	100–119	120–139
Frequency	8	14	33	6	5	3	1
Score	$\leqslant 19$	$\leqslant 39$	$\leqslant 59$	$\leqslant 79$	$\leqslant 99$	$\leqslant 119$	$\leqslant 139$
Cumulative frequency							

a) How many innings did he play ?

b) In how many innings did he score less than 60 ?

c) In how many innings did he score 40 or more ?

4. The table is based on a golfer's scores on the professional circuit one summer.

Score	67	68	69	70	71	72
Frequency	2	4	9			
Score	$\leqslant 67$	$\leqslant 68$	$\leqslant 69$	$\leqslant 70$	$\leqslant 71$	$\leqslant 72$
Cumulative frequency	2	6	15	24	36	51

Score	73	74	75	76	77	78
Frequency						
Score	$\leqslant 73$	$\leqslant 74$	$\leqslant 75$	$\leqslant 76$	$\leqslant 77$	$\leqslant 78$
Cumulative frequency	64	72	77	85	91	95

Complete this table and hence find

a) the number of rounds in which he scored 73

b) the number of rounds in which he scored 75 or more.

5. A school organises a Grand Prize Draw to raise money to buy a minibus. Tickets are sold at 50 p per book and pupils are encouraged to sell as many books as possible by the award of inducement prizes, including a first prize of £ 20 to the pupil who sells the most books. The table shows the distribution of the numbers of books sold by the pupils in the school.

Number of books sold	0–5	6–10	11–15	16–20	21–25
Frequency	77	124			
Number of books sold	$\leqslant 5$	$\leqslant 10$	$\leqslant 15$	$\leqslant 20$	$\leqslant 25$
Cumulative frequency			383	611	775

Number of books sold	26–30	31–35	36–40	41–45	46–50
Frequency		73	32	22	9
Number of books sold	$\leqslant 30$	$\leqslant 35$	$\leqslant 40$	$\leqslant 45$	$\leqslant 50$
Cumulative frequency	867				

Complete the table and hence find

a) the number of pupils who sold more than 30 books

b) the number of pupils who sold fewer than 21 books

c) the number of pupils who sold more than 10 books but fewer than 31 books.

Was the £ 20 inducement prize won by one pupil or could it have been shared ?

CUMULATIVE FREQUENCY CURVE

When we have cumulative tables like those given in the previous exercise we can draw a graph by plotting the cumulative frequency against the mark or score.

The data for question 2 of the previous exercise can be set out as given below.

Mark	⩽ 10	⩽ 20	⩽ 30	⩽ 40	⩽ 50	⩽ 60	⩽ 70	⩽ 80	⩽ 90	⩽ 100
Cumulative frequency	7	21	39	72	108	151	172	187	195	200

If we plot each cumulative frequency at the *upper value* of each interval the marks can either be joined by straight lines, in which case the graph is called the *cumulative frequency polygon,* or we can draw a smooth curve through them to obtain a *cumulative frequency curve.*

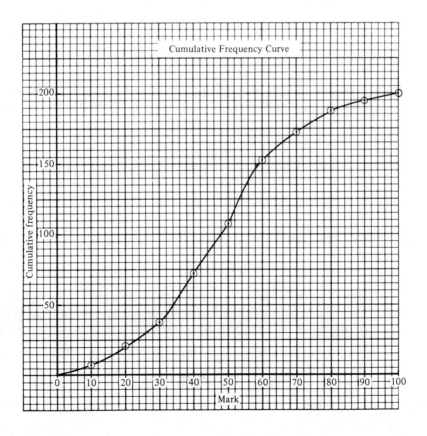

EXERCISE 13d

Use the cumulative frequency tables from questions 1 to 4 of Exercise 13c to draw a cumulative frequency curve for each set of data.

FINDING THE MEDIAN

Remember that when we need one number to represent a set then, depending on the circumstances, we can use either the mean, or the mode, or the median (see Book 3A, Chapter 26).

The *mean,* or arithmetic average, of a set of n numbers is the sum of the numbers divided by n.

The *mode* of a set of numbers is the number that occurs most often.

For example, given the numbers 3, 4, 5, 5, 5, 8, 9, 9

$$\text{the mean is } \frac{3+4+5+5+5+8+9+9}{8} = 6$$

$$\text{the mode is } 5$$

The *median* of a set of numbers is the number in the middle when they are arranged in order of size. If there are n numbers in the set the median is the $\left(\dfrac{n+1}{2}\right)$th number.

When n is even there is no actual $\left(\dfrac{n+1}{2}\right)$th number, so we take the average of the numbers on each side of $\dfrac{n+1}{2}$, e.g. for 10 numbers, the $\left(\dfrac{n+1}{2}\right)$th number is the $5\frac{1}{2}$th number and there is no such number, so we take the average of the 5th and 6th.

The median can easily be found from the cumulative frequency curve. At the middle value of the cumulative frequency we draw a line across to meet the curve, and read off the corresponding value of the mark.

In our example the middle value of the cumulative frequency is the $\left(\dfrac{200+1}{2}\right)$th value, i.e. the $100\frac{1}{2}$th value.

We approximate this to the 100th value.

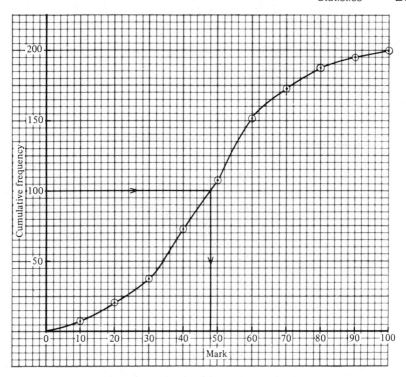

From the graph the median mark is 48.

EXERCISE 13e

1. Find the median from each cumulative frequency curve drawn for the questions in Exercise 13d.

2. Use the cumulative frequency table that follows to draw the cumulative frequency curve for the prices of all the houses advertised in a property magazine one weekend.

Price (thousands of £s)	$\leqslant 30$	$\leqslant 40$	$\leqslant 50$	$\leqslant 60$	$\leqslant 70$
Cumulative frequency	10	22	60	128	170

Price (thousands of £s)	$\leqslant 80$	$\leqslant 90$	$\leqslant 100$	$\leqslant 110$	$\leqslant 120$
Cumulative frequency	187	197	203	208	210

Use your graph to estimate the median 'asking price' price for a house.

3. The cumulative frequency curve for the marks in an English test is given below. Use the graph to find

a) the number of pupils sitting the test   b) the median mark.

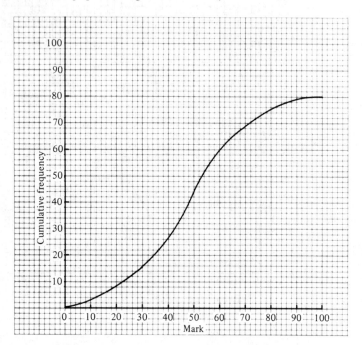

4. Use the following cumulative frequency table to draw the corresponding cumulative frequency curve for the marks obtained by candidates in an examination.

Marks	⩽9	⩽19	⩽29	⩽39	⩽49
Cumulative frequency	7	16	28	47	80

Marks	⩽59	⩽69	⩽79	⩽89	⩽99
Cumulative frequency	125	174	202	212	220

Use your graph to estimate the median mark.

5. The number of cars using a cross-channel ferry on each trip during a particular month was noted and the results are given in the following table.

Number of cars	40	41	42	43	44	45	46	47	48	49	50
Number of crossings	2	4	6	10	10	12	8	6	2	1	1

Give the corresponding cumulative frequency table and hence draw the cumulative frequency curve. Use your graph to estimate the median number of cars making the crossing. How many crossings did the ferry make during the month ?

6. A traffic survey counted the number of cars per hour passing Southwood Post Office each hour of the day from 8 a.m. to 6 p.m. for a week. The results are given in the table.

	8 a.m. –9 a.m.	9 a.m. –10 a.m.	10 a.m. –11 a.m.	11 a.m. –12 noon	12 noon –1 p.m.
Monday	39	37	46	36	41
Tuesday	16	31	40	39	42
Wednesday	24	39	37	45	44
Thursday	19	33	32	34	42
Friday	30	37	36	41	48
Saturday	28	38	46	39	42
Sunday	3	7	42	14	11

	1 p.m. –2 p.m.	2 p.m. –3 p.m.	3 p.m. –4 p.m.	4 p.m. –5 p.m.	5 p.m. –6 p.m.
Monday	34	33	32	22	23
Tuesday	43	39	37	24	17
Wednesday	39	38	36	29	27
Thursday	38	37	39	25	27
Friday	47	40	43	35	34
Saturday	48	42	40	31	33
Sunday	33	36	35	27	26

Use groups 0–5, 6–10, 11–15, etc. to make a frequency table and a cumulative frequency table. Draw the cumulative frequency curve and use it to estimate the median number of cars passing Southwood Post Office per hour.

RANGE

So far we have described a distribution by finding where its centre is, but we also need to know how widely the distribution is spread. One measure of spread, or *dispersion*, is the range.

The *range* is the difference between the two extreme values. It is considered to be of little use since it tells us nothing about all the other values in between, and it can be distorted by one or two extreme values.

Consider a student who scores marks of 54, 93, 86, 75, 8, 59, 73, 83, 55, 64, 73, 52, 74, 64 and 70 in fifteen examinations. The range is from 8 to 93, whereas every mark apart from the 8 is more than 50.

QUARTILES

A much better measure of spread is found by using the range of the middle 50% of the values. To find this we use the *quartiles*.

First arrange the n values in ascending order.

The *lower quartile* is the $\left(\dfrac{n+1}{4}\right)$th value, and the *upper quartile* is the $3\left(\dfrac{n+1}{4}\right)$th value.

The difference between the upper quartile and the lower quartile is called the *interquartile range*.

If Q_1 denotes the lower quartile and Q_3 the upper quartile, the interquartile range is $Q_3 - Q_1$.

When the fifteen examination marks given on page 237 are written in ascending order they are

$$8, 50, 54, 55, 59, 64, 64, 70, 73, 73, 74, 75, 83, 86, 93$$

Q_1 is the $\left(\dfrac{15+1}{4}\right)$th value, i.e. the 4th value

$\therefore$ $Q_1 = 55$

Q_3 is the $3\left(\dfrac{15+1}{4}\right)$th value, i.e. the 12th value

$\therefore$ $Q_3 = 75$

$\therefore$ the interquartile range is $Q_3 - Q_1$

$$= 75 - 55$$

$$= 20$$

Sometimes it is convenient to use the semi-interquartile range which is defined as $\dfrac{Q_3 - Q_1}{2}$.

In our example, the semi-interquartile range is $\dfrac{20}{2}$, i.e. 10.

When the number of values is large it is convenient to make certain approximations. If $n = 200$, Q_1 is the $\left(\dfrac{200+1}{4}\right)$th value, i.e. the $50\frac{1}{4}$th value, and Q_3 is the $150\frac{3}{4}$th value. We use the 50th value and the 150th value.

The cumulative frequency curve for the English test scores, given on page 233 is reproduced below.

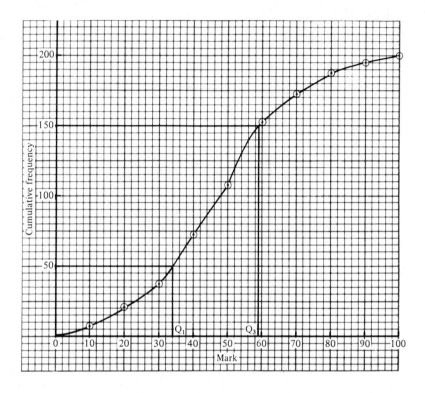

From the curve $Q_1 = 34$

       and $Q_3 = 59$

The interquartile range is therefore $59 - 34 = 25$, and the semi-interquartile range is $12\frac{1}{2}$.

EXERCISE 13f

1. Use the cumulative frequency curves obtained in questions 4 to 6 of Exercise 13e to find, for each set of data,

a) the upper and lower quartiles

b) the interquartile range.

2. The cumulative frequency curve given below shows the weekly earnings, in pounds, of a group of teenagers.

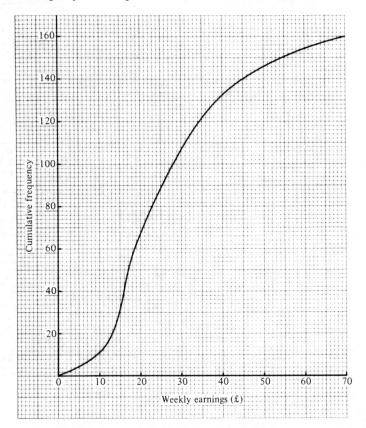

Use the graph to find   a) the median   b) the upper and lower quartiles. Hence find the interquartile range.

3. The table shows the distribution of the ages of people attending a public concert.

Age range	0–19	20–39	40–59	60–79	80–99
No. of people attending concert	8	26	110	128	56

Copy and complete the following cumulative frequency table and use it to draw a cumulative frequency curve.

Age range	< 20	< 40	< 60	< 80	< 100
No. of people attending concert					

Hence find

a) the number of people attending the concert

b) the median age

c) the upper and lower quartile ages, and the interquartile range.

4. One hundred people were chosen at random and each was allowed to fire 50 shots from a gun at a target. The number of bulls scored by each person was noted and the following frequency table was constructed.

Number of bulls	Frequency	Number of of bulls	Cumulative frequency
1–5	1	$\leqslant 5$	
6–10	3	$\leqslant 10$	
11–15	5	$\leqslant 15$	
16–20	7		
21–25	15		
26–30	25		
31–35	20		
36–40	12		
41–45	8		
46–50	4		

Copy this table and complete the third and fourth columns. Draw the cumulative frequency curve using a scale of 2 cm to represent 10 bulls on one axis and 2 cm to represent a cumulative frequency of 10 on the other axis. Use your graph to estimate

a) the median   b) the upper and lower quartiles.

5. The marks obtained by the pupils sitting a test are given in the following table.

Marks	0–9	10–19	20–29	30–39	40–49	50–59	60–69	70–79
Frequency	9	13	27	43	28	20	12	8

Illustrate these figures by drawing a cumulative frequency curve. Use 2 cm to represent 10 marks on the one axis and a cumulative frequency of 20 on the other axis. Use your graph to estimate

a) the median

b) the upper and lower quartiles, and hence the interquartile range

c) the pass mark if three-quarters of the pupils pass.

6. In the first round of a golf tournament the following scores were recorded:

```
70   68   71   67   74   69   69   71   68   70
71   70   72   69   69   68   71   70   70   72
72   69   68   70   68   69   67   71   69   70
68   67   70   70   73   69   71   67   69   68
```

a) Construct a frequency table for these scores.

b) Use this to give a cumulative frequency table.

c) How many rounds of less than 70 were there ?

d) How many rounds of more than 69 were there ?

e) Use your cumulative frequency table to draw a cumulative frequency curve and use it to find the median score.

7. The table is based on a cricketer's scores in 100 innings.

Score	0–10	11–20	21–30	31–40	41–50	51–60
Frequency	7	9	11	13	16	18

Score	61–70	71–80	81–90	91–100	101–110	111–120
Frequency	11	7	4	2	1	1

a) Construct a cumulative frequency table for these scores and use it to draw a cumulative frequency curve.

b) How many scores did he have that were 50 or less than 50 ?

c) How many scores did he have that were more than 70 ?

d) Use the curve to estimate the median score, the upper and lower quartiles, and the interquartile range.

8. A botanist measured the lengths of 120 leaf specimens from a certain species of tree. The results were as follows:

Length (cm)	< 9	< 9.5	< 10	< 10.5	< 11	< 11.5	< 12
Cumulative frequency	2	6	14	23	35	50	73

Length (cm)	< 12.5	< 13	< 13.5	< 14	< 14.5	< 15
Cumulative frequency	92	103	112	116	119	120

Use this data to draw a cumulative frequency graph. From your curve find

a) the median length

b) the values of the upper and lower quartiles.

MIXED QUESTIONS ON STATISTICS AND PROBABILITY

The following exercise contains questions on work covered in Book 3A, together with work covered in this chapter.

EXERCISE 13g

1. The following cumulative frequency table gives the percentage marks of 250 pupils in an English examination.

Mark	10	20	30	40	50	60	70	80	90	100
Number of pupils scoring up to and including this mark	5	15	29	52	89	142	197	223	240	250

a) How many pupils scored a mark of more than 70 ?

b) How many pupils scored a mark from 41 to 60 ?

c) Plot the values from the table on a graph and draw a smooth curve through your points. (Use a scale of 2 cm to represent 20 marks on the one axis and 2 cm to represent a cumulative frequency of 25 on the other axis.)

d) Use your graph to estimate
   i) the median   ii) the upper and lower quartiles.

e) State the probability that a pupil chosen at random will have a mark.
   i) less than or equal to 50   ii) greater than 60.

2. The following cumulative frequency table gives the result of a survey into the masses (in kilograms) of 80 boys.

Mass (kg)	$\leqslant 45$	$\leqslant 50$	$\leqslant 55$	$\leqslant 60$	$\leqslant 65$	$\leqslant 70$
Cumulative frequency	7	11	14	19	25	32

Mass (kg)	$\leqslant 75$	$\leqslant 80$	$\leqslant 85$	$\leqslant 90$	$\leqslant 95$
Cumulative frequency	42	58	71	78	80

a) Calculate how many boys have a mass of more than 80 kg.

b) Calculate how many boys have a mass of 65 kg or less but more than 50 kg.

c) Using a vertical scale of 2 cm to represent 10 boys and a horizontal scale of 2 cm to represent 10 kg, plot these values on graph paper and draw a smooth curve through your points.

d) Use your graph to estimate the median mass and the upper and lower quartile masses.

e) State the probability that a boy chosen at random will have a mass in excess of 70 kg.

3. The histogram illustrates the distribution of the weekly pocket money of the 240 pupils in the fourth year of a school.

a) How many pupils received from £6 to £10 inclusive ?

b) Half the pupils received more than £x per week. Estimate the value of x.

c) The line AB indicates that the value of the lower quartile of the distribution is £1.50. What does this mean ?

d) The value of the interquartile range is £2.70. What is the value of the upper quartile ? What information does the interquartile range give us about the weekly pocket money of the group ?

e) Estimate the total amount of pocket money received by the fourth year pupils.

f) Hence estimate the mean amount of pocket money received by the fourth year pupils.

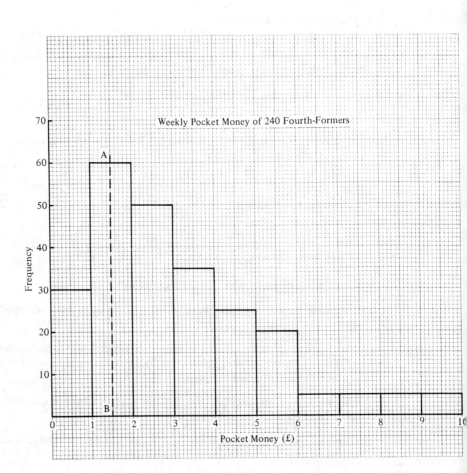

4. The following marks were obtained by the 80 candidates in an English test which was marked out of 60.

```
54  52  31  47  24  36  27  15  44  26
 8  20  46  32  27  31  33  57  39  32
43  32  23  33  31  21  38  28  40  19
52  37  38  39   9  30  47  29   8  13
33  35  48  18  36  39  23  58  34  35
16  21  32  38  34  13  27  32  37  23
37  49  25  38  24  27  48  36  45  18
41  34  43  12  47  24   8  29  37  33
```

Use this data to complete the table below.

Interval	Tally	Frequency	Mark	Cumulative frequency
0–9			$\leqslant 9$	
10–19			$\leqslant 19$	
20–29			$\leqslant 29$	
30–39				
40–49				
50–60				

Use the information in your table to draw a cumulative frequency curve and from it estimate

a) the median mark

b) the upper and lower quartiles

c) the number of candidates who passed if the pass mark was 40

d) the pass mark if 70% of the candidates passed

e) the probability that a pupil selected at random scored less than 30.

5. The marks of 4000 candidates in a history examination are summarised in the table.

Mark	$\leqslant 20$	$\leqslant 30$	$\leqslant 40$	$\leqslant 50$	$\leqslant 60$	$\leqslant 70$	$\leqslant 80$	$\leqslant 90$	$\leqslant 100$
Number of candidates	230	450	750	1400	2400	3300	3800	3950	4000

a) Draw a cumulative frequency diagram to represent this data. (Use 2 cm to represent 20 marks on the *x*-axis and 2 cm to represent 500 candidates on the cumulative frequency axis.)

b) Use your cumulative frequency diagram to find
   i) the number of candidates who scored 75 marks or less
   ii) the median mark
   iii) the interquartile range
   iv) the percentage of candidates who scored more than 65%.

c) What is the probability that the score of a candidate chosen at random is
   i) 40 or less
   ii) from 41 to 60 inclusive ?

6. The ages, in completed years, of the forty applicants for a teaching post are given in the following table.

Age (years)	21–24	25–28	29–32	33–36	37–44
Frequency	3	4	8	12	13

(Note that an applicant aged 36 years and 8 months belongs to the 33–36 group.)

a) Draw up a suitable cumulative frequency table and hence draw a cumulative frequency curve. Use 2 cm to represent 2 years on the horizontal axis and 2 cm to represent 5 on the cumulative frequency axis.

b) Use your graph to find the interquartile range.

c) What is the probability that an applicant drawn at random
   i) belongs to the 29–32 group
   ii) is 33 years of age or older ?

d) If two applicants are selected at random from all the applicants, what is the probability that
   i) both come from the 29–32 age group ?
   ii) the first comes from the 29–32 age group and the second from the 37–44 age group ?

14 MATRIX TRANSFORMATIONS

Matrices can be used for several different purposes, for example they can be used for solving simultaneous equations and for processing information. Now we will see how they can be used for defining some transformations.

THE POSITION VECTOR OF A POINT

If a point has coordinates $(2, 4)$, then the vector $\overrightarrow{OA}$ is $\begin{pmatrix} 2 \\ 4 \end{pmatrix}$ and this is called the *position vector* of A relative to the original O.

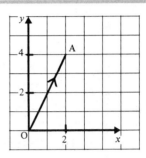

EXERCISE 14a

Give the position vector of the point $A(6, -1)$. Illustrate with a sketch.

A is the point $(6, -1)$

$$\overrightarrow{OA} = \begin{pmatrix} 6 \\ -1 \end{pmatrix}$$

Give the position vectors of the points in questions 1 to 6. Illustrate each with a sketch.

1. $(4, 5)$ **3.** $(-7, 5)$ **5.** $(5, 3)$

2. $(3, -2)$ **4.** $(-3, -5)$ **6.** $(-5, 2)$

Give the coordinates of the points whose position vectors are given in questions 7 to 12. Illustrate each with a sketch.

7. $\begin{pmatrix} 5 \\ 2 \end{pmatrix}$ **9.** $\begin{pmatrix} -2 \\ -4 \end{pmatrix}$ **11.** $\begin{pmatrix} -6 \\ 2 \end{pmatrix}$

8. $\begin{pmatrix} 1 \\ -3 \end{pmatrix}$ **10.** $\begin{pmatrix} 2 \\ -3 \end{pmatrix}$ **12.** $\begin{pmatrix} 2 \\ -6 \end{pmatrix}$

THE IMAGE OF A POSITION VECTOR

EXERCISE 14b

Find the image of the position vector $\begin{pmatrix} 3 \\ 5 \end{pmatrix}$ under a reflection in the *y*-axis.

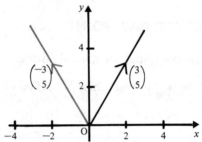

The image is the vector $\begin{pmatrix} -3 \\ 5 \end{pmatrix}$.

For each of the following questions, draw *x* and *y* axes, marking values from −5 to 5 on each axis.

1. Find the image of the position vector $\begin{pmatrix} 5 \\ 2 \end{pmatrix}$ under a rotation of 90° clockwise about the origin.

2. Find the image of the position vector $\begin{pmatrix} -4 \\ 3 \end{pmatrix}$ under a reflection in the *x*-axis.

3. Find the image of the position vector $\begin{pmatrix} 4 \\ -2 \end{pmatrix}$ under a rotation of 180° about the origin.

4. Find the image of the position vector $\begin{pmatrix} 3 \\ -5 \end{pmatrix}$ under a rotation of 90° clockwise about the origin.

5. Find the image of the position vector $\begin{pmatrix} 5 \\ 3 \end{pmatrix}$ under a reflection in the line $y = x$.

6. Find the image of the position vector $\begin{pmatrix} 2 \\ 1 \end{pmatrix}$ under an enlargement with scale factor 2, centre the origin.

TRANSFORMATION MATRIX

Consider the transformation which is a reflection in the x-axis. If the object is the position vector $\begin{pmatrix} 3 \\ 2 \end{pmatrix}$, the image is $\begin{pmatrix} 3 \\ -2 \end{pmatrix}$

We can say that this transformation changes $\begin{pmatrix} 3 \\ 2 \end{pmatrix}$ to $\begin{pmatrix} 3 \\ -2 \end{pmatrix}$

This transformation changes any position vector in the same way: it leaves the x coordinate alone but it changes the sign of the y coordinate, i.e.,

it changes $\begin{pmatrix} a \\ b \end{pmatrix}$ to $\begin{pmatrix} a \\ -b \end{pmatrix}$

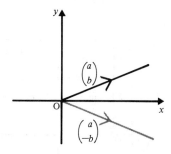

We also know that premultiplying by a matrix changes a vector,

e.g. $\begin{pmatrix} 1 & 0 \\ 0 & -1 \end{pmatrix} \begin{pmatrix} 4 \\ 3 \end{pmatrix} = \begin{pmatrix} 4 \\ -3 \end{pmatrix}$ and $\begin{pmatrix} 1 & 0 \\ 0 & -1 \end{pmatrix} \begin{pmatrix} a \\ b \end{pmatrix} = \begin{pmatrix} a \\ -b \end{pmatrix}$

So we can use the matrix $\begin{pmatrix} 1 & 0 \\ 0 & -1 \end{pmatrix}$ to define the transformation 'reflection

in the x-axis'. We call $\begin{pmatrix} 1 & 0 \\ 0 & -1 \end{pmatrix}$ a *transformation matrix*.

FINDING THE IMAGE

If we are given a transformation matrix $\begin{pmatrix} 2 & 1 \\ 1 & 1 \end{pmatrix}$ and a point A(2, 3),

then we can find the image A′ under this transformation, by multiplying the position vector of A by the transformation matrix.

$$\overset{}{} \quad \overset{A}{} \quad \overset{A'}{}$$

i.e. $\qquad \begin{pmatrix} 2 & 1 \\ 1 & 1 \end{pmatrix} \begin{pmatrix} 2 \\ 3 \end{pmatrix} = \begin{pmatrix} 7 \\ 5 \end{pmatrix}$

Note that the transformation matrix *must* come first.

The position vector of A' is then $\begin{pmatrix} 7 \\ 5 \end{pmatrix}$ and A' is the point (7, 5).

EXERCISE 14c

Find the image, A', of the point A(1, 2) under the transformation defined by the matrix $\begin{pmatrix} 3 & 1 \\ 1 & 1 \end{pmatrix}$. Illustrate with a sketch.

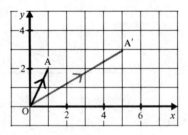

The position vector of A is $\begin{pmatrix} 1 \\ 2 \end{pmatrix}$

$$\overset{}{} \quad \overset{A}{} \quad \overset{A'}{}$$

$$\begin{pmatrix} 3 & 1 \\ 1 & 1 \end{pmatrix} \begin{pmatrix} 1 \\ 2 \end{pmatrix} = \begin{pmatrix} 5 \\ 3 \end{pmatrix}$$

The position vector of A' is $\begin{pmatrix} 5 \\ 3 \end{pmatrix}$, i.e. A' is the point (5, 3).

Find the image, A', of the given point A under the transformation defined by the given matrix. Illustrate with a diagram

1. The point A is (1, 2) and the transformation matrix is $\begin{pmatrix} 1 & 2 \\ 3 & 4 \end{pmatrix}$

2. The point A is (4, 1) and the transformation matrix is $\begin{pmatrix} 2 & 1 \\ 1 & 2 \end{pmatrix}$

3. The point A is (−2, 3) and the transformation matrix is $\begin{pmatrix} 1 & 2 \\ 1 & 1 \end{pmatrix}$

4. The point A is (−1, −3) and the transformation matrix is $\begin{pmatrix} -1 & 1 \\ 2 & 1 \end{pmatrix}$

5. The point A is (2, 3) and the transformation matrix is $\begin{pmatrix} 4 & -1 \\ -1 & 2 \end{pmatrix}$

6. The point A is (2, −1) and the transformation matrix is $\begin{pmatrix} 1 & 3 \\ 0 & 1 \end{pmatrix}$

Sometimes, there are several object and image points on one diagram. If so, then it is clearer to mark only the points and to leave out the lines representing the position vectors.

Find the images, A′ and B′, of the points A(3, 1) and B(1, 4) under the transformation defined by the matrix $\begin{pmatrix} 0 & 1 \\ 1 & 0 \end{pmatrix}$. Mark the points on a sketch. Join AB and A′B′.

$$\begin{matrix} & A & A' \\ \begin{pmatrix} 0 & 1 \\ 1 & 0 \end{pmatrix} & \begin{pmatrix} 3 \\ 1 \end{pmatrix} & = \begin{pmatrix} 1 \\ 3 \end{pmatrix} \end{matrix}$$

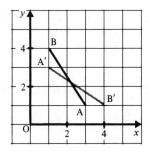

$$\begin{matrix} & B & B' \\ \begin{pmatrix} 0 & 1 \\ 1 & 0 \end{pmatrix} & \begin{pmatrix} 1 \\ 4 \end{pmatrix} & = \begin{pmatrix} 4 \\ 1 \end{pmatrix} \end{matrix}$$

A′ is the point (1, 3) and B′ is the point (4, 1).

In questions 7 to 12 you are given the coordinates of two points A and B and a transformation matrix. Find the coordinates of the images, A' and B', of A and B under the transformation defined by the matrix. Mark all the points on the diagram, but do not draw the position vectors. In each case join AB and A'B'.

7. A is the point $(1, 1)$, B is the point $(3, 2)$ and the transformation matrix is

$$\begin{pmatrix} -1 & 0 \\ 0 & 1 \end{pmatrix}$$

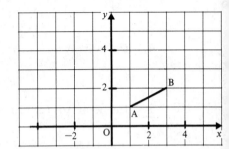

8. A is the point $(1, -1)$, B is the point $(2, 0)$ and the transformation matrix is

$$\begin{pmatrix} 1 & 2 \\ 2 & 3 \end{pmatrix}$$

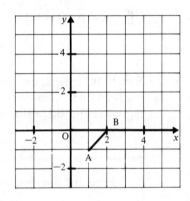

9. A is the point $(1, 3)$, B is the point $(1, -2)$ and the transformation matrix is $\begin{pmatrix} 1 & 3 \\ 0 & 1 \end{pmatrix}$

10. A is the point $(1, 1)$, B is the point $(-2, 0)$ and the transformation matrix is $\begin{pmatrix} 3 & 0 \\ 0 & 3 \end{pmatrix}$

11. A is the point $(1, 4)$, B is the point $(4, 1)$ and the transformation matrix is $\begin{pmatrix} 1 & -1 \\ -2 & 1 \end{pmatrix}$

12. A is the point $(3, 2)$, B is the point $(-3, 2)$ and the transformation matrix is $\begin{pmatrix} 1 & 2 \\ 2 & -1 \end{pmatrix}$

IDENTIFYING A TRANSFORMATION

To find out whether a transformation is a reflection, a rotation, an enlargement or some other transformation, we need a simple object to which the transformation can be applied.

A rectangle or a triangle is usually the most convenient.

REFLECTIONS

EXERCISE 14d

A, B, C and D are the points $(1, 0)$, $(3, 0)$, $(3, 3)$ and $(1, 3)$. Draw a diagram, mark the given points and join them up.

Find the image of each point under the transformation defined by the matrix $\begin{pmatrix} -1 & 0 \\ 0 & 1 \end{pmatrix}$, marking the points on the diagram.

Join up the image points in order. What is the transformation?

$$\begin{matrix} & A & & A' \\ \begin{pmatrix} -1 & 0 \\ 0 & 1 \end{pmatrix} & \begin{pmatrix} 1 \\ 0 \end{pmatrix} & = & \begin{pmatrix} -1 \\ 0 \end{pmatrix} \end{matrix}$$

$$\begin{matrix} & B & & A' \\ \begin{pmatrix} -1 & 0 \\ 0 & 1 \end{pmatrix} & \begin{pmatrix} 3 \\ 0 \end{pmatrix} & = & \begin{pmatrix} -3 \\ 0 \end{pmatrix} \end{matrix}$$

$$\begin{matrix} & C & & C' \\ \begin{pmatrix} -1 & 0 \\ 0 & 1 \end{pmatrix} & \begin{pmatrix} 3 \\ 3 \end{pmatrix} & = & \begin{pmatrix} -3 \\ 3 \end{pmatrix} \end{matrix}$$

$$\begin{matrix} & D & & D' \\ \begin{pmatrix} -1 & 0 \\ 0 & 1 \end{pmatrix} & \begin{pmatrix} 1 \\ 3 \end{pmatrix} & = & \begin{pmatrix} -1 \\ 3 \end{pmatrix} \end{matrix}$$

The transformation is a reflection. The mirror line is the *y*-axis.

Draw x and y axes, each using a scale from -4 to 5. Mark the given points and join them up in order. Find the image of each point under the transformation defined by the given matrix and join up the image points in order. You will see that the transformation is a reflection. What is the mirror line?

1. The given points are A(-2, 1), B(2, 1), C(3, 2) and D(-1, 2).

The transformation matrix is $\begin{pmatrix} 1 & 0 \\ 0 & -1 \end{pmatrix}$

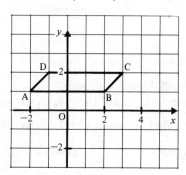

2. The given points are A(1, 1), B(4, 1) and C(4, 2).

The transformation matrix is $\begin{pmatrix} 0 & 1 \\ 1 & 0 \end{pmatrix}$

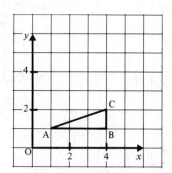

3. The given points are A(2, -3), B(5, -3) and C(3, 2).

The transformation matrix is $\begin{pmatrix} -1 & 0 \\ 0 & 1 \end{pmatrix}$

4. The given points are A(4, 1), B(3, 3) and C(2, 0).

The transformation matrix is $\begin{pmatrix} 0 & -1 \\ -1 & 0 \end{pmatrix}$

To save writing so many matrices, we can combine two or three or more position vectors into one matrix.

Find the images of A(2, 0), B(3, 3) and C(−1, 1) under the transformation defined by the matrix $\begin{pmatrix} -1 & 0 \\ 0 & 1 \end{pmatrix}$. Mark the object and the image points on a diagram. What is the transformation ?

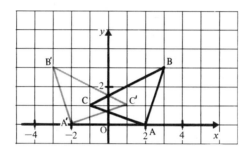

$$\begin{pmatrix} -1 & 0 \\ 0 & 1 \end{pmatrix} \overset{\text{A \ B \ C}}{\begin{pmatrix} 2 & 3 & -1 \\ 0 & 3 & 1 \end{pmatrix}} = \overset{\text{A' \ B' \ C'}}{\begin{pmatrix} -2 & -3 & 1 \\ 0 & 3 & 1 \end{pmatrix}}$$

The transformation is a reflection.
The mirror line is the *y*-axis.

5. The given points are A(1, 1), B(3, 1), C(3, 2) and D(1, 2).

The transformation matrix is $\begin{pmatrix} 0 & 1 \\ 1 & 0 \end{pmatrix}$

6. The given points are A(2, 0), B(4, 0), C(4, 2) and D(2, 2).

The transformation matrix is $\begin{pmatrix} 0 & 1 \\ 1 & 0 \end{pmatrix}$

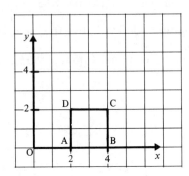

7. The given points are A(1, 1), B(2, 1), C(2, 2) and D(1, 2).

The transformation matrix is $\begin{pmatrix} 0 & -1 \\ -1 & 0 \end{pmatrix}$

8. The given points are A(1, 0), B(4, 0) and C(4, 2).

The transformation matrix is $\begin{pmatrix} -1 & 0 \\ 0 & 1 \end{pmatrix}$

9. The given points are A(2, 1), B(3, 1), C(3, 4) and D(2, 4).

The transformation matrix is $\begin{pmatrix} 1 & 0 \\ 0 & -1 \end{pmatrix}$

10. The given points are A(1, 1), B(3, 1), C(4, 3) and D(3, 3).

The transformation matrix is $\begin{pmatrix} 0 & 1 \\ 1 & 0 \end{pmatrix}$

11. The given points are A(2, 4), B(4, 5) and C(3, 2).

The transformation matrix is $\begin{pmatrix} -1 & 0 \\ 0 & 1 \end{pmatrix}$

ROTATIONS

EXERCISE 14e

A, B and C are the points $(1, 0)$, $(3, 0)$ and $(3, 1)$. Draw a diagram, mark the points and join them up. Find the image of each point under the transformation defined by the matrix $\begin{pmatrix} 0 & -1 \\ 1 & 0 \end{pmatrix}$. Mark the image points on the diagram and join them up. What is the transformation?

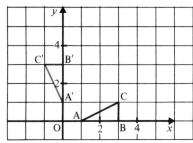

$$\begin{pmatrix} 0 & -1 \\ 1 & 0 \end{pmatrix} \overset{\text{A B C}}{\begin{pmatrix} 1 & 3 & 3 \\ 0 & 0 & 1 \end{pmatrix}} = \overset{\text{A' B' C'}}{\begin{pmatrix} 0 & 0 & -1 \\ 1 & 3 & 3 \end{pmatrix}}$$

The transformation is a rotation.
Its centre is O. The angle of rotation is 90° anticlockwise.

Draw x and y axes, marking values from -4 to 4 on each axis. Mark the given points and join them up in order. Find the image of each point under the transformation defined by the given matrix and join up the image points. You will see that the transformation is a rotation. Describe the rotation.

1. The given points are $A(1, 1)$, $B(4, 1)$, $C(4, 3)$ and $D(1, 3)$.

The transformation matrix is $\begin{pmatrix} 0 & 1 \\ -1 & 0 \end{pmatrix}$

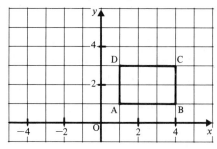

2. The given points are A(1, 1), B(4, 1), C(4, 2) and D(1, 2).

The transformation matrix is $\begin{pmatrix} -1 & 0 \\ 0 & -1 \end{pmatrix}$

3. The given points are A(1, 0), B(3, 0) and C(4, 4).

The transformation matrix is $\begin{pmatrix} 0 & -1 \\ 1 & 0 \end{pmatrix}$

<u>4.</u> The given points are A(1, 1), B(4, 1) and C(4, 4).

The transformation matrix is $\begin{pmatrix} 0 & 1 \\ -1 & 0 \end{pmatrix}$

<u>5.</u> The given points are A(3, 2), B(4, 3) and C(1, 4).

The transformation matrix is $\begin{pmatrix} -1 & 0 \\ 0 & -1 \end{pmatrix}$

ENLARGEMENTS

EXERCISE 14f

A, B, C and D are the points (1, 0), (3, 0), (3, 3) and (1, 3). Draw a diagram, mark the points and join them up in order. Find the image of each point under the transformation defined by the matrix $\begin{pmatrix} 2 & 0 \\ 0 & 2 \end{pmatrix}$ and mark each point on the diagram. Join up the image points. What is the transformation?

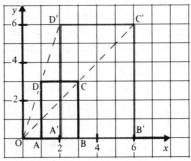

$$\begin{array}{cc} & \begin{array}{cccc} A & B & C & D \end{array} \\ \begin{pmatrix} 2 & 0 \\ 0 & 2 \end{pmatrix} & \begin{pmatrix} 1 & 3 & 3 & 1 \\ 0 & 0 & 3 & 3 \end{pmatrix} \end{array} = \begin{array}{c} \begin{array}{cccc} A' & B' & C' & D' \end{array} \\ \begin{pmatrix} 2 & 6 & 6 & 2 \\ 0 & 0 & 6 & 6 \end{pmatrix} \end{array}$$

The transformation is an enlargement, centre O, with scale factor 2.

Draw *x* and *y* axes, marking values from 0 to 10 on each. Mark the given points and join them up in order. Find the image of each of the given points under the transformation defined by the given matrix. Mark the image points and join them up in order. Describe the enlargement.

1. The given points are A(1, 0), B(3, 0) and C(3, 3).

The transformation matrix is $\begin{pmatrix} 2 & 0 \\ 0 & 2 \end{pmatrix}$

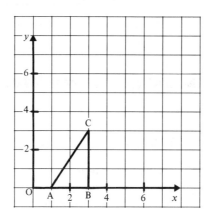

2. The given points are A(0, 1), B(−2, 1), C(−2, 0) and O(0, 0).

The transformation matrix is $\begin{pmatrix} 3 & 0 \\ 0 & 3 \end{pmatrix}$

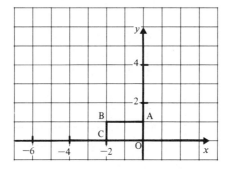

3. The given points are A(2, 2), B(2, 4), C(4, 4) and D(4, 2).

The transformation matrix is $\begin{pmatrix} 1\frac{1}{2} & 0 \\ 0 & 1\frac{1}{2} \end{pmatrix}$

4. The given points are A(4, 2), B(4, 4) and C(−4, 4).

The transformation matrix is $\begin{pmatrix} 2\frac{1}{2} & 0 \\ 0 & 2\frac{1}{2} \end{pmatrix}$

For questions 5 and 6, mark the axes with values from −5 to 5.

5. The given points are O(0, 0), A(0, 1), B(−1, 1) and C(−1, 0).

The transformation matrix is $\begin{pmatrix} -2 & 0 \\ 0 & -2 \end{pmatrix}$

6. The given points are A(0, 2), B(3, 2), C(3, 5) and D(0, 5).

The transformation matrix is $\begin{pmatrix} -1 & 0 \\ 0 & -1 \end{pmatrix}$

Is there another transformation which produces the same image ?

OTHER TRANSFORMATIONS – ONE-WAY STRETCH

EXERCISE 14g

A, B, C and D are the points (0, 1), (0, 3), (2, 3) and (2, 1). Draw a diagram, mark the points and join them up. Find the images of the given points under the transformation defined by the matrix $\begin{pmatrix} 4 & 0 \\ 0 & 1 \end{pmatrix}$. Mark the points and join them up. What is the transformation ?

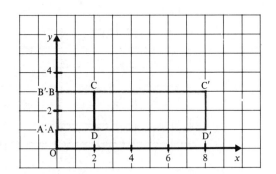

$$\begin{pmatrix} 4 & 0 \\ 0 & 1 \end{pmatrix} \begin{matrix} A & B & C & D \\ \begin{pmatrix} 0 & 0 & 2 & 2 \\ 1 & 3 & 3 & 1 \end{pmatrix} \end{matrix} = \begin{matrix} A' & B' & C' & D' \\ \begin{pmatrix} 0 & 0 & 8 & 8 \\ 1 & 3 & 3 & 1 \end{pmatrix} \end{matrix}$$

The transformation is a stretch parallel to the *x*-axis, with scale factor 4.

Draw x and y axes marking the values indicated on each. Mark the given points and join them up. Find the image of each of the given points under the transformation defined by the given matrix. Mark in the points and join them up. You will see that each transformation is a one-way stretch. Describe the transformation.

1. $0 \leqslant x \leqslant 10$, $-3 \leqslant y \leqslant 4$. The given points are A(1, 0), B(3, 0), C(3, 2) and D(1, 2). The transformation matrix is $\begin{pmatrix} 3 & 0 \\ 0 & 1 \end{pmatrix}$

2. $0 \leqslant x \leqslant 5$, $0 \leqslant y \leqslant 5$. The given points are A(1, 0), B(3, 0), C(3, 2) and D(1, 2). The transformation matrix is $\begin{pmatrix} 1 & 0 \\ 0 & 2 \end{pmatrix}$

<u>3.</u> $0 \leqslant x \leqslant 7$, $0 \leqslant y \leqslant 3$. The given points are A(1, 1), B(4, 1), C(4, 2) and D(1, 2). The transformation matrix is $\begin{pmatrix} 1\frac{1}{2} & 0 \\ 0 & 1 \end{pmatrix}$

<u>4.</u> $-3 \leqslant x \leqslant 3$, $0 \leqslant y \leqslant 7$. The given points are A(-2, 1), B(1, 1), C(1, 2) and D(-2, 2). The transformation matrix is $\begin{pmatrix} 1 & 0 \\ 0 & 3 \end{pmatrix}$

TRANSFORMATIONS THAT CANNOT BE DESCRIBED SIMPLY

Some transformation matrices define transformations which are different from any of the previous transformations and which sometimes cannot be described adequately. The next exercise gives some examples of these.

EXERCISE 14h

Draw x and y axes, marking values from -8 to 8 on each. Mark the given points and join them up. Find the image of each point under the transformation defined by the given matrix. Mark the image points and join them up. Do *not* try to describe the transformation.

1. The given points are A(-1, 0), B(1, 0), C(1, 2) and D(-1, 2). The transformation matrix is $\begin{pmatrix} 1 & 2 \\ 3 & 1 \end{pmatrix}$

2. The given points are A(-1, 0), B(1, 0), C(1, 2) and D(-1, 2). The transformation matrix is $\begin{pmatrix} 1 & -2 \\ -3 & 1 \end{pmatrix}$

3. The given points are A($-2, -1$), B($1, -1$), C($1, 2$) and D($-2, 2$).

The transformation matrix is $\begin{pmatrix} 2 & 0 \\ 0 & 3 \end{pmatrix}$

4. The given points are A($-2, -1$), B($1, -1$), C($1, 1$) and D($-2, 1$).

The transformation matrix is $\begin{pmatrix} 2 & 4 \\ 1 & 2 \end{pmatrix}$

5. The given points are A($-2, -1$), B($2, -1$), C($2, 1$) and D($-2, 1$).

The transformation matrix is $\begin{pmatrix} -1 & 1 \\ 2 & -2 \end{pmatrix}$

6. The given points are A($-2, -2$), B($1, -1$), C($1, 2$) and D($-2, 2$).

The transformation matrix is $\begin{pmatrix} 0 & 0 \\ 0 & 0 \end{pmatrix}$

7. The given points are A($1, 0$), B($3, 0$) and C($2, 2$).

The transformation matrix is $\begin{pmatrix} 1 & 2 \\ 0 & 1 \end{pmatrix}$

8. The given points are A($-2, 0$), B($2, 0$), C($2, 2$) and D($-2, 2$).

The transformation matrix is $\begin{pmatrix} 1 & -2 \\ 0 & 1 \end{pmatrix}$

MIXED TRANSFORMATIONS

EXERCISE 14i

In each of the questions 1 to 12, O is point ($0, 0$), A is ($2, 0$), B is ($2, 1$) and C is ($0, 1$). The rectangle OABC is the object. Draw x and y axes, marking values from -8 to 8 on each axis. Find the image of OABC under the transformation defined by the given matrix and (where possible) describe the transformation.

1. $\begin{pmatrix} 1 & 0 \\ 0 & -1 \end{pmatrix}$ **5.** $\begin{pmatrix} 2 & -3 \\ 3 & 2 \end{pmatrix}$ **9.** $\begin{pmatrix} 1 & 0 \\ 0 & 3 \end{pmatrix}$

2. $\begin{pmatrix} 1 & 1\frac{1}{2} \\ 0 & 1 \end{pmatrix}$ **6.** $\begin{pmatrix} 2 & 0 \\ 0 & 1 \end{pmatrix}$ **10.** $\begin{pmatrix} \frac{1}{2} & 0 \\ 0 & \frac{1}{2} \end{pmatrix}$

3. $\begin{pmatrix} 0 & -1 \\ -1 & 0 \end{pmatrix}$ **7.** $\begin{pmatrix} 4 & 0 \\ 0 & 4 \end{pmatrix}$ **11.** $\begin{pmatrix} 2 & 2 \\ 1 & 3 \end{pmatrix}$

4. $\begin{pmatrix} -3 & 0 \\ 0 & 3 \end{pmatrix}$ **8.** $\begin{pmatrix} 1 & 2 \\ 1 & 4 \end{pmatrix}$ **12.** $\begin{pmatrix} 1 & 0 \\ 2 & 1 \end{pmatrix}$

13. What are the simplest objects you could use to identify a transformation? Find and describe the transformation given by $\begin{pmatrix} 1 & -3 \\ 0 & 1 \end{pmatrix}$, using as simple an object as you can.

14. Draw x and y axes, marking values from -5 to 5 on each axis. Use $1\,cm$ to 1 unit.
The object is the quadrilateral OABC where O is $(0, 0)$, A is $(2, 0)$, B is $(4, 2)$ and C is $(2, 2)$.
Find and draw the eight images of OABC under the transformations defined by the following eight matrices:

a) $\begin{pmatrix} 1 & 0 \\ 0 & -1 \end{pmatrix}$ d) $\begin{pmatrix} 0 & 1 \\ 1 & 0 \end{pmatrix}$ g) $\begin{pmatrix} 0 & -1 \\ -1 & 0 \end{pmatrix}$

b) $\begin{pmatrix} -1 & 0 \\ 0 & -1 \end{pmatrix}$ e) $\begin{pmatrix} 0 & -1 \\ 1 & 0 \end{pmatrix}$ h) $\begin{pmatrix} 1 & 0 \\ 0 & 1 \end{pmatrix}$

c) $\begin{pmatrix} -1 & 0 \\ 0 & 1 \end{pmatrix}$ f) $\begin{pmatrix} 0 & 1 \\ -1 & 0 \end{pmatrix}$

15. Find the images of the following objects under the transformations defined by the matrix $\begin{pmatrix} 1 & 0 \\ 0 & 1 \end{pmatrix}$

a) OABC: $O(0, 0)$, $A(2, 0)$, $B(2, 2)$ and $C(0, 2)$
b) $\triangle$PQR: $P(-1, 1)$, $Q(-3, 1)$ and $R(-3, 4)$
c) parallelogram WXYZ: $W(1, -1)$, $X(0, -3)$, $Y(-3, -3)$ and $Z(-2, -1)$.
What do you notice about the results?

16. A is the point with position vector $\begin{pmatrix} 1 \\ 0 \end{pmatrix}$ and B is the point with position

vector $\begin{pmatrix} 0 \\ 1 \end{pmatrix}$

A' and B' are the images of A and B under the transformations defined by the following matrices:

a) $\begin{pmatrix} 1 & 0 \\ 0 & -1 \end{pmatrix}$ b) $\begin{pmatrix} 2 & 0 \\ 0 & 2 \end{pmatrix}$ c) $\begin{pmatrix} 1 & 2 \\ 0 & 1 \end{pmatrix}$ d) $\begin{pmatrix} 2 & 5 \\ 4 & -1 \end{pmatrix}$

In each case write down the position vectors of A' and B' and illustrate with a diagram. What do you notice about the position vectors of A' and B' and the columns of the matrix which produced them?

THE IDENTITY TRANSFORMATION

We saw in questions 14 and 15 in the last exercise that, under the transformation defined by the unit matrix $\begin{pmatrix} 1 & 0 \\ 0 & 1 \end{pmatrix}$ the image is the same as the object.

If the image is identical to the object the transformation is called an *identity* transformation.

A rotation of 360° about the origin is an example of an identity transformation.

TRANSFORMATIONS AND IMAGES

Remember that a transformation is the *operation* or *process* that changes an object into its image; it is *not* the resulting image. If we use the same matrix to transform several different objects, we will obtain different images but the *transformation* is the same in each case.

A transformation transforms the whole space we are using and carries the object with it to become the image.

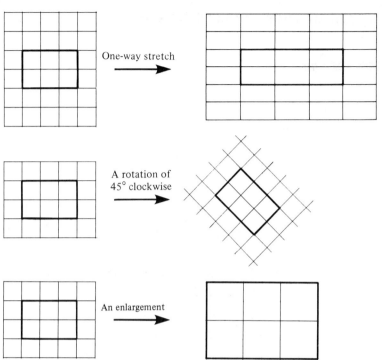

One-way stretch

A rotation of 45° clockwise

An enlargement

INVERSE TRANSFORMATIONS

An inverse transformation is one that will map an image back to its object.

Suppose, for example, that we start with an enlargement of scale factor 2. An enlargement of scale factor $\frac{1}{2}$ will then shrink the image down to the size of the object again.

If we produce an image by rotating an object through 60° anticlockwise about a point P, then a rotation of 60° clockwise will return it to its original position.

EXERCISE 14j

1. What is the inverse of a rotation of 90° clockwise about the origin?

2. What is the inverse of an enlargement of scale factor 3 and centre the origin?

3. What is the inverse of a reflection in the x-axis?

4. What is the inverse of a rotation of 45° anticlockwise about the origin?

INVERSE MATRIX TRANSFORMATIONS

EXERCISE 14k

1. Draw x and y axes, marking values from -4 to 4 on each axis. A is the point $(1, 0)$, B is $(3, 0)$ and C is $(3, 3)$.

M is the matrix $\begin{pmatrix} 0 & -1 \\ 1 & 0 \end{pmatrix}$

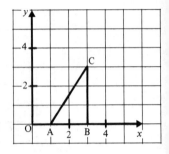

a) Transform $\triangle ABC$ using the matrix **M** and label the image A'B'C'.

b) Describe the transformation.

c) Find the inverse of the matrix **M**.

d) Use the inverse matrix to transform $\triangle A'B'C'$. What happens?

e) Describe the transformation defined by the inverse matrix.

2. Draw x and y axes, marking values from 0 to 6 on each axis. A is the point $(1, 1)$, B is $(2, 1)$, C is $(2, 2)$ and D is $(1, 2)$.

M is the matrix $\begin{pmatrix} 3 & 0 \\ 0 & 3 \end{pmatrix}$

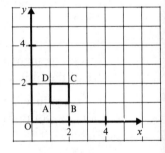

a) Transform the square ABCD using the matrix **M** and label the image A'B'C'D'.

b) Describe the transformation.

c) Find the inverse of the matrix **M**.

d) Use the inverse matrix to transform A'B'C'D'. What happens?

e) Describe the transformation defined by the inverse matrix. Is this the inverse of the transformation described in (b)?

3. Draw x and y axes, marking values from -4 to 4 on each axis. Mark the points A($1, 0$), B($3, 1$), C($3, 2$) and D($1, 1$).

a) Transform the parallelogram using the matrix $\begin{pmatrix} 0 & 1 \\ -1 & 0 \end{pmatrix}$ and label the image A′B′C′D′.

b) Describe the transformation.

c) Find the inverse of the matrix $\begin{pmatrix} 0 & 1 \\ -1 & 0 \end{pmatrix}$

d) Use the inverse matrix to transform A′B′C′D′. What happens?

e) Describe the transformation defined by the inverse matrix. Is this the inverse of the transformation defined by $\begin{pmatrix} 0 & 1 \\ -1 & 0 \end{pmatrix}$?

4. Draw x and y axes, marking values from 0 to 9 on each axis. Mark the points A($1, 1$), B($3, 3$) and C($1, 3$).

a) Transform $\triangle$ABC using the matrix $\begin{pmatrix} 1 & 2 \\ 0 & 1 \end{pmatrix}$. Label the image A′B′C′.

b) Find the inverse of the matrix $\begin{pmatrix} 1 & 2 \\ 0 & 1 \end{pmatrix}$

c) Use the inverse matrix to transform $\triangle$A′B′C′. What happens?

5. Draw x and y axes, marking values from 0 to 13 on each. Mark the points A($1, 0$), B($3, 0$), C($3, 2$) and D($1, 2$).

a) Transform the square ABCD using the matrix $\begin{pmatrix} 1 & 1 \\ 3 & 2 \end{pmatrix}$

b) Find the inverse of the matrix $\begin{pmatrix} 1 & 1 \\ 3 & 2 \end{pmatrix}$

c) Use the inverse matrix to transform A′B′C′D′. What happens?

6. Draw x and y axes, marking values from 0 to 10 on each. Mark the points O($0, 0$), A($1, 0$), B($1, 2$) and C($0, 2$).

a) Find the image of rectangle OABC under the transformation defined by the matrix $\begin{pmatrix} 2 & 4 \\ 1 & 2 \end{pmatrix}$. What happens?

b) Find, if possible, the inverse of the matrix $\begin{pmatrix} 2 & 4 \\ 1 & 2 \end{pmatrix}$

c) Comment on your answers to (a) and (b). Does the transformation in (a) have an inverse?

INVERSE MATRICES AND INVERSE TRANSFORMATIONS

We conclude that if a transformation is defined by a matrix **M**, the inverse transformation is defined by the inverse matrix $\mathbf{M}^{-1}$.

If $\mathbf{M}^{-1}$ does not exist then the transformation does not have an inverse.

AN INVARIANT POINT

There is one point which is invariant under every transformation defined by a matrix. This is found in the next exercise.

EXERCISE 14I

For each question draw x and y axes, marking values from -5 to 5 on each axis. Mark the points O($0, 0$), A($2, 0$), B($2, 2$) and C($0, 2$) and use the square OABC as the object.

1. Find the image of OABC under the transformation defined by the matrix $\begin{pmatrix} 1 & 2 \\ 0 & 1 \end{pmatrix}$. Which of the four points are invariant?

2. Find the image of OABC under the transformation defined by the matrix $\begin{pmatrix} 2 & 0 \\ 0 & 2 \end{pmatrix}$. Which of the points is invariant?

3. Find the image of OABC under the transformation defined by the matrix $\begin{pmatrix} 1 & 0 \\ 0 & -1 \end{pmatrix}$. Which of the four points are invariant?

4. Find the image of OABC under the transformation defined by the matrix $\begin{pmatrix} 2 & 1 \\ 1 & 2 \end{pmatrix}$. Which point is invariant?

5. Which one point is always invariant whichever transformation is used? Find the image of this point under a transformation defined by a matrix of your choice. Is it still invariant?

We see from the last exercise that, for any transformation defined by a 2×2 matrix, *the origin is invariant.*

TRANSFORMATIONS NOT USING MATRICES

Some of the transformations that can be defined by matrices are:

rotations with centres at the origin
reflections whose mirror lines pass through the origin
shears with invariant lines which pass through the origin
enlargements whose centres are at the origin.

There is no transformation matrix that will produce a rotation about $(1, 1)$ or a reflection in the line $x = 2$ or an enlargement with centre $(0, 6)$, because in each of these cases, the origin changes.

In a translation in particular, the origin is not an invariant point and therefore a translation cannot be produced by a matrix. We can describe a translation only by stating what the movement or *displacement* is. The easiest way to do this is to give the vector that describes the displacement.

EXERCISE 14m

Describe the transformation that maps ABCD to A'B'C'D'.

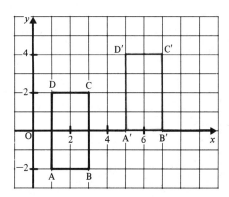

(Consider the displacement from D to D')

The transformation is a translation given by the vector $\begin{pmatrix} 4 \\ 2 \end{pmatrix}$

Describe the transformations in questions 1 to 4.

1.

3.

2.

4.

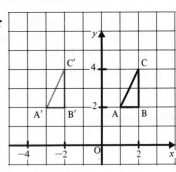

In questions 5 to 8, find the image of the given object under a translation defined by the given vector.

5.

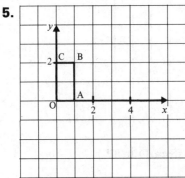

The vector is $\begin{pmatrix} 3 \\ 1 \end{pmatrix}$

6.

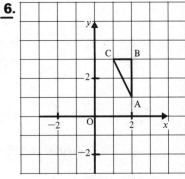

The vector is $\begin{pmatrix} -3 \\ -3 \end{pmatrix}$

7.

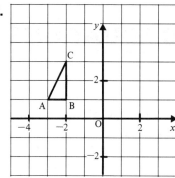

The vector is $\begin{pmatrix} 4 \\ -2 \end{pmatrix}$

8.

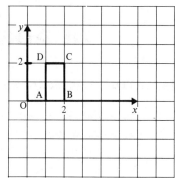

The vector is $\begin{pmatrix} -1 \\ 1 \end{pmatrix}$

9. Describe the inverse of the transformations given in questions 1 to 8.

15 QUADRATIC EQUATIONS

COMPLETING THE SQUARE

The numbers 9 and 25 can be written as 3^2 and 5^2, whereas 7 and 11 cannot be written as the square of another exact number. Because 9 and 25 can be written in this way they are called *perfect squares*.

Other examples are $\frac{9}{4}$ which is $\left(\frac{3}{2}\right)^2$ and $\frac{121}{169}$ which is $\left(\frac{11}{13}\right)^2$.

In a similar way, because we can write $x^2 + 2x + 1$ as $(x+1)^2$ and $4x^2 + 12x + 9$ as $(2x+3)^2$, we say that $x^2 + 2x + 1$ and $4x^2 + 12x + 9$ are perfect squares.

EXERCISE 15a

Express $x^2 + 12x + 36$ in the form $(x+a)^2$

$$x^2 + 12x + 36 = (x+6)(x+6)$$
$$= (x+6)^2$$

Express each of the following expressions in the form $(x+a)^2$.

1. $x^2 + 6x + 9$

2. $a^2 + 4a + 4$

3. $p^2 - 10p + 25$

4. $s^2 - 12s + 36$

5. $x^2 - 5x + \frac{25}{4}$

6. $b^2 + 3b + \frac{9}{4}$

7. $x^2 + 9x + \frac{81}{4}$

8. $a^2 - a + \frac{1}{4}$

9. $x^2 - \frac{1}{2}x + \frac{1}{16}$

10. $x^2 + 8x + 16$

11. $x^2 + x + \frac{1}{4}$

12. $x^2 + \frac{2}{3}x + \frac{1}{9}$

13. $p^2 + 18p + 81$

15. $t^2 - \frac{3}{2}t + \frac{9}{16}$

17. $x^2 - 2cx + c^2$

14. $a^2 - \frac{4}{5}a + \frac{4}{25}$

16. $x^2 + 2bx + b^2$

18. $x^2 + \frac{b}{a}x + \frac{b^2}{4a^2}$

Express $4x^2 + 12x + 9$ in the form $(ax + b)^2$

$$4x^2 + 12x + 9 = (2x + 3)(2x + 3)$$
$$= (2x + 3)^2$$

Express the following expressions in the form $(ax + b)^2$.

19. $9x^2 + 6x + 1$

22. $9x^2 - 24x + 16$

25. $9x^2 - 6x + 1$

20. $4x^2 - 12x + 9$

23. $4x^2 - 4x + 1$

26. $4x^2 + 2x + \frac{1}{4}$

21. $100x^2 - 60x + 9$

24. $25x^2 + 20x + 4$

27. $\frac{9x^2}{4} + 2x + \frac{4}{9}$

FORMING A PERFECT SQUARE

To make $x^2 + 6x$ into a perfect square we must add 9 to it.

Then $\qquad\qquad x^2 + 6x + 9 = (x + 3)^2$

and to make $x^2 - 3x$ into a perfect square we must add $\frac{9}{4}$ to it.

Then $\qquad\qquad x^2 - 3x + \frac{9}{4} = \left(x - \frac{3}{2}\right)^2$

More generally, to make $x^2 + px$ into a perfect square we take half the coefficient of x $\left(\text{i.e.} \frac{p}{2}\right)$, square it $\left(\text{i.e.} \frac{p^2}{4}\right)$ and add this to $x^2 + px$.

Then $x^2 + px + \frac{p^2}{4}$ is a perfect square and can be written $\left(x + \frac{p}{2}\right)^2$

EXERCISE 15b

> What must be added to $x^2 + 6x$ to make it into a perfect square?
>
> The coefficient of x is 6
>
> Half of this is 3
>
> The square of 3 is 9
>
> 9 must be added to $x^2 + 6x$ to make it into a perfect square.

What must be added to each of the following expressions to make it into a perfect square?

1. $x^2 + 4x$

2. $a^2 + 8a$

3. $x^2 - 12x$

4. $p^2 - 14p$

5. $x^2 - 3x$

6. $x^2 + 20x$

7. $c^2 + 7c$

8. $b^2 - \frac{1}{2}b$

9. $a^2 - \frac{3}{2}a$

10. $x^2 + x$

11. $x^2 + 2hx$

12. $x^2 + \frac{b}{a}x$

Now consider $9x^2 + 12x$. If we want to make this into a perfect square we first take out the factor 9

i.e.
$$9x^2 + 12x = 9\left(x^2 + \tfrac{12}{9}x\right)$$
$$= 9\left(x^2 + \tfrac{4}{3}x\right)$$

To complete the square within the bracket find the coefficient of x $\left(\text{i.e. } \tfrac{4}{3}\right)$, find half of it $\left(\tfrac{2}{3}\right)$, square this value $\left(\tfrac{4}{9}\right)$, and add it to the expression within the bracket.

Then
$$9\left(x^2 + \tfrac{4}{3}x + \tfrac{4}{9}\right) = 9x^2 + 12x + 4$$
$$= (3x + 2)^2$$

which is in the form $(ax + b)^2$

EXERCISE 15c

What must be added to each of the following expressions to make it into a perfect square ?

1. $9x^2 + 12x$

2. $4x^2 + 12x$

3. $36a^2 + 60a$

4. $100x^2 - 60x$

5. $25x^2 - 20x$

6. $4x^2 + 20x$

7. $49a^2 - 28a$

8. $\dfrac{a^2}{4} - 2a$

9. $\dfrac{4}{9}a^2 - \dfrac{2a}{3}$

QUADRATIC EQUATIONS

Now consider the equation $(x+1)^2 = 4$

If we take the square root of each side we get

$$x + 1 = \pm\sqrt{4}$$
$$= \pm 2$$
$$\text{If } x + 1 = 2$$
$$x = 1$$
$$\text{and if } x + 1 = -2$$
$$x = -3$$

These two values of x satisfy the equation $(x+1)^2 = 4$.

EXERCISE 15d

Solve the equations:

1. $(x+1)^2 = 9$

2. $(x-2)^2 = 16$

3. $(x-3)^2 = 25$

4. $(x+6)^2 = 100$

5. $(x+7)^2 = 1$

6. $(x-1)^2 = 25$

7. $(x+2)^2 = 49$

8. $(x-5)^2 = 16$

9. $(x-7)^2 = 4$

10. $(x+4)^2 = 16$

11. $(x+3)^2 = 25$

12. $(x-9)^2 = 36$

13. $(x+1)^2 = \dfrac{1}{4}$

14. $(x-2)^2 = \dfrac{9}{4}$

15. $(x-\dfrac{1}{2})^2 = \dfrac{25}{4}$

Solve the equation $(2x + 3)^2 = 4$

Taking the square root of each side we get

$$2x + 3 = \pm 2$$

i.e. $2x + 3 = 2$ or $2x + 3 = -2$

$2x = -1$ or $2x = -5$

$x = -\frac{1}{2}$ or $x = -\frac{5}{2}$

Solve the equations:

16. $(2x - 1)^2 = 16$ **20.** $(7x + 2)^2 = 100$ **24.** $(4x - 3)^2 = 1$

17. $(3x + 2)^2 = 25$ **21.** $(2x + 1)^2 = 36$ **25.** $(9x - 5)^2 = 4$

18. $(5x - 1)^2 = 36$ **22.** $(3x - 4)^2 = 49$ **26.** $(5x + 3)^2 = 16$

19. $(3x - 4)^2 = 1$ **23.** $(5x + 2)^2 = 25$ **27.** $(7x - 5)^2 = 81$

SOLUTION OF QUADRATIC EQUATIONS BY COMPLETING THE SQUARE

In Book 3A, Chapter 13, we were able to solve some quadratic equations by factorising the left-hand side and using the fact that if $A \times B = 0$ then either $A = 0$ or $B = 0$ (or A and B are both zero).

There are other equations which cannot be solved in this way because the left-hand side will not factorise. We can solve these equations by expressing them in the form $(x + a)^2 = c$ and taking the square roots of both sides. This is called the method of *completing the square*.

Consider the equation $x^2 - 6x + 2 = 0$

Subtract 2 from each side $x^2 - 6x = -2$

Complete the square on the LHS by adding 9 and add the same quantity to the RHS.

$$x^2 - 6x + 9 = -2 + 9$$

i.e. $(x - 3)^2 = 7$

Take the square root of each side $\qquad x - 3 = \pm 2.646$

$$x = 3 \pm 2.646$$

$$= 5.646 \text{ or } 0.354$$

i.e. $\quad x = 5.65$ or 0.35 correct to 2 d.p.

These values of x are called the *roots* of the equation.

EXERCISE 15e

Solve the equation $x^2 + 5x - 3 = 0$ by completing the square.

$$x^2 + 5x - 3 = 0$$

$$x^2 + 5x = 3$$

$$x^2 + 5x + \frac{25}{4} = 3 + \frac{25}{4}$$

$$\left(x + \frac{5}{2}\right)^2 = \frac{12 + 25}{4}$$

$$\left(x + \frac{5}{2}\right)^2 = \frac{37}{4}$$

$$x + \frac{5}{2} = \pm \frac{\sqrt{37}}{2}$$

$$x = -\frac{5}{2} \pm \frac{6.083}{2}$$

$$= \frac{1.083}{2} \text{ or } \frac{-11.083}{2}$$

$$= 0.5415 \text{ or } -5.5415$$

i.e. $\quad x = 0.54$ or -5.54 correct to 2 d.p.

Solve the following equations by completing the square.

1. $x^2 + 4x = 5$ $\qquad$ **5.** $x^2 - 4x + 1 = 0$ $\qquad$ **9.** $x^2 - 7x + 5 = 0$

2. $x^2 - 6x = 7$ $\qquad$ **6.** $x^2 + 8x = 3$ $\qquad$ **10.** $x^2 - x - 4 = 0$

3. $x^2 + 10x = 11$ $\qquad$ **7.** $x^2 - 4x = 9$ $\qquad$ **11.** $x^2 + 9x - 3 = 0$

4. $x^2 + 8x + 3 = 0$ $\qquad$ **8.** $x^2 + 9x + 4 = 0$ $\qquad$ **12.** $x^2 + 8x + 4 = 0$

Previously, when solving linear equations, we have frequently divided both sides by a non-zero number. When solving a quadratic equation by completing the square *always* divide both sides by the non-zero coefficient of x^2.

Solve equation $2x^2 + 6x - 5 = 0$ by completing the square.

$$2x^2 + 6x - 5 = 0$$

$$x^2 + 3x - \tfrac{5}{2} = 0$$

$$x^2 + 3x = \tfrac{5}{2}$$

$$x^2 + 3x + \tfrac{9}{4} = \tfrac{5}{2} + \tfrac{9}{4}$$

$$\left(x + \frac{3}{2}\right)^2 = \frac{10 + 9}{4}$$

$$\left(x + \frac{3}{2}\right)^2 = \frac{19}{4}$$

$$x + \frac{3}{2} = \pm\frac{\sqrt{19}}{2}$$

$$x = -\frac{3}{2} \pm \frac{4.359}{2}$$

$$x = \frac{1.359}{2} \quad \text{or} \quad \frac{-7.359}{2}$$

$$= 0.6795 \quad \text{or} \quad -3.6795$$

i.e. $x = 0.68$ or -3.68 correct to 2 d.p.

Solve the following equations by completing the square.

13. $2x^2 + 6x = 9$

14. $6x^2 - 12x = 5$

15. $4x^2 + 8x = 3$

16. $2x^2 - 3x - 4 = 0$

17. $3x^2 + 12x - 8 = 0$

18. $3x^2 - 5x = 1$

19. $5x^2 - 5x = 4$

20. $5x^2 + 8x + 2 = 0$

21. $4x^2 - 7x - 3 = 0$

22. $6x^2 - 5x - 1 = 0$

23. $7x^2 + 7x - 4 = 0$

24. $3x^2 - 9x = 2$

SOLUTION OF QUADRATIC EQUATIONS BY FORMULA

If we apply the method of completing the square to the general quadratic equation $ax^2 + bx + c = 0$, where a, b and c are positive or negative numbers, we can establish a formula for solving the equation.

Consider the general equation

$$ax^2 + bx + c = 0$$

Divide both sides by a

$$x^2 + \frac{b}{a}x + \frac{c}{a} = 0$$

Subtract $\frac{c}{a}$ from each side

$$x^2 + \frac{b}{a}x = -\frac{c}{a}$$

Complete the square on the LHS and add the same quantity to the RHS.

$$x^2 + \frac{b}{a}x + \frac{b^2}{4a^2} = -\frac{c}{a} + \frac{b^2}{4a^2}$$

Therefore

$$\left(x + \frac{b}{2a}\right)^2 = \frac{-4ac + b^2}{4a^2}$$

Take square roots of each side

$$x + \frac{b}{2a} = \pm \frac{\sqrt{b^2 - 4ac}}{2a}$$

Subtract $\frac{b}{2a}$ from each side

$$x = -\frac{b}{2a} \pm \frac{\sqrt{b^2 - 4ac}}{2a}$$

i.e.

$$x = \frac{-b \pm \sqrt{b^2 - 4ac}}{2a}$$

This is called the *formula* for solving quadratic equations. It gives values of x, or roots of the equation, for any given values of a, b and c (provided that $b^2 - 4ac$ is not negative).

Remember that a is the coefficient of x^2
b is the coefficient of x
c is the constant number term.

Since the two values of x are

$$-\frac{b}{2a} + \frac{\sqrt{b^2 - 4ac}}{2a} \quad \text{and} \quad -\frac{b}{2a} - \frac{\sqrt{b^2 - 4ac}}{2a}$$

the sum of the two roots is always $\left(\frac{-b}{2a}\right) + \left(\frac{-b}{2a}\right) = -\frac{b}{a}$

This provides a useful check that your answers are correct.

EXERCISE 15f

Use the formula to solve the equation $x^2 - 9x - 2 = 0$ giving your answers correct to two decimal places.

$$x^2 - 9x - 2 = 0$$

$$a = 1, \quad b = -9, \quad c = -2$$

$$x = \frac{-b \pm \sqrt{b^2 - 4ac}}{2a}$$

$$= \frac{-(-9) \pm \sqrt{(-9)^2 - 4(1)(-2)}}{2 \times 1}$$

$$= \frac{9 \pm \sqrt{81 + 8}}{2}$$

$$= \frac{9 \pm \sqrt{89}}{2}$$

$$= \frac{9 \pm 9.434}{2}$$

$$= \frac{18.434}{2} \quad \text{or} \quad \frac{-0.434}{2}$$

$$= 9.217 \quad \text{or} \quad -0.217$$

$$\therefore \quad x = 9.22 \quad \text{or} \quad -0.22 \quad \text{correct to 2 d.p.}$$

Check: Sum of roots is $9.22 + (-0.22) = 9$

and $\dfrac{-b}{a} = \dfrac{-(-9)}{1} = 9$

confirming the results.

Use the formula to solve the following quadratic equations.

1. $x^2 + 6x + 3 = 0$ **5.** $x^2 + 4x - 3 = 0$ **9.** $x^2 + 6x - 6 = 0$

2. $x^2 + 7x + 4 = 0$ **6.** $x^2 + 9x + 12 = 0$ **10.** $x^2 + 9x - 1 = 0$

3. $x^2 + 5x + 5 = 0$ **7.** $x^2 + 8x + 13 = 0$ **11.** $x^2 + 3x - 5 = 0$

4. $x^2 + 7x - 2 = 0$ **8.** $x^2 + 10x - 15 = 0$ **12.** $x^2 + 4x - 7 = 0$

13. $x^2 - 4x + 2 = 0$ **17.** $x^2 - 5x - 5 = 0$ **21.** $x^2 - 9x - 2 = 0$

14. $x^2 - 7x + 3 = 0$ **18.** $x^2 - 5x + 2 = 0$ **22.** $x^2 - 4x - 9 = 0$

15. $x^2 - 6x + 6 = 0$ **19.** $x^2 - 3x + 1 = 0$ **23.** $x^2 + 7x - 2 = 0$

16. $x^2 - 4x - 3 = 0$ **20.** $x^2 - 7x - 3 = 0$ **24.** $x^2 + 8x + 5 = 0$

Solve the equation $3x^2 + 7x - 2 = 0$ giving your answers correct to two decimal places.

$$3x^2 + 7x - 2 = 0$$

$$a = 3, \quad b = 7, \quad c = -2$$

$$x = \frac{-b \pm \sqrt{b^2 - 4ac}}{2a}$$

$$= \frac{-7 \pm \sqrt{7^2 - 4(3)(-2)}}{2 \times 3}$$

$$= \frac{-7 \pm \sqrt{49 + 24}}{6}$$

$$= \frac{-7 \pm \sqrt{73}}{6}$$

$$= \frac{-7 \pm 8.544}{6}$$

$$= \frac{1.544}{6} \text{ or } -\frac{15.544}{6}$$

$$= 0.257 \text{ or } -2.591$$

$$= 0.26 \text{ or } -2.59 \quad \text{correct to 2 d.p.}$$

Check: Sum of roots is $0.26 + (-2.59) = -2.33$

and $\dfrac{-b}{a} = \dfrac{-7}{3} = -2.33$ (to 2 d.p.)

confirming the results.

---

25. $2x^2 + 7x + 2 = 0$ **27.** $3x^2 + 7x + 3 = 0$

26. $2x^2 + 7x + 4 = 0$ **28.** $4x^2 + 7x + 1 = 0$

29. $5x^2 + 9x + 2 = 0$ **32.** $5x^2 - 9x + 2 = 0$

30. $2x^2 - 7x + 4 = 0$ **33.** $3x^2 + 5x - 3 = 0$

31. $4x^2 - 7x + 1 = 0$ **34.** $3x^2 + 9x - 1 = 0$

EXERCISE 15g

Solve the equation $4x^2 = 7x + 1$ giving your answers correct to two decimal places.

$$4x^2 = 7x + 1$$

(First arrange the equation in the form $ax^2 + bx + c = 0$)

$$4x^2 - 7x - 1 = 0$$

$$a = 4, \quad b = -7, \quad c = -1$$

$$x = \frac{-b \pm \sqrt{b^2 - 4ac}}{2a}$$

$$= \frac{-(-7) \pm \sqrt{(-7)^2 - 4(4)(-1)}}{2 \times 4}$$

$$= \frac{7 \pm \sqrt{49 + 16}}{8}$$

$$= \frac{7 \pm \sqrt{65}}{8}$$

$$= \frac{7 \pm 8.062}{8}$$

$$= \frac{15.062}{8} \text{ or } \frac{-1.062}{8}$$

$$= 1.883 \text{ or } -0.133$$

$$= 1.88 \text{ or } -0.13 \quad \text{correct to 2 d.p.}$$

Check: Sum of roots is $1.88 + (-0.13) = 1.75$

and $\dfrac{-b}{a} = \dfrac{-(-7)}{4} = \dfrac{7}{4} = 1.75$

confirming the results.

1. $2x^2 = 8x + 11$

2. $4x^2 = 8x + 3$

3. $3x^2 = 3 - 5x$

4. $5x^2 = x + 3$

5. $4x^2 + 2 = 7x$

6. $3x^2 = 12x + 2$

7. $2x^2 = 3x + 1$

8. $4x^2 = 5 - 3x$

9. $3x^2 + 2 = 9x$

10. $6x^2 - 9x = 4$

11. $2x^2 = 5x + 5$

12. $3x^2 + 4x = 1$

13. $4x^2 = 4x + 1$

14. $3x^2 + 7x = 2$

15. $5x^2 = 5x - 1$

16. $8x^2 = x + 1$

EXERCISE 15h

In this exercise try the method of factorising first. If factors cannot be found use the formula.

1. $2x^2 + 3x - 2 = 0$

2. $3x^2 + 6x + 2 = 0$

3. $6x^2 + 7x + 2 = 0$

4. $2x^2 + 3x - 3 = 0$

5. $3x^2 - 8x + 2 = 0$

6. $3x^2 - 8x - 3 = 0$

7. $2x^2 - 3x - 3 = 0$

8. $8x^2 + 10x - 3 = 0$

9. $6x^2 + 7x - 2 = 0$

10. $4x^2 - 3x - 2 = 0$

11. $7x^2 + 8x - 2 = 0$

12. $5x^2 - 3x - 1 = 0$

13. $3x^2 = 7x - 2$

14. $11x^2 + 12x + 3 = 0$

15. $20x^2 = 3 - 11x$

16. $3x^2 - 14x + 15 = 0$

17. $5x^2 + 8x + 2 = 0$

18. $2x^2 = 7x + 3$

19. $2x^2 + 9x = 5$

20. $6x^2 = 5x + 2$

HARDER EQUATIONS

EXERCISE 15i

Solve the equation $\dfrac{1}{x+1} + \dfrac{2}{x-3} = 4$ giving your answers correct to two decimal places.

$$\frac{1}{x+1} + \frac{2}{x-3} = 4$$

Multiply both sides by $(x+1)(x-3)$

$$(x-3) + 2(x+1) = 4(x+1)(x-3)$$

$$x - 3 + 2x + 2 = 4(x^2 - 2x - 3)$$

$$3x - 1 = 4x^2 - 8x - 12$$

i.e. $$4x^2 - 11x - 11 = 0$$

$$a = 4, \quad b = -11, \quad c = -11$$

$$x = \frac{-b \pm \sqrt{b^2 - 4ac}}{2a}$$

$$= \frac{11 \pm \sqrt{121 - 4(4)(-11)}}{8}$$

$$= \frac{11 \pm \sqrt{121 + 176}}{8}$$

$$= \frac{11 \pm \sqrt{297}}{8}$$

$$= \frac{11 \pm 17.234}{8}$$

$$= \frac{28.234}{8} \text{ or } \frac{-6.234}{8}$$

$$= 3.529 \text{ or } -0.779$$

i.e. $$x = 3.53 \text{ or } -0.78 \quad \text{correct to 2 d.p.}$$

Solve the following equations; give answers correct to two decimal places.

1. $x + \dfrac{2}{x} = 11$

5. $\dfrac{2}{x+5} + \dfrac{3}{x-2} = 4$

2. $x - \dfrac{5}{x} = 3$

6. $\dfrac{2}{x} + \dfrac{1}{x+1} = 4$

3. $x + \dfrac{2}{x} = 7$

7. $\dfrac{3}{x-1} - \dfrac{2}{x+3} = 1$

4. $\dfrac{3}{x+2} - \dfrac{1}{x+4} = 2$

8. $\dfrac{5}{x} - 2x = 5$

PROBLEMS INVOLVING QUADRATIC EQUATIONS

EXERCISE 15j

The sum of two numbers is 13 and the sum of their squares is 97. Find the numbers.

Let one number be x then the other number is $13 - x$

and
$$(13 - x)^2 + x^2 = 97$$
$$169 - 26x + x^2 + x^2 = 97$$
$$2x^2 - 26x + 169 = 97$$
$$2x^2 - 26x + 72 = 0$$
$$x^2 - 13x + 36 = 0$$
$$(x - 4)(x - 9) = 0$$
$$x - 4 = 0 \text{ or } x - 9 = 0$$

i.e.
$$x = 4 \text{ or } x = 9$$

If
$$x = 4, \ 13 - x = 9$$

If
$$x = 9, \ 13 - x = 4$$

The two numbers are therefore 4 and 9.

The following problems lead to quadratic equations that factorise.

1. The sum of two numbers is 13 and the sum of their squares is 85. Find them.

2. The difference between two positive numbers is 2 and the sum of their squares is 20. Find the numbers.

3. The sum of the squares of two consecutive positive numbers is 61. Find two numbers.

4. One side of a rectangle is 4 cm longer than the other. Find the sides if the area of the rectangle is 45 cm².

5. The perimeter of a rectangle is 26 cm and its area is 40 cm². Find the sides.

6. Two positive whole numbers differ by 3, and the sum of their squares is 89. If the smaller number is x form an equation in x and solve it to find the numbers.

7. The sides of a right-angled triangle are x cm, $(x+7)$ cm and $(x+8)$ cm. Find them.

8. A rectangle is 6 cm longer than it is wide. If its area is the same as that of a square of side 4 cm find its dimensions.

9. The sides of a right-angled triangle are x cm, $(x-2)$ cm and $(x-4)$ cm. Find them.

10. The hypotenuse of a right-angled triangle is 10 cm. Find the other two sides if their sum is 14 cm.

11. The product of two numbers is 84. If these numbers differ by 5, find them.

12. One number is 3 more than another. If their product is 88, find them.

13. The length of a rectangle is 5 cm more than its width. If the area of the rectangle is 36 cm² find its dimensions.

14. The base of a triangle is 5 cm more than its perpendicular height. If the area of the triangle is 42 cm² find
a) the length of its base
b) its perpendicular height.

15.

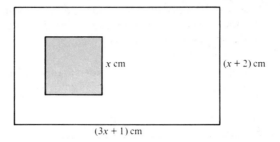

(3x + 1) cm

A square of side x cm is removed from a rectangular piece of cardboard measuring $(3x + 1)$ cm by $(x + 2)$ cm. If the area of card remaining is 62 cm^2 form an equation in x and solve it to find the dimensions of the original card.

16.

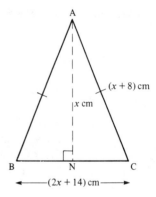

N is the midpoint of the base BC of a triangle ABC. If AB = AC, AN = x cm, BC = $(2x + 14)$ cm and AC = $(x + 8)$ cm form an equation in x and solve it. Hence find the length of the base and height of the triangle ABC.

EXERCISE 15k

The following questions may lead to quadratic equations that do not factorise. Always check whether a quadratic equation will factorise before using the formula. If an answer is not exact give it correct to 3 s.f.

1. The sum of two numbers is 10 and the sum of their squares is 80. Find them.

2. The sum of two numbers is 9 and the difference between their squares is 60. Find them.

3. Find a number such that the sum of the number and its reciprocal is 20. In this case give the answers correct to 2 decimal places.

4. One side of a rectangle is 3 cm longer than another. Find the sides if the area of the rectangle is 20 cm^2.

5. Find the length of the hypotenuse of a right-angled triangle whose sides are x cm, $(x + 1)$ cm and $(x + 3)$ cm.

6. The parallel sides of a trapezium are $(x-2)$cm and $(x+4)$cm long. If the distance between the parallel sides is x cm and the area of the trapezium is 42 cm^2 find its dimensions.

7. A rectangular block is 2 cm wider than it is high and twice as long as it is wide. If its total surface area is 190 cm^2 find its dimensions.

8. Sally is x years old. Her mother's age is (x^2-4) years and her father is 6 years older than her mother. If the combined age of all three is 76 years form an equation in x and solve it. How old is her father?

HARDER PROBLEMS

EXERCISE 15I

A coach is due to reach its destination 30 kilometres away at a certain time. Its start is delayed by 18 minutes, but by increasing the average speed by 5 km/h the driver arrives on time. How long did the journey actually take? What was the intended average speed?

Let the intended average speed be x km/h. (The information can then be set out in table form taking care to work in compatible units.)

	Speed in km/h	Distance in km	Time in hours
Intended journey	x	30	$\dfrac{30}{x}$
Actual journey	$x+5$	30	$\dfrac{30}{x+5}$

Since the actual time is 18 minutes, i.e. $\dfrac{3}{10}$ hour, shorter than the intended time, then

$$\frac{30}{x} - \frac{30}{x+5} = \frac{3}{10}$$

Multiply both sides by $10x(x+5)$

$$300(x+5) - 300x = 3x(x+5)$$

$$100(x+5) - 100x = x^2 + 5x$$

$$100x + 500 - 100x = x^2 + 5x$$

$$0 = x^2 + 5x - 500$$

i.e. $$x^2 + 5x - 500 = 0$$

$$(x+25)(x-20) = 0$$

∴ $$x = -25 \text{ or } 20$$

But -25 is unacceptable as the average speed has to be positive.

∴ $$x = 20$$

i.e. the intended speed is 20 km/h and the time actually

taken is $\dfrac{30}{20+5}$ hours $= \dfrac{30}{25}$ hours   i.e. 1 hour 12 min.

---

1. When its average speed increases by 10 m.p.h. the time taken for a car to make a journey of 105 miles is reduced by 15 minutes. Find the original average speed of the car.

2. Find the price of potatoes per kilogram if, when the price rises by 5 p per kg, I can buy 1 kg less for £2.10.

3. Tickets are available for a concert at two prices, the dearer ticket being £3 more than the cheaper one. Find the price of each ticket if a youth group can buy ten more of the cheaper tickets than the dearer tickets for £180.

4. In order to go on holiday Peter converts £300 into French francs. Had he bought three months earlier he would have received the same number of francs for £50 less, since the rate of exchange was two francs to the £ more then than on the day he bought them. Find the present rate of exchange.

5. From a piece of wire 42 cm long, a length $10x$ cm is cut off and bent into a rectangle whose length is one and a half times its width. The remainder is bent to form a square. If the combined area of the rectangle and square is 63 cm^2 find their dimensions.

6. The members of a club hire a coach for the day at a cost of £210. Seven members withdraw which means that each member who makes the trip must pay an extra £1. How many members originally agreed to go?

16 USING MONEY

MONEY

In many respects money is similar to any other commodity. Foreign currencies can be bought and sold in much the same way that cars can be bought and sold. Money can be lent and borrowed in a manner similar to hiring out or renting, say, a scaffold tower.

EXCHANGE RATES

When we shop abroad, prices quoted in the local currency often give us little idea of value so we tend to convert prices into sterling (£). To do this we need to know the exchange rate, i.e. how many units of the local currency are equivalent to one pound sterling.

For example, using an exchange rate of 9.95 Ff to £1

means that $£100 = 100 \times 9.95\,\text{Ff} = 995\,\text{Ff}$

and that $99.5\,\text{Ff} = £\dfrac{99.5}{9.95} = £10$

A reasonable idea of cost is given by rounding off the exchange rate to make the arithmetic easy, but skill in mental arithmetic is useful! For example, a price of 250 Ff could be approximately converted to sterling by rounding $9.95\,\text{Ff} \equiv £1$ to $10\,\text{Ff} \equiv £1$.

Then $250\,\text{Ff} \approx £\dfrac{250}{10} = £25$ to the nearest £1

A more accurate conversion can be made using a conversion graph or a calculator.

EXERCISE 16a

If £1 is equivalent to 2630 Italian Lire (L), estimate the sterling equivalent of

a) 5000 L   b) 1000 L

    a)   (Approximating the exchange rate to 2500 L = £1 makes the arithmetic simple.)

$$5000\,L \approx £\frac{5000}{2500} = £2$$

    b)

$$1000\,L \approx £\frac{1000}{2500} = £\tfrac{2}{5} = 40\,p$$

This table gives the equivalent of £1 in various currencies.

£	French franc (Ff)	Spanish peseta (pta)	Italian lire (L)	Irish punt (pt)
1	9.95	180	2180	1.20

Use this table to   a) estimate   b) calculate (to the nearest penny) the sterling equivalent of

1. 200 Ff	**8.** 40 pta	**15.** 900 L
2. 20 Ff	**9.** 600 pta	**16.** 2.50 pt
3. 2500 Ff	**10.** 3810 pta	**17.** 4.80 pt
4. 5 Ff	**11.** 3000 L	**18.** 10.00 pt
5. 450 Ff	**12.** 10 000 L	**19.** 25.00 pt
6. 5000 pta	**13.** 250 L	**20.** 1.60 pt
7. 100 pta	**14.** 12 500 L	**21.** 3.70 pt

Use the table on page 291 to find how many pesetas are equivalent to 1 Ff.

From the table   9.95 Ff = 180 pta

$$\therefore \qquad\qquad 1\,Ff = \frac{180}{9.95}\,pta$$

$$= 18.09\,pta$$

Use the table given at the beginning of the exercise to make the following conversions. Use your own judgement on how accurately your answers should be given.

22. 1 pt to Ff

23. 100 pta to Ff

24. 1 Ff to L

25. 100 L to pta

26. 10 pta to L

27. 3.50 pt to Ff

28. 650 pta to Ff

29. 25 Ff to L

30. 4500 L to pta

31. 280 pta to L

32. 84 Ff to L

33. 3800 L to pta

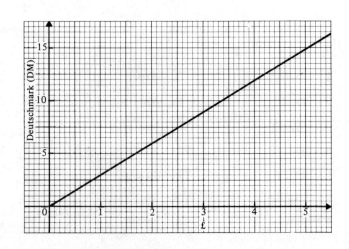

Use the conversion graph on page 292 to find

34. £3 in DM   **36.** £1.40 in DM   **38.** 8 DM in £

35. £2.50 in DM   **37.** 12 DM in £   **39.** 2.50 DM in £

40. Using an exchange rate of 1.80 U.S. dollars ($) to the pound sterling, make a conversion graph with a scale of 1 cm for £1 on the horizontal axis and a scale of 1 cm for $1 on the vertical axis. Use your graph to make the following conversions.

a) £2.50 to $ b) £4.75 to $ c) $4.20 to £.

EXCHANGE CROSS RATES

Institutions dealing with several foreign currencies need the exchange rate from any one foreign currency to any other. This information is published daily by the *Financial Times* in an exchange cross rate table.

EXCHANGE CROSS RATES

Nov. 6	£	$	DM	Yen	Ff	Sfr	Nfl	Lira	C$	Bfr	Ecu
£	1	1.772	2.908	230.0	9.935	2.568	3.275	2178	1.993	59.75	1.422
$	0.564	1	1.641	129.8	5.607	1.449	1.848	1229	1.125	33.72	0.802
DM	0.344	0.609	1	79.09	3.416	0.883	1.126	749.0	0.685	20.55	0.489
Yen (per 1000)	4.348	7.704	12.64	1000	43.20	11.17	14.24	9470	8.665	259.8	6.183
Ff (per 10)	1.007	1.784	2.927	231.5	10	2.585	3.296	2192	2.006	60.14	1.431
Sfr	0.389	0.690	1.132	89.56	3.869	1	1.275	848.1	0.776	23.27	0.554
Nfl	0.305	0.541	0.888	70.23	3.034	0.784	1	665.0	0.609	18.24	0.434
Lira (per 1000)	0.459	0.814	1.335	105.6	4.562	1.179	1.504	1000	0.915	27.43	0.653
C$	0.502	0.889	1.459	115.4	4.985	1.289	1.643	1093	1	29.98	0.713
Bfr (per 100)	1.674	2.966	4.867	384.9	16.63	4.298	5.481	3645	3.336	100	2.380
Ecu	0.703	1.246	2.045	161.7	6.987	1.806	2.303	1532	1.402	42.02	1

The left-hand column refers to 1 unit of currency unless otherwise stated.

Hence the first row of figures gives the equivalent of £1 in other currencies. The fourth row gives the equivalent of 1000 yen in other currencies, e.g. 1000 yen = 11.17 Sf (Swiss francs).

EXERCISE 16b

Use the table to give the following exchange rates:

1. £ to Canadian Dollars (C $)
2. DM to Lire
3. Belgian Francs (Bf) to Yen
4. Dutch Florins (N Fl.) to $
5. $ to Yen

6. Swiss Francs (Sf) to £
7. $ to £
8. Bf to $
9. DM to $
10. N Fl. to £

BUYING AND SELLING FOREIGN CURRENCY

In the previous section we assumed that there is just one exchange rate between two currencies. For most holiday and business travel purposes it is reasonable to work with a single exchange rate. However, when changing sterling into foreign currency before going on holiday and then changing what is left of that currency back into sterling on return, we find that we have to deal with two exchange rates. High Street banks offering exchange display their rates under two headings: 'Bank Buys' and 'Bank Sells'. (Exchange rates vary slightly from bank to bank in much the same way that the cost of a packet of tea varies from shop to shop.) A typical display of exchange rates looks like this.

	Bank Buys	Bank Sells
Belgian f.	62.65	58.65
French f.	10.38	9.68
Deutschmark	3.035	2.835
Italian Lire	2280	2130
Spanish pta	190	177
Swiss f.	2.66	2.49
US $	1.835	1.710

This means that if we are exchanging French francs and sterling,

the bank will sell us French francs at 9.68 Ff to £1,

the bank will buy French francs from us at 10.38 Ff to £1.

Hence if we want to change £100 into French francs, then we will get

$$100 \times 9.68 \, \text{Ff} = 968 \, \text{Ff}.$$

If we want to change 968 Ff into sterling then we will get

$$£\frac{968}{10.38} = £93.25$$

In addition to the differential exchange rate, banks normally charge a commission on each transaction and this is typically 1% of the sterling value. Hence the first transaction of changing £100 into Ff is subject to a charge of 1% of £100, i.e. £1, so the cost of the 968 Ff is £101.

Similarly the second transaction is subject to a charge of 1% of £95, i.e. 95 p. Therefore, for our 968 Ff we would get £93.25 – 93 p, i.e. £92.32.

EXERCISE 16c

Use the table on page 294 to answer the following questions.

1. If I change £100 into deutschmarks, how many will I get?

2. If I come back from holiday with 250 DM how much sterling will the bank exchange them for?

3. What will it cost me in sterling to buy 1 000 000 lire from the bank?

4. How much will the bank pay me in sterling for U.S. $ 500?

5. How many pesetas will £500 buy?

6. A company exporting goods to Belgium is paid in Belgian francs and receives a cheque for 5000 Bf. How much in sterling will the company receive from its bank if the bank charges a commission of $1\frac{1}{2}$%?

7. Holiday flats in France are offered for rent at 2000 Ff a week. I rent one for two weeks and pay for it by writing out a cheque in French francs. How much does it cost me in sterling if the bank charges 1% commission?

8. Lesley Smith changed £100 into US $ for a business trip, but didn't spend any of the dollars. On return she changed the dollars back into sterling. If 1% commission was deducted on each transaction, how much did she lose?

9. A leather bag in an Italian shop is offered for sale at 125 000 L. A tourist, whose lire were bought in England at a charge of $1\frac{1}{2}$% commission, buys the bag. What is the cost in pounds of the bag to the tourist?

10. Mr and Mrs Edwards rented a flat in Spain for one week and paid 45 000 pta. On return they were given a refund of 5000 pta. If the bank charged them 1% commission on currency exchanges, find the cost in pounds of the rental, giving your answer correct to the nearest pound.

INVESTMENTS

Most people who have money that they do not need to spend immediately, invest it. Investing money means that the money is lent to an institution to use until such time as the owner wants it back. The institution pays the owner for the use of the money; this payment is called *interest*.

The most familiar forms of investment are Building Society accounts, Bank deposit accounts, Post Office savings accounts and Saving Certificates.

The interest payable on any investment is usually given as a percentage rate per annum, e.g. 8% p.a.

EXERCISE 16d

Give answers correct to the nearest penny.

An ordinary share account in a Building Society offers an interest rate of 8% p.a. payable half-yearly. If £100 is invested in this account and the interest is not withdrawn, find the amount in the account after 1 year.

Interest for the first 6 months is $\frac{1}{2}$ of 8% of £100 $= \dfrac{4}{100} \times £100$

$$= £4$$

(As the interest is not withdrawn, there is £104 invested for the second six months.)

Interest for the second 6 months is $\frac{1}{2}$ of 8% of £104 $= \dfrac{4}{100} \times £104$

$$= £4.16$$

After one year there is £108.16 in the account.

(Note that if the society paid the interest only yearly, the rate would have to be 8.16% p.a. to give the same amount. This rate of 8.16% is called the *compounded annual rate* (c.a.r.) and is often quoted by Building Societies along with their ordinary rate.)

1. £100 is invested in a Building Society. Assuming that no capital or interest is withdrawn find the amount in the account after 1 year when the rate of interest is

a) 5% p.a. payable half-yearly

b) 4% p.a. payable quarterly (every 3 months).

2. £100 is invested in a bank deposit account. If no capital or interest is withdrawn find the amount in the account after 1 year when the rate of interest is

a) 9% p.a. payable half-yearly

b) 9.2% p.a. payable yearly.

3. A savings account pays interest at the rate of 7% p.a. payable half-yearly. £200 is invested in this account. Find

a) the amount in the account after 1 year

b) the compounded annual rate.

4. £100 is invested in a Building Society at an interest rate of 10% p.a. payable half-yearly. Assuming that no capital or interest is withdrawn find

a) the amount in the account after 1 year

b) the compounded annual rate

c) the amount in the account after 2 years.

5. Savings Certificates are advertised by the statement '£100 becomes £120 in two years'. A building society offers interest at the rate of 9% p.a. payable half-yearly. If £100 was invested in the building society, what would this become after two years, and how does it compare with the Savings Certificates?

6. A Building Society offers a two-year bond of £1000 at a rate of 10% p.a. (A bond is a form of investment where the capital cannot be withdrawn during the term of the bond which in this case is two years.). The interest is paid direct to the investor every six months and cannot be credited to the bond. How much interest is paid over the two year term?

If, instead of buying one of these bonds, £1000 is invested in an account paying an interest rate of 8% p.a. payable half-yearly and if the interest is left in the account, how much would be in the account after two years?

7. A local authority offers a five-year bond of £1000, at a rate of 9% p.a. payable yearly. A bank offers a 'gold' savings account at a rate of 8.5% p.a. payable quarterly.

Tom Jones has £1000 to invest. If he wants to withdraw the interest only once a year, which of these two investments will give him the greater return?

INTEREST AND TAX

Interest from investments is called investment income and is subject to tax in much the same way as earned income is.

Building societies and banks pay interest which is net of tax to standard rate tax payers, i.e. they pay money direct to the Inland Revenue, so the investor does not have to pay standard rate tax on the interest.

Sometimes interest rates are published in the form

8% p.a. net = 11.4% p.a. gross.

The gross rate is the interest the bank would have to pay to enable the investor to get the same amount of interest after paying the tax himself.

Some investments pay the gross rate of interest, so the investor has to pay any tax due.

EXERCISE 16e

A bank deposit account pays 8% p.a. net. Find the gross rate if standard rate tax is 35%.

On £100, 8% p.a. net gives interest of £8. The gross rate must give an amount which leaves £8 *after* tax of 35% is paid.

$$\therefore \qquad £8 = (100 - 35)\% \text{ of gross interest}$$

$$\text{i.e.} \qquad £8 = \frac{65}{100} \times (\text{gross interest})$$

$$£\frac{8 \times 100}{65} = \text{gross interest}$$

$\therefore$ gross interest on £100 is £12.31

$\therefore$ the gross interest rate is 12.31%.

1. A bank deposit account pays 7% p.a. net.
   Find the gross rate if standard rate tax is 29%.

2. A building society account pays $9\frac{1}{4}$% p.a. net.
   Find the gross rate if standard rate tax is 25%.

Complete the following table, giving answers correct to 2 d.p.

	Net rate of interest	Standard rate of income tax	Gross rate of interest
3.	5%	20%	
4.	6%	30%	
5.	8%		10%
6.	4%		5.5%
7.		40%	12.5%

8. A savings account offers interest of 8% p.a. gross, payable yearly. A building society offers interest of 6% p.a. net, payable yearly. If the standard rate of tax is 30%, which investment gives the bigger return to a tax payer and by how much?

9. An investor has £2000 to invest. He can choose from either an account paying 10% p.a. gross or an account paying 8% p.a. net. The standard rate of tax is 33%. Which choice gives him the better return and by how much if

a) he is a tax payer   b) he does not have to pay tax?

COMPOUND INTEREST

Suppose that £1000 is invested in an account that pays interest at 9% p.a. each year. If the capital and the interest are left in the account then, using the methods in the investment section successively for each year, we could find the amount in the account after, say, 7 years.

Alternatively, as the interest rate is 9% p.a. we can say that each year the account increases by $\frac{9}{100}$, or 0.09, of its value at the beginning of the year,

i.e.   its new value is   its original value + 0.09 of its original value,

i.e.   its new value is   1.09 of its original value.

Therefore the amount in the account after
    1 year is $1.09 \times £1000$
    2 years is $1.09 \times (1.09 \times £1000) = (1.09)^2 \times £1000$
    3 years is $1.09 \times (1.09)^2 \times £1000 = (1.09)^3 \times £1000$
    . . .
    7 years is $(1.09)^7 \times £1000$

1.09^7 can be found using a calculator as follows

1	.	0	9	y^x	7	=

Therefore, after 7 years the amount is $1.828 \times £1000$

$$= £1828$$

The increase, £828, is called the *compound interest*.

1.09 is called the multiplying factor for 1 year and $(1.09)^7$ is the multiplying factor for 7 years.

If £500 is invested at an interest rate of 12 % p.a. the multiplying factor for 1 year is 1.12.

After 9 years, the multiplying factor is $(1.12)^9$ i.e. in 9 years, the original £500 becomes

$$(1.12)^9 \times £500$$

$$= 2.773 \times £500$$

$$= £1387 \text{ (correct to the nearest £)}$$

APPRECIATION AND DEPRECIATION

Certain possessions such as houses and antiques tend to increase in value, or appreciate, as time passes. When the appreciation is expressed as a percentage rate per annum, the calculation is basically the same as for compound interest.

For example, suppose that a house bought for £20 000 in 1980 appreciates each year by 5 % of its value at the beginning of that year, then the yearly multiplying factor is 1.05,
i.e. in 1981 the house is worth $1.05 \times £20 000$.

By 1990 the house has been appreciating for 10 years so its value then will be $(1.05)^{10} \times £20 000$.

Other possessions such as cars and motor cycles tend to decrease in value, or depreciate, as time passes.

For example, if a car is bought for £8000 in 1980 and depreciates each year by 8 % its value at the beginning of that year, then after 1 year it is worth 92 % of £8000.

i.e. $0.92 \times £8000$

This time the multiplying factor is 0.92 for 1 year. After 7 years, the value of the car is $(0.92)^7 \times £8000$.

EXERCISE 16f

Give answers correct to the nearest penny when necessary.

1.   £1000 is invested for 2 years at 5% p.a. compound interest. Find the compound interest.

2.   £500 is invested for 2 years at 6% p.a. compound interest. How much is it then worth?

3.   £3000 is invested for 3 years at 8% p.a. compound interest. Find the compound interest.

4.   £1500 is invested for 3 years at 10% p.a. compound interest. Find the compound interest.

Use your calculator to find the following, giving your answers correct to four significant figures.

5. 1.12^8 **7.** 0.85^8 **9.** 1.11^5 **11.** 0.92^{10}

6. 1.08^8 **8.** 0.95^9 **10.** 1.15^{20} **12.** 0.87^{12}

13.   £2000 is invested for 6 years at 8% p.a. compound interest. How much is it then worth?

14.   £9000 is invested at 9% p.a. compound interest. How much is it worth after
a) 3 years   b) 10 years?

15.   £8500 is invested at 5% p.a. compound interest. How much is it worth after 6 years?

16.   Find the compound interest on £5000 invested for 8 years at   a) 9% p.a.
b) $8\frac{1}{2}$% p.a.

17.   Find the compound interest on £6700 invested for 7 years at   a) 6.5% p.a.
b) 7.25% p.a.

18.   Mr and Mrs Castrano buy a house for £60 000. What will it be worth, to the nearest £100, in   a) 2 years   b) 5 years, if it appreciates at 10% each year?

19.   Miss Green buys a flat for £50 000. What will it be worth to the nearest £100, in   a) 4 years   b) 6 years, if its value increases each year by 8%?

20.   John White pays £50 for a postage stamp for his collection. If its value appreciates by 15% each year what will it be worth in 5 years time?

21. A motorcycle bought for £1500 depreciates in value by 10% each year. Find its value, to the nearest £100, after   a) 3 years   b) 5 years.

22. When scientific calculators came on the market they were expensive, but in recent years have become much cheaper. In 1975 a good calculator cost £60. Assuming that the price of such a calculator reduced by 30% each year how much, to the nearest 10p, would one cost 4 years later?

23. The population of Mauritania is estimated to increase by 5% each year. If the population in 1990 was 1 500 000, estimate the population in 2000 giving your answer correct to the nearest hundred thousand.

COMPOUND GROWTH TABLE

In the previous exercise we needed to work out $(1.12)^8$ and other similar values. For convenience these multiplying factors are gathered together in Compound Growth Tables, and are frequently used commercially to show how sums of money, populations, sales, etc., grow at given percentage rates of increase over various periods of time.

The following table shows the multiplying factors for rates of growth from 6% to 15% over a 10 year period.

Rate of Growth	Number of Years									
	1	2	3	4	5	6	7	8	9	10
6%	1.060	1.124	1.191	1.262	1.338	1.419	1.504	1.594	1.689	1.791
7%	1.07	1.145	1.225	1.311	1.403	1.501	1.606	1.718	1.838	1.967
8%	1.08	1.166	1.260	1.360	1.469	1.587	1.714	1.851	1.999	2.159
9%	1.090	1.188	1.295	1.412	1.539	1.677	1.828	1.993	2.172	2.367
10%	1.100	1.210	1.331	1.464	1.611	1.772	1.949	2.144	2.358	2.594
11%	1.110	1.232	1.368	1.518	1.685	1.870	2.076	2.305	2.558	2.839
12%	1.120	1.254	1.405	1.574	1.762	1.974	2.211	2.476	2.770	3.106
13%	1.130	1.277	1.443	1.631	1.842	2.082	2.353	2.658	3.004	3.395
14%	1.140	1.300	1.482	1.689	1.925	2.195	2.502	2.853	3.252	3.707
15%	1.150	1.323	1.521	1.749	2.011	2.313	2.660	3.059	3.518	4.046

The table shows that the multiplying factor for a population growing at 8% for 8 years is 1.851 and that the multiplying factor for a sum of money growing at 12% for 9 years is 2.770.

EXERCISE 16g

In this exercise use the compound growth table on page 302. Give all answers correct to 4 significant figures.

What sum of money will £250 grow to if invested for 7 years at 12%?

From the table the multiplying factor is 2.211

i.e.   £250 will grow to $2.211 \times £250$

$= £552.75$

---

1. What sum will £10 grow to if invested for 3 years at 8%?

2. What sum will £20 grow to if invested for 6 years at 11%?

3. The population of Downtown is 2000. What will this increase to in 10 years if the growth rate is 6%?

4. Sally's wages have increased by 7% each year for the last 8 years. Eight years ago she was earning £100 per week. What is her present weekly wage?

5. Sales of Topmeat have increased steadily at 12% per year since it was introduced some years ago. Five years ago the company was selling 5000 tins a week. Find the present weekly sales.

Find the compound interest on

6. £300 invested for 10 years at 13%

7. £500 invested for 7 years at 7%

8. £700 invested for 9 years at 10%

9. £800 invested for 5 years at 12%

10. £400 invested for 8 years at 15%

Find the sum which, when invested for 8 years at 8% compound interest, will grow to £925.50.

£1 invested for 8 years at 8% compound interest will grow to £1.851

i.e.   £1.851 is what £1 will grow into in 8 years at 8%

∴   £925.50 is what £$\dfrac{925.50}{1.851}$, i.e. £500, will grow into in 8 years at 8%.

11.   Find the sum which, when invested for 6 years at 14%, will grow to £439.

12.   Find the sum which, when invested for 10 years at 9%, will grow to £1183.50.

13.   Find the sum which, when invested for 7 years at 6%, will grow to £1353.60.

14.   Find the population which, when growing at 12% for 5 years, will become 7048.

15.   My weekly wage has grown by a steady 6% each year for the past 10 years. I earn £235 each week now. What was my weekly wage 10 years ago??

In how many years will £800 grow to £1473.60 if invested at 13% compound interest?

If £800 grows to £1473.60 at 13% in the given time then

£1 grows to £$\dfrac{1473.60}{800}$ = £1.842 at 13% in the given time.

Using the table, go down to 13% and then go across until 1.842 is found.
This shows that the period of investment was 5 years.

In questions 16 to 20, how many years will it take

16. £300 to grow to £472.20 at 12 % p.a. compound interest?

17. £500 to grow to £925.50 at 8 % p.a. compound interest?

18. £800 to grow to £2046.40 at 11 % p.a. compound interest?

19. a population of 75 000 to grow to 89 325 at an annual growth rate of 6 %?

20. annual sales figures of 25 000 to grow to 62 550 at a steady annual growth rate of 14 %?

21. If a population of 7400 grows to 14 245 in five years at a steady annual rate of x %, find x.

22. When £400 is invested for x years at 10 % compound interest it amounts to £532.40. Find x.

CREDIT

Most of us need to borrow money at some time in our lives. When we buy goods or services and pay for them over an extended period of time we have obtained credit, (i.e. borrowed money). There are many ways of borrowing money and almost as many names for the different forms of loan.

MORTGAGES

Money borrowed to pay for a house or flat is called a mortgage. Mortgages are available from Building Societies, banks and some local authorities.

A mortgage is a long-term loan repayable, usually monthly, over several years. The deeds of the property are held by the lender for the duration of the mortgage. The charge for the loan is called interest. Mortgage interest rates are newsworthy because they fluctuate frequently and repayments form a large part of many people's expenditure.

When negotiating a mortgage, most people are interested in the size of the monthly repayments. These are frequently quoted per £1000 borrowed and vary with the interest rate and the number of years over which the loan is to be repaid.

CREDIT SALES AND BANK LOANS

When buying items such as cars, furniture and larger electrical appliances, credit is available in the form of bank loans or credit sales.

A bank loan is a straightforward loan of money for a fixed term (typically between two and five years) with fixed monthly repayments. The goods that you buy with it are yours from the start, although security for the loan, such as deeds, or share certificates, is often required.

A credit sale is similar to a bank loan in that the goods are yours from the time of purchase and payment is usually by monthly instalments for a fixed term, typically 3 months to 2 years. Credit sale agreements are usually operated by the company supplying the goods, and security is not required. There is usually a charge for all these credit arrangements and by law this has to be clearly printed as an annual percentage rate (APR).

CREDIT CARDS

Credit cards like Access and Visa operate in a different way from traditional forms of credit. Each card holder is allocated a credit limit. Suppose that it is £500. This means that the card holder can use the card to pay for goods and services up to the total value of £500.

A statement is issued each month detailing how much has been spent and demanding a minimum payment towards this debt (this is usually £5 or 5% of the debt, whichever is the greater). The cardholder must pay at least the minimum figure but may pay more, or even pay off the full debt in which case no interest is charged.

If a part payment only is made there is a charge of about 2% per month on the outstanding debt from the date of the statement. This interest charge sounds low, but 2% per month is equivalent to 26.8% p.a.

EXERCISE 16h

(Where necessary work to the nearest penny.)

1. The Newtown Building Society offers a twenty-year mortgage for monthly payments of £11.50 per £1000 borrowed. What are the monthly repayments on a £50 000 mortgage?

2. Jean and Michael Black want a mortgage of £60 000. The Redbrick Building Society offers them a 25-year mortgage with monthly repayments of £10.25 per £1000 borrowed. The Red Lion Bank offers them a 15-year mortgage with monthly repayments of £11.00 per £1000 borrowed.
For the full term of the mortgage, how much would they have to pay to
a) the building society   b) the bank?

3. Elizabeth Wood obtains a 95% mortgage on a house costing £60 000. Her monthly repayments are £13.60 per £1000 borrowed.

a) What are her monthly repayments?

b) If the mortgage runs for 25 years, what are her total repayments?

4. Mr and Mrs Smith have a mortgage on which the outstanding balance is £28 000. The interest rate is $12\frac{1}{2}$% p.a. What monthly payment would just cover the interest charges?

5. Zia Koren has a mortgage. When the outstanding debt is £9000 the interest rate rises from 10% p.a. to 11% p.a. The monthly repayments were £80 per month. Will it be necessary to increase these payments to stop the debt increasing, and if so by how much?

A motorcycle is priced at £2150. The credit sale terms are 25% deposit plus 24 monthly payments of £82.50. Find the cost of the motorcycle if it is bought by credit sale.

$$\text{Deposit} = 25\% \text{ of } £2150$$
$$= £537.50$$
$$\text{Total repayments} = 24 \times £82.50$$
$$= £1980$$
$$\text{Therefore HP cost} = £1980 + £537.50$$
$$= £2517.50$$

---

6. A hi-fi system is advertised at £520. If bought on credit, the terms are £50 deposit plus 18 monthly payments of £32. Find the credit cost.

7. A dining table and set of chairs is offered for £850 cash or on credit terms of 12 monthly payments of £81.50. Find the difference between the cash price and the credit price.

8. A freezer, advertised at £250, is offered for sale at either 2% discount for cash or on credit terms of 6 monthly repayments of £50.

a) How much is saved by paying cash?

b) What is the credit sale cost?

9. Mr Johnson wants to buy a car costing £7500, but cannot afford to pay cash. The following options for paying are available

a) A bank loan of £7500 repayable over 36 months at £281.38 per month.

b) A credit agreement of a deposit of 25% of the cash price followed by 30 monthly repayments of £254.17.

What is the cost of the car under each of these options?

10. A microcomputer package for business use is available under the following terms:

Either   a rental scheme costing £120 per month under which all service and repairs are free.

or   extended credit terms requiring payments of £220 per month for 18 months but any necessary service and repairs have to be paid for.

A company had one of these packages for three years, during which time it required service and repairs to the value of £400. The company chose the rental scheme. If instead they had chosen to buy the package on extended credit, would they have saved money or lost money and what is the difference?

11. When Tariq received his credit card statement the balance was £362.20. The minimum payment demanded is £5 or 5% of the balance whichever is the greater. What must Tariq pay?

12. James had a credit limit of £600 on his credit card. At the beginning of the month his balance was nil. He used the card during the month to pay £29.00 for petrol, £160 for clothes, £46 for a meal, £320 for a video recorder and £18.20 for records. He then offered his card for payment of a garage bill of £150. The garage checked with the credit card company. Did they give the garage authorisation to accept the card? Give a reason for your answer.

17 GRADIENTS AND AREAS

TANGENT TO A CURVE

The graph shows the curve whose equation is $y = \frac{1}{2}x(5-x)$

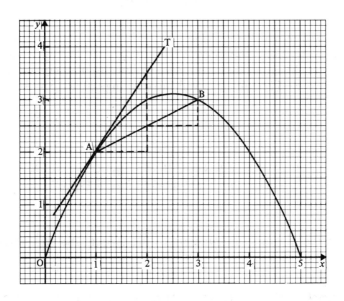

A line joining two points on a curve is a *chord*.

The line AB is a chord of the curve shown.

A line which touches a curve at a point is a *tangent* to the curve at that point.

In the diagram, AT is a tangent to the curve at A.

GRADIENTS

The gradient of a straight line is found by taking two points on the line and, moving left to right from one point to the other, evaluating the fraction

$$\frac{\text{distance moved up}}{\text{distance moved across}}$$

If you have to move down, the gradient is negative.

309

When choosing two points on the line, it is sensible to make the distance across a whole number of units.

If the coordinates of the two points are known, the gradient is given by

$$\frac{\text{difference in } y \text{ coordinates}}{\text{difference in } x \text{ coordinates}}$$

In the diagram, the gradient of the chord AB is $\frac{1}{2}$.

When moving along a curve, the gradient changes continuously. Imagine moving along the curve in the diagram, starting from O. When you get to A imagine that you stop following the curve and move on in a constant direction: you will move along the tangent AT.

Therefore

the gradient of a curve at a point is defined as the gradient of the tangent to the curve at this point.

In the diagram, the gradient of the tangent AT is $\frac{3}{2}$, therefore the gradient of the curve at A is $\frac{3}{2}$.

Finding a gradient by drawing and measurement means that the curve must be accurately drawn and then the tangent must be positioned carefully. Using a transparent ruler helps and, as a rough guide, the tangent should be approximately at the same 'angle' to the curve on each side of the point of contact.

EXERCISE 17a

1. Draw x and y axes from -6 to $+6$ using a scale of $1\,\text{cm}$ for 1 unit on both axes.

   Plot the points A$(1, 1)$, B$(3, 2)$, C$(-4, -1)$, D$(-5, 1)$, E$(1, 6)$, F$(4, -5)$.

   Find, where possible, the gradient of

   a) AB   b) BC   c) DE
   d) EF   e) AD   f) AE

2.

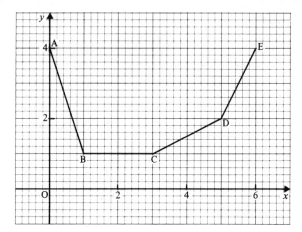

Find the gradient of the line
a) AB   b) BC   c) CD   d) DE

3. Copy and complete the table for $y = \dfrac{x^2}{10}$

x	0	1	2	3	4	5	6	7	8
y	0	0.1	0.4						

Use a scale of 2 cm for 1 unit on both axes and draw the curve.

a) P is the point on the curve where $x = 2$ and Q is the point on the curve where $x = 4$. Draw the chord PQ and find its gradient.

b) Draw, as accurately as possible, the tangents to the curve at the points where $x = 1, 4, 6$.

c) Find the gradients of the tangents to the curve at the points where $x = 1, 4, 6$.

4. Copy and complete the table for $y = \dfrac{10}{x}$, giving values of y correct to 1 d.p.

x	1	1.5	2	3	4	5	6	7	8
y	10	6.7	5	3.3	2.5				

Use a scale of 2 cm for 1 unit on both axes and draw the curve for values of x from 1 to 8.

a) A is the point on the curve where $x = 1$ and B is the point on the curve where $x = 4$. Find the gradient of the chord AB.

b) Find the gradients of the tangents to the curve at A and B.

c) Find the gradient of the tangent to the curve at the point where $x = 3$.

UNEQUAL SCALES

In the many practical applications of graphs it is rarely possible to have the same scales on both axes.

If the scales are not the same, care must be taken to read vertical measurements from the scale on the vertical axis and horizontal measurements from the scale on the horizontal axis.

EXERCISE 17b

The table shows the girth (w cm) of a pumpkin, n days after being fed with fertilizer.

n	1	2	3	4	5	6	7
w	15	17	20	24	29	35	41

Use a scale of 2 cm for 1 day and 2 cm for 10 cm of girth to draw the graph illustrating this information.

a) Find the gradient of the chord joining the points where $n = 3$ and $n = 7$ and interpret the result.

b) Find the gradient of the tangent at the point where $n = 3$ and interpret the result.

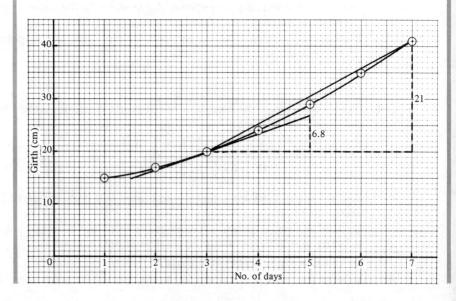

a) Gradient of chord $= \dfrac{21}{4} = 5.25$

This shows that the girth of the pumpkin is increasing by an average of 5.25 cm per day over the four-day period

b) Gradient of tangent $\approx \dfrac{6.8}{2} = 3.4$

This shows that the girth of the pumkin is increasing by 3.4 cm per day at the time of measurement on the third day.

1. The number of ripe strawberries on a particular strawberry plant were counted on Monday, Wednesday, Friday, Saturday and Sunday during one week. The results were recorded and plotted to give the following graph.

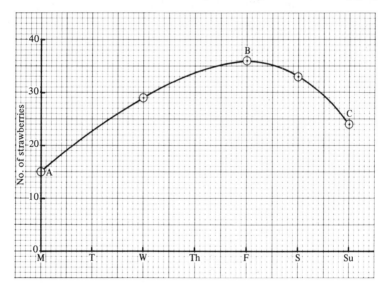

a) How many ripe strawberries were there on
   i) Wednesday   ii) Saturday?

b) How many strawberries were probably ripe on Thursday?

c) Find the gradient of the chord joining the points A and B and interpret the result.

d) Find the gradient of the chord joining B and C and interpret the result.

2. Draw a *y*-axis from 0 to 50 using a scale of 2 cm to 10 units and an *x*-axis from 0 to 6 using a scale of 2 cm to 1 unit.

Plot the points A(2, 10), B(1, 12), C(4, 25), D(0, 30), E(6, 45).

Find the gradients of the lines AB, BC, CD, DE.

3. The table shows the population of an island at 10 year intervals from 1900 to 1980.

Date (D)	1900	1910	1920	1930	1940	1950	1960	1970	1980
No. of people (N)	500	375	280	210	160	120	90	65	50

Using scale of $2\,\text{cm} \equiv 10$ years and $2\,\text{cm} \equiv 50$ people draw the graph illustrating this information.

a) Find the gradient of the chord joining the points on the curve where $D = 1910$ and $D = 1940$. Interpret your result.

b) Find the gradient of the tangent to the curve where $D = 1910$ and interpret the result.

4. The table shows the sales of 'Jampot' jam for 5 months following an advertising campaign.

Month (M)	1	2	3	4	5
Sales (No. of jars)	2000	2500	3500	5000	7000

Using a scale of $2\,\text{cm} \equiv 1$ month and $2\,\text{cm} \equiv 1000$ jars draw the graph illustrating this information.

a) Find the gradient of the tangent to the curve where $M = 2$ and interpret the result.

b) Find the gradient of the tangent to the curve where $M = 4$ and interpret the result.

5. Draw the graph of $y = x^3$ for values of x from 0 to 4 using a scale of $2\,\text{cm}$ for 1 unit on the x-axis and $1\,\text{cm}$ for 5 units on the y-axis.

Find the gradient of the curve at the points where

a) $x = 1$ b) $x = 3$

6. Copy and complete the following table of values for $y = 3x(4-x)$

x	0	1	2	2.5	3	4
y	0	9				

Using a scale of $2\,\text{cm}$ for 1 unit on the x-axis and $1\,\text{cm}$ for 1 unit on the y-axis draw the graph of $y = 3x(x-4)$.

Use the graph to find the gradient of the tangent to the curve where

a) $x = 2$ b) $x = 2.5$ c) $x = 3$

FINDING AREAS BOUNDED BY CURVES

It is sometimes necessary to find the area of a shape with curved boundaries. If the curve is part of a circle we can use the formula for the area of a circle. For other curves we can use approximate methods.

COUNTING SQUARES

For this method, the area required is drawn on squared paper using a suitable scale. (A grid of small squares produces a more accurate result than a grid of larger squares.)

For example, a survey of a village green resulted in the following scale drawing on 5 mm squared paper.

A square is included in the count if more than half of it is enclosed.

The number of squares enclosed in the diagram is 81.

Each square has a side of 5 mm and therefore an area of 25 mm².

Therefore the area of the scale drawing is $81 \times 25 \text{ mm}^2$

$$= 2025 \text{ mm}^2$$

$$= 20.25 \text{ cm}^2$$

Each square on the drawing represents a square of side 10 m on the village green (i.e. an area of 100 m²),

therefore the area of the green is $81 \times 100 \text{ m}^2$

$$= 8100 \text{ m}^2$$

EXERCISE 17c

The following shapes are drawn on 5 mm squared paper. For each question find the area of

a) the shape drawn

b) the actual shape represented by the scale drawing (use the scale given).

1.

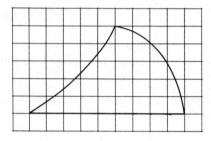

Scale: 5 mm ≡ 50 cm

2.

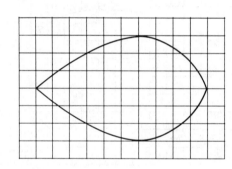

Scale: 5 mm ≡ 2 m

3.

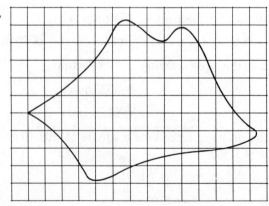

Scale: 5 mm ≡ 1 km

4. Draw a circle of radius 5 cm on 5 mm squared paper. Find the area of the circle

    a) by counting squares

    b) by using the formula $A = \pi r^2$ and a calculator.

AREAS UNDER GRAPHS

This graph shows the line $y = \frac{1}{3}(11 - 2x)$ drawn for values of x from 1 to 4.

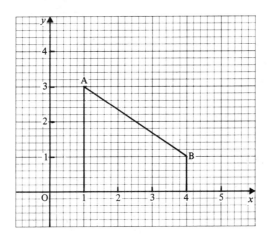

Consider the area enclosed by the section AB of the line, the x-axis, and the lines $x = 1$ and $x = 4$ (these are called *ordinates*). This is a trapezium and its area is given by

$$\tfrac{1}{2}(\text{sum of parallel sides}) \times (\text{distance between them})$$

The lengths of the parallel sides are 3 units and 1 unit, and the distance between them is 3 units.

Therefore the area under the line AB is

$$\tfrac{1}{2}(3 + 1) \times 3 \text{ square units} = 6 \text{ square units.}$$

Notice that, although 1 cm represents 1 unit on each axis we do not know what those units are, so the area is given as a number of square units.

When the scales on the two axes are different, care must be taken to read vertical lengths in units from the vertical scale and horizontal lengths in units from the horizontal scale.

EXERCISE 17d

Find the area between the line $y = 20 - 5x$, the x-axis and the ordinate $x = 1$.

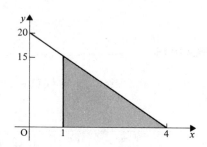

(Notice that a sketch of the graph is sufficient to show the area required; an accurate graph is not necessary.)

When $x = 1$, $y = 15$

The required area is a triangle of base 3 units and height 15 units.

Therefore area $= \frac{1}{2}(\text{base} \times \text{height})$

$\qquad\qquad = \frac{1}{2} \times 3 \times 15$ square units

$\qquad\qquad = 22.5$ square units.

In each case find, in square units, the area enclosed by the x-axis, the given line and the given ordinates.

1. $y = 1 + x$, $x = 0$, $x = 4$

2. $y = 5 - x$, $x = 0$

3. $y = 3 + 2x$, $x = 1$, $x = 5$

4. $y = 8 - 2x$, $x = 1$

5. $y = 20 - x$, $x = 4$ and $x = 10$

6. $y = 4 + 6x$, $x = 2$ and $x = 6$

7. $y = 15$, $x = 5$ and $x = 9$

8. $y = \frac{1}{2}(15 - x)$, $x = 3$ and $x = 12$

USING TRAPEZIUMS TO FIND THE AREA UNDER A CURVE ――――

A curve can be approximated to by a series of straight lines.

To find the area between a curve and the *x*-axis, the area is divided into a convenient number of vertical strips. A chord is drawn across the top of each strip to give a set of trapeziums.

The sum of the areas of these trapeziums is then found and this is approximately equal to the required area.

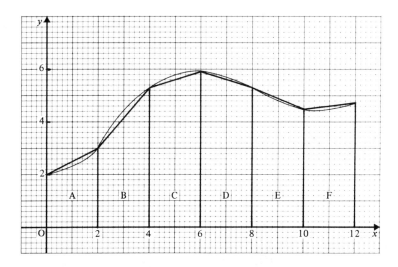

The area under this curve is divided into six strips each of width 2 units. Drawing the chords across the top of each strip gives six trapeziums.

Reading from the graph,

for trapezium A, the lengths of the parallel sides are 2 units and 3 units and the distance between them is 2 units,

therefore   area A $= \frac{1}{2}$ (sum of parallel sides) × (distance between them)

$$= \tfrac{1}{2}(2+3)\times(2) \text{ sq units}$$

$$= 5 \text{ sq units.}$$

Finding the sum of the areas of all six trapeziums gives the total area as

$$5 + 8.2 + 11.1 + 11.2 + 9.8 + 9.1 \text{ sq units}$$

$$= 54.4 \text{ sq units.}$$

Notice that all the strips are the same width. Although it is not necessary to use equal width strips, it is usually convenient.

EXERCISE 17e

Use the trapezium rule to find the area between each of the following curves and the *x*-axis. Use the given number of *equal width* strips.

1.

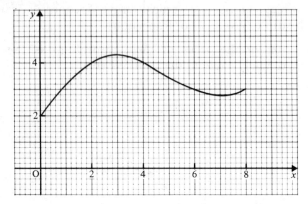

Use   a) two strips   b) four strips
Comment on your answers to parts (a) and (b).

2.

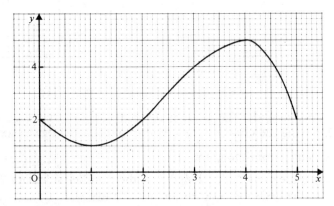

Use five strips.
Comment on the result if two strips were used.

3. A curve passes through the points given in the table

x	0	1	2	3	4
y	1	2	4	4	2

Use a scale of 1 cm for 1 unit on each axis and draw the curve for values of *x* from 0 to 4.
Use four strips to find approximately the area between this curve and the *x*-axis.

Use five strips to find, approximately, the area under the curve passing through the points given in the table for values of x from 1 to 11.

x	1	3	5	7	9	11
y	2	10	20	25	20	15

(A sketch graph is sufficient to give the necessary information.)

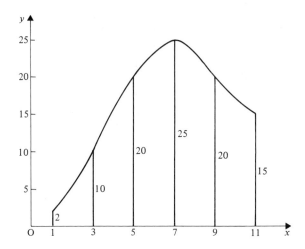

Area $\approx \frac{1}{2}(2+10)(2) + \frac{1}{2}(10+20)(2) + \frac{1}{2}(20+25)(2)$
$$+ \frac{1}{2}(25+20)(2) + \frac{1}{2}(20+15)(2) \text{ sq units}$$

$= 12 + 30 + 45 + 45 + 35$ sq units

$= 167$ sq units

4. A curve goes through the points given in the table.

x	0	1	2	3	4
y	10	6	4	6	10

Draw a rough sketch of the curve.
Use four strips to find the area under the curve. Is your answer greater than or less than the true value?

5. Sketch the graph of the parabola $y = 3x^2$ from $x = 0$ to $x = 3$.

a) Divide the area under the curve into three strips and mark the values of the ordinates on your sketch. Hence find, approximately, the area under your curve.

b) Repeat part (a) using six strips.

6. A river is 40 metres wide and its depth was measured from one bank to the other bank at 5-metre intervals across its width. The values obtained are shown in the table.

Distance from bank (m)	0	5	10	15	20	25	30	35	40
Depth (m)	2	5	6	6.5	6	5	4	2.5	1.5

a) Draw a rough sketch of the cross-section of the river.

b) Use eight strips to estimate the area of the cross-section.

c) The speed of the water at this point of the river is measured as 0.25 m/s. How many litres of water (to the nearest 10ℓ) pass through this cross-section in one second?

d) How many litres of water flow through the cross-section in one hour? Give your answer to the nearest 1000 litres.

18 TRAVEL GRAPHS

DISTANCE, SPEED AND TIME

In the metric system distance is measured in kilometres or metres while miles and feet are the most common Imperial units.

Time is measured in hours, minutes or seconds.

Speed is measured in distance units per time unit, e.g. a speed could be given in km per min.

Remember that
$$\text{distance} = \text{speed} \times \text{time}$$

and when using this formula, units must be consistent. For example, if a speed of 8 km/h and a time of 5 minutes are given then one quantity must be changed so that the time unit is the same for both.

EXERCISE 18a

Change a speed of 20 m/s to
a)   m/min   b)   km/h

     a) $20 \text{ m/s} = 20 \times 60 \text{ m/min}$

                               $= 1200 \text{ m/min}$

     b) $20 \text{ m/s} = \dfrac{20}{1000} \text{ km/s}$

                               $= 0.02 \text{ km/s}$

                               $= 0.02 \times 60 \times 60 \text{ km/h}$

                               $= 72 \text{ km/h}$

1. Change 33 km/h to   a) km/min   b) m/h

2. Change 100 m/s to   a) km/s   b) m/min

3. Change 40 m.p.h. to   a) miles/min   b) miles/s

4. Change 90 km/h to   a) km/s   b) m/s

5. Change 100 m/s to   a) m/h   b) km/h

Find, in metres per second, the average speed for a journey of 5 km in 4 minutes.

(For a speed in m/s, we need the distance in metres and the time in seconds.)

$$5 \text{ km} = 5000 \text{ m}$$
$$4 \text{ min} = 240 \text{ s}$$

$$\text{Using } D = S \times T \quad \text{gives} \quad S = \frac{D}{T}$$

$$\text{Speed} = \frac{5000}{240} \text{ m/s}$$
$$= 20.8 \text{ m/s}$$

Find the unknown quantity in the following table, giving your answers in the units indicated.

	Distance	Speed	Time
6.	m	5 km/s	0.5 s
7.	90 m	m/s	4 min
8.	5 miles	m.p.h.	10 min
9.	2 km	4 km/h	min
10.	km	8 m/s	2 min

11.	miles	20 m.p.h.	5 min
12.	30 km	m/s	10 min
13.	120 m	m/s	5 min
14.	km	20 m/s	3 min
15.	1 km	25 m/s	s

DISTANCE-TIME GRAPHS

If a train travels from York at 40 km/h for 3 hours, stops for half an hour and then returns to York at 50 km/h, we can draw a graph to illustrate this journey.

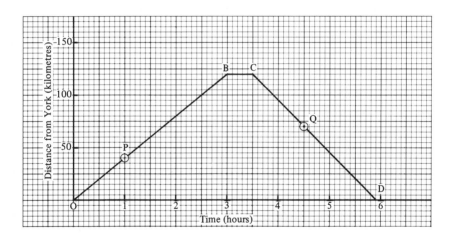

Time, as the independent variable, always goes on the horizontal axis.

OB represents the first part of the journey. The train starts at York and one hour later it is 40 km away. The point P, 1 hour along the time axis and 40 km along the distance axis is marked, and a straight line is drawn through O and P to B where the time is three hours.

BC represents the next part of the journey. The train is at rest for half an hour so a line, 0.5 h along the time axis, is drawn horizontally through B.

CD represents the last part of the journey. The train returns to York at 50 km/h so the line comes down, passing through the point Q which is 1 hour from C and 50 km down from C.

From the graph we see that the train returns to York 5.9 hours after leaving it.

EXERCISE 18b

Draw travel graphs to show the following journeys.

1. A cyclist leaves home and rides at 15 km/h for 2 hours. He rests for $\frac{1}{2}$ hour and then continues riding away from home at 12 km/h for $1\frac{1}{2}$ hours. He has another rest of $\frac{1}{2}$ hour before returning home, without stopping, at 20 km/h. For how long is the cyclist away from home?
Use 1 cm for 1 hour and 1 cm for 10 km.

2. A bus leaves the bus station at 10.00 a.m. It travels at 30 km/h for $\frac{1}{2}$ hour, then stops for 12 minutes, before continuing at 40 km/h for 2 hours. How far has the bus travelled from the bus station now? Use 2 cm for 1 hour and 1 cm for 10 km.

3. A family travel by car from a town A to a town B 50 km away, in 48 minutes. They stop in town B for 1 hour and then continue to a village C, which is 70 km from B, at a speed of 50 km/h. The family stop at C for 2 hours and then return, without stopping, along the same route to A at 60 km/h. Use 3 cm for 1 hour and 1 cm for 10 km.
a) What is the speed of the journey from A to B?
b) What is the time taken for the return journey from C to A?

4. A bead is threaded on a straight wire, AB, 50 m long. The bead starts at A and travels to B at 20 m/s. It is held at B for 10 seconds and then returns to A at 10 m/s. Use 1 cm for 5 seconds and 1 cm for 10 metres.

What time elapses between the bead leaving A and returning to A?

5. A funfair train runs on a track that is 200 m long. The track has three sections, A to B which is 50 m long, B to C which is 100 m long and C to the end D. The train travels at 5 m/s on the first section, 2 m/s on the second section and 4 m/s on the last section.
Use 1 cm for 5 seconds and 1 cm for 10 metres.

How long does the train take to travel the full length of the track?

6. A lift, starting from the ground floor, travels up at 2 m/s for 12 seconds, to the top floor. It then stops for 20 seconds before descending to the ground floor. The descent takes 8 seconds.
Use 1 cm for 5 seconds and 1 cm for 5 metres.
a) How far above the ground floor is the top floor?
b) What is the speed of the lift on its descent?

AVERAGE SPEED

The average speed for a journey can be found from a distance–time graph.

Remember that $$\text{average speed} = \frac{\text{total distance}}{\text{total time}}$$

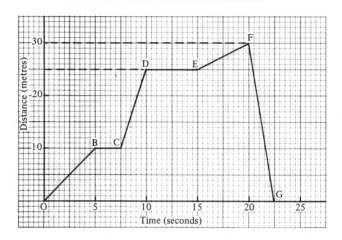

For the journey illustrated in the graph,

the section represented by O to D, a distance of 25 m, is covered in a time of 10 seconds,

therefore the average speed for this section is $\dfrac{25}{10}$ m/s = 2.5 m/s.

For the section represented by O to F, a distance of 30 m is covered in a time of 20 seconds,

therefore the average speed for this section is $\dfrac{30}{20}$ m/s = 1.5 m/s.

For the whole journey represented by O to G, a distance of 60 m (30 m away from the start and 30 m back again) is covered in 22.5 seconds.

therefore the average speed for the whole journey is $\dfrac{60}{22.5}$ m/s = 2.7 m/s.

EXERCISE 18c

Use the travel graphs drawn for Exercise 18b to find the average speed for

a) the journey during the first half of the time taken

b) the whole journey.

Give answers correct to 3 s.f. where necessary.

CURVED DISTANCE-TIME GRAPHS

When an object moves with constant speed, the distance–time graph representing its motion is a straight line. However, when an object moves so that its speed is constantly changing (e.g. a car or a big-dipper) then the distance–time graph representing its motion is a curved line. To draw such a graph, we need a relation between the time and the distance travelled.

Consider, for example, a rocket fired from the ground so that its distance (*d* metres) from the launching pad after *t* seconds is given by

$$d = 80t - 5t^2$$

Taking values of *t* from 0 to 8, at two-second intervals, gives the following table.

t	0	2	4	6	8
$80t$	0	160	320	480	640
$5t^2$	0	20	80	180	320
$d\ (= 80t - 5t^2)$	0	140	240	300	320

Plotting these values and drawing a smooth curve through the points gives the distance–time graph.

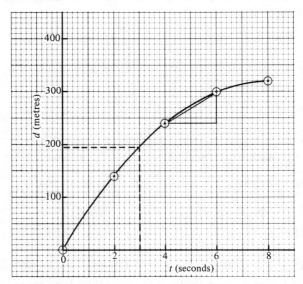

From this graph we can see that

3 seconds after launching, the rocket is 195 m above the launch pad.

We can also find the average speed of the rocket over any interval of time.

Consider, for example, the motion during the fifth and sixth seconds.
The rocket moves $(300 - 240)$ m, i.e. 60 m, in these 2 seconds.
Therefore the average speed for the interval from $t = 4$ to $t = 6$

$$\text{is } \frac{60}{2} \text{ m/s} = 30 \text{ m/s}$$

Notice that the chord joining the points on the curve where $t = 4$ and
$t = 6$, has a gradient of $\dfrac{60}{2} = 30$.

EXERCISE 18d

1. A car moves away from a set of traffic lights. The table shows the distance, d metres, of the car from the lights after t seconds.

t	0	1	2	3	4	5
d	0	2	8	18	32	50

Draw the distance–time graph using scales of $1\,\text{cm} \equiv \frac{1}{2}$ second and $1\,\text{cm} \equiv 5\,\text{m}$.

From your graph find
a) the distance of the car from the lights after $2\frac{1}{2}$ seconds
b) the average speed of the car during the 2nd second
c) the average speed of the car during the first five seconds.

2. A rocket is launched and the table shows the distance travelled, d metres, after a time t seconds from lift-off.

t	0	1	2	3	4	5
d	0	5	40	135	320	625

Draw the distance–time graph using scales of $2\,\text{cm} \equiv 1$ second and $1\,\text{cm} \equiv 100\,\text{m}$.

Use your graph to find
a) the distance of the rocket from the launch pad $4\frac{1}{2}$ seconds after lift-off
b) the average speed of the rocket for the first 4 seconds of its journey
c) the average speed of the rocket during the fourth second.

VELOCITY

Consider a bead threaded on a straight wire AB.

If we are told that the bead is moving along the wire at 5 m/s, we know something about the motion of the bead but we do not know which way the bead is moving.

If we are told that the bead is moving from A to B at 5 m/s we know *both* the direction of motion *and* the speed of the bead.

Velocity is the name given to the quantity that includes the speed *and* the direction of motion.

When an object moves along a straight line, like the bead, there are only two possible directions of motion. In this case a positive sign is used to indicate motion in one direction and a negative sign is used to indicate motion in the opposite direction.

Taking the direction A to B as positive, we can illustrate velocities of +5 m/s and −5 m/s on a diagram.

Velocity = +5 m/s   Velocity = −5 m/s

EXERCISE 18e

1. For each of the following statements state whether it is the velocity or the speed of the object that is given.

a) A train travels between London and Watford at 70 km/h.

b) A train travels from London to Watford at 70 km/h.

c) A ball rolls down a hill at 5 m/s.

d) A ball rolls along a horizontal groove at 3 m/s.

e) A lift moves between floors at 2 m/s.

f) A lift moves up from the ground floor at 2 m/s.

g) A ferry crosses the channel from Dover to Calais at 15 knots (nautical miles per hour).

2. A bead moves along a horizontal wire AB. Taking the direction from A to B as positive, draw a diagram to illustrate the motion of the bead if its velocity is

a) $-2\,\text{m/s}$ b) $4\,\text{m/s}$ c) $-10\,\text{m/s}$ d) 0

3.

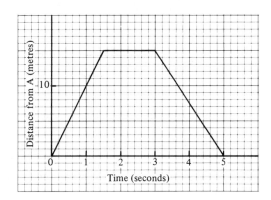

The graph illustrates the motion of a bead along a straight wire AB as the bead moves from A to B, stops at B, and moves back to A again.

Taking the direction $\overrightarrow{AB}$ as a positive, find

a) the speed of the bead as it moves from A to B

b) the velocity of the bead as it moves from A to B

c) the speed of the bead as it moves from B to A

d) the velocity of the bead as it moves from B to A

e) the average speed for the whole motion.

4.

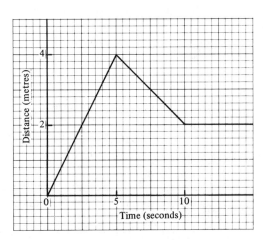

The graph illustrates the motion of a ball rolling in a straight line along horizontal ground. Taking the direction of the first part of the motion as positive, describe the motion of the ball, giving its velocity for each section of the motion.

5.

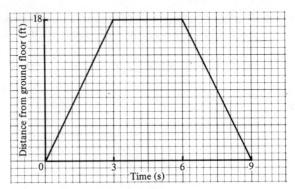

The graph above illustrates the motion of a lift which travels from the ground floor to the first floor and then returns to the ground floor. Taking the upward direction as positive, state which of the following statements *must* be true.

a) The velocity of the lift is the same on both the upward and downward journeys.

b) On the downward journey the speed is 6 ft/s.

c) The average speed of the lift between leaving the ground floor and returning to it, is zero.

d) On the upward journey the velocity of the lift is 6 ft/s.

e) The velocity of the lift is zero for three seconds.

FINDING VELOCITY FROM A DISTANCE-TIME GRAPH

This distance–time graph illustrates the motion of a ball thrown upwards from the ground.

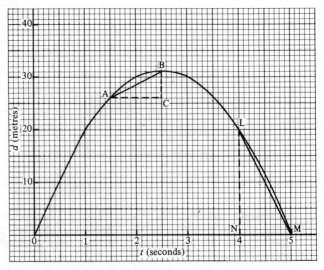

Taking the upward direction as positive we see that, up to the point where $t = 2\frac{1}{2}$, the distance of the ball from the ground is increasing,
i.e. the ball has a positive velocity (the ball is going up).
From $t = 2\frac{1}{2}$ to $t = 5$, the distance of the ball from the ground is decreasing, i.e. the ball has a negative velocity (the ball is going down).

Average velocity is defined as $\dfrac{\text{increase in distance}}{\text{time taken}}$

Therefore the average velocity of the ball in the interval from $t = 1.5$ to $t = 2.5$ is

$$\frac{\text{increase in distance from } t = 1.5 \text{ to } t = 2.5}{2.5 - 1.5} \text{ m/s} = \frac{5}{1} \text{ m/s}.$$

On the graph this is represented by $\dfrac{\text{BC}}{\text{AC}}$ which is the gradient of the

chord AB.

Similarly the average velocity of the ball from $t = 4$ to $t = 5$ is

$$\frac{\text{the increase in distance in this time}}{5 - 4} \text{ m/s} = \frac{-20}{1} \text{ m/s}$$

On the graph this is represented by $\dfrac{-\text{LN}}{\text{NM}}$ which is the gradient of the
chord LM.

Therefore on a distance–time graph,

> the average velocity from t_1 to t_2 given by the gradient of the chord joining the points on the curve where $t = t_1$ and $t = t_2$.

The average velocity during any time interval can now be found using this fact, as the following example shows.

From $t = 1\frac{1}{2}$ to $t = 4$ the average velocity is given by the gradient of the chord AL, i.e.

$$\frac{-6}{2.5} \text{ m/s} = -2.4 \text{ m/s}$$

VELOCITY AT AN INSTANT

Consider again the distance–time graph on page 332.

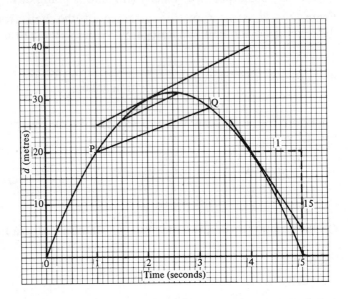

Suppose that we want to find the velocity of the ball at the instant when $t = 2$.

We can get an approximate value for this velocity by finding the average velocity from, say, $t = 1$ to $t = 3.2$, i.e. by finding the gradient of the chord PQ.

A better approximation is obtained by taking a smaller interval of time, say $t = 1.5$ to $t = 2.6$, i.e. by making the ends of the chord closer together.

The best answer is obtained when the interval of time is as small as possible, i.e. when the ends of the chord coincide. When this happens the chord becomes a tangent to the curve at the point where $t = 2$.

Therefore the velocity of the ball at the instant when $t = 2$ is given by the gradient of the tangent to the curve at the point where $t = 2$.

By drawing and measurement, the velocity is 5 m/s. Similarly, at the point where $t = 4$, the gradient of the tangent is found to be -15. Therefore the velocity when $t = 4$ is -15 m/s.

In general

> the velocity at the instant when $t = T$ is given by the gradient of the tangent to the distance–time curve at the point where $t = T$.

EXERCISE 18f

1. Use the graph drawn for question 1 in Exercise 18d, page 329 to find
a) the average velocity during the first three seconds
b) the velocity of the car 2 seconds after leaving the lights
c) the velocity of the car 4 seconds after leaving the lights.

2. Use the graph drawn for question 2 of Exercise 18d to find
a) the average velocity of the rocket during the time from $t = 2$ to $t = 4$
b) the average velocity of the rocket over the interval $t = 2$ to $t = 3$
c) the velocity of the rocket when $t = 2$
d) the velocity of the rocket when $t = 2.5$.

3. The table shows the distance, d metres, of a ball from its starting position, t seconds after being thrown into the air.

t	0	1	2	3	4	5	6
d	0	25	40	45	40	25	0

Use scales of $2 \, \text{cm} \equiv 1$ second and $1 \, \text{cm} \equiv 5 \, \text{m}$ and draw the graph of d against t.

From your graph find
a) when the ball returns to the starting point
b) the average velocity of the ball from $t = 1$ to $t = 2$
c) the average velocity of the ball from $t = 1$ to $t = 1.5$
d) the velocity of the ball when $t = 1$
e) the velocity of the ball when $t = 4$
f) the velocity of the ball when $t = 5$.

4. Use the graph at the foot of page 332 to find

a) the velocity when $t = 1$

b) the average velocity during the first second

c) the average velocity during the first four seconds

d) the greatest height of the ball

e) the average velocity for the time between $t = 3$ and $t = 5$.

5. A particle moves in a straight line so that t seconds after leaving a fixed point O on the line, its distance, d metres, from O is given by

$$d = 8t - 2t^2$$

a) Copy and complete the following table

t	0	1	2	3	4
$8t$	0	8			
$-2t^2$	0	-2			
d	0	6			

b) Use scales of $2\,\text{cm} \equiv 1\,\text{second}$ and $1\,\text{cm} \equiv 2\,\text{m}$ and draw the distance–time graph.

c) From your graph find the velocity of the particle when $t = 2$ and when $t = 3$.

d) What is the greatest distance of the particle from its starting point?

ACCELERATION

When the speed of a moving object is increasing we say that the object is accelerating.

If a train moves away from a station A and accelerates from rest so that its speed increases by $2\,\text{m/s}$ each second then

1 second after leaving A the train has a speed of $2\,\text{m/s}$
2 seconds after leaving A the train has a speed of $4\,\text{m/s}$
3 seconds after leaving A the train has a speed of $6\,\text{m/s}$.

The train is said to have an acceleration of $2\,\text{m/s}$ per second and this is written as $2\,\text{m/s/s}$ or $2\,\text{m/s}^2$.

If the speed of the train decreases it is said to be decelerating.

Suppose that the speed of the train decreases by 1 m/s each second, then we say that the deceleration is 1 m/s per second or 1 m/s^2.

We can also say that the train has an acceleration of −1 m/s^2, i.e. a deceleration is a negative acceleration.

Consider a car that accelerates from rest at 5 m/s^2 for 10 seconds and then decelerates at 2 m/s^2 back to rest.

An acceleration of 5 m/s^2 means that the speed of the car increases by 5 m/s each second. Therefore after 10 seconds its speed is 50 m/s. A deceleration of 2 m/s^2 means that the speed of the car reduces by 2 m/s each second. Therefore, the speed of 50 m/s is reduced by 2 m/s each second, and this means that the car takes 25 seconds to stop.

EXERCISE 18g

1. A train accelerates from rest at 1 m/s^2 for 30 seconds. How fast is the train moving at the end of the 30 seconds ?
If the train now decelerates back to rest at 0.5 m/s^2 how long does it take for the train to stop ?

2. A train accelerates from rest at 2 m/s^2. How fast is the train moving after
a) 2 seconds   b) 30 seconds   c) 1 minute ?

3. A bus moves away from rest at a bus stop with an acceleration of 4 m/s^2 for 5 seconds; it then has to decelerate to rest at 2 m/s^2. How long after leaving the bus stop is the bus again stationary ?

4. The speed of a lift increases from 6 m/s to 20 m/s in 7 seconds. Find the acceleration.

5. A train accelerates from rest at 0.5 km/minute^2. How fast (in km/h) is the train moving after
a) 3 minutes   b) 10 minutes   c) 45 seconds ?

6. The speed of a car increases from 10 km/h to 80 km/h in 5 seconds. Find the acceleration.

7. Find, in m/s^2, the acceleration of a motor bike when its speed increases from 10 km/h to 50 km/h in 4 seconds.

VELOCITY-TIME GRAPHS

A car accelerates from rest at $5 \, \text{m/s}^2$ for 6 seconds and then travels at a constant speed for 10 seconds after which it decelerates to rest at $3 \, \text{m/s}^2$.

This information can be shown on a graph by plotting velocity against time. This is called a velocity–time graph.

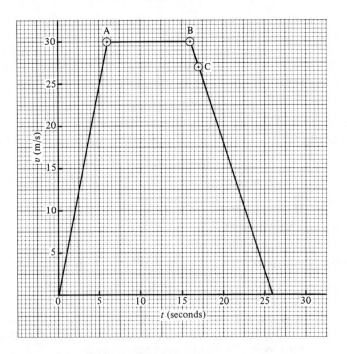

After 6 seconds, the car is moving at 30 m/s, so we draw a straight line from O to the point A, where $t = 6$ and $v = 30$.
Notice that the gradient of OA represents the acceleration.
The line AB (zero gradient) represents the car moving at constant speed.

The last section of the journey is represented by the line drawn from B through C to the time axis, where C is 1 unit along the time axis and 3 units down the velocity axis from B.
Notice that the gradient of BC is -3 and this represents the deceleration of 3 m/s.

> In general, acceleration is represented by the gradient of the velocity–time graph.

EXERCISE 18h

1.

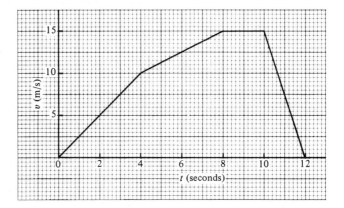

This velocity–time graph illustrates the journey of a car between a set of traffic-lights and a zebra crossing.

a) What is the car's acceleration for the first 4 seconds ?

b) What happens when $t = 4$?

c) For how long is the car moving at a constant speed ?

d) For how long is the car braking ?

e) What is the deceleration of the car ?

f) For how long is the car moving ?

2.

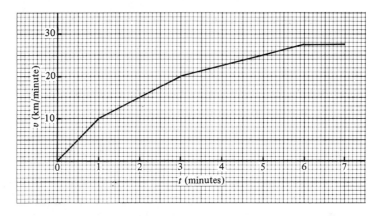

This velocity–time graph illustrates the first 7 minutes of the flight of a rocket.

a) What is the initial acceleration of the rocket ?

b) What is the speed of the rocket 2 minutes after its launch ?

c) What steady speed is obtained by the rocket ?

d) What is the acceleration of the rocket during the fourth minute of its flight ?

3.

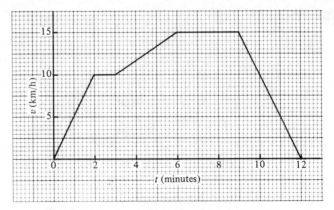

This velocity–time graph illustrates the journey of a train between two stations.

a) What is the acceleration for the first 2 minutes?

b) What is the greatest speed of the train?

c) For how long is the train travelling at constant speed?

d) What is the acceleration during the third minute?

e) What is the deceleration of the train?

Draw a velocity–time graph to illustrate the following journeys.
Use scales of $1\,\text{cm} \equiv 2$ seconds and $1\,\text{cm} = 5\,\text{m/s}$.

4. A car accelerates steadily from rest reaching a speed of $12\,\text{m/s}$ in 10 seconds.

5. A train accelerates from rest reaching a speed of $8\,\text{m/s}$ in 5 seconds and then immediately decelerates to rest in 4 seconds.

6. A motorbike accelerates from rest to a speed of $20\,\text{m/s}$ in 4 seconds, maintains this steady speed for 8 seconds and then decelerates to rest in 5 seconds.

Sketch a velocity–time graph for each of the following journeys.

7. A bullet is fired into a block of wood at $100\,\text{m/s}$ and comes to rest 3 seconds later.

8. A car accelerates from rest at $2\,\text{m/s}^2$ for 5 seconds, then moves with constant speed for 15 seconds before decelerating back to rest at $4\,\text{m/s}^2$.

9. A train accelerates from rest at $1\,\text{m/s}^2$ for 3 seconds, $2\,\text{m/s}^2$ for 3 seconds and then $5\,\text{m/s}^2$ for 5 seconds.

10. A car accelerates from rest at $10\,\text{m/s}^2$ for 2 seconds, $5\,\text{m/s}^2$ for 5 seconds and then $2\,\text{m/s}^2$ for 3 seconds. The car then travels at constant speed for 10 seconds before decelerating at $8\,\text{m/s}^2$ back to rest.

11. A bullet is fired at 50 m/s into sand which retards the bullet at 10 m/s².

12. A car travels at 30 m/s for 5 seconds, then decelerates at 4 m/s² for 3 seconds and travels at constant speed for another 10 seconds.

13. A block of wood is thrown straight down into the sea. The wood enters the water at 50 m/s and sinks for 6 seconds.

FINDING THE DISTANCE FROM A VELOCITY-TIME GRAPH

This velocity-time graph shows a car accelerating from a speed of 4 m/s to a speed of 20 m/s in 9 seconds.

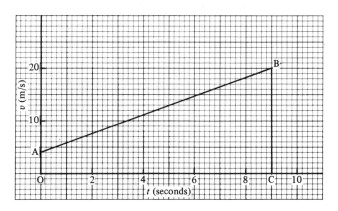

The time for which the car is accelerating is represented by the line OC. The speed of the car increases from 4 m/s to 20 m/s.

Therefore the average speed of the car is $\frac{1}{2}(4+20)$ m/s.

On the graph, this average speed is represented by $\frac{1}{2}(OA+BC)$.

Now   average speed $= \dfrac{\text{distance covered}}{\text{time}}$

so   distance covered = average speed × time

On the graph this is represented by $\frac{1}{2}(OA+BC) \times OC$.

This is the area of the trapezium OABC, i.e.

> the distance travelled is represented by the area under the velocity-time graph.

EXERCISE 18i

The velocity–time graph illustrates a train journey between two stations.

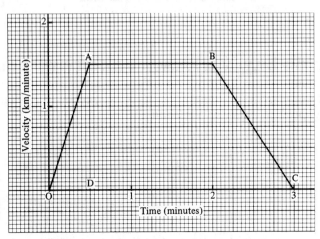

a) What is the maximum speed of the train in km/h?
b) What is the train's acceleration in the first half minute?
c) How far does the train travel in the first 30 seconds?
d) What is the distance between the stations?

a) From the graph, the maximum speed is 1.5 km/min

$$= 1.5 \times 60 \, \text{km/h}$$

$$= 90 \, \text{km/h}$$

b) The acceleration is given by the gradient of OA, which is $\dfrac{1.5}{0.5} = 3$

Therefore the acceleration is 3 km/minute².

c) The distance travelled in the first 30 seconds is given by the area of △OAD

area △OAD $= \frac{1}{2}(\text{OD}) \times (\text{AD})$

$$= 0.5 \times (0.5) \times (1.5)$$

$$= 0.375$$

Therefore the train travels 0.375 km in the first 30 seconds.

d) The distance between the stations is represented by the area of trapezium OABC.

$$\text{area OABC} = \tfrac{1}{2}(\text{OC} + \text{AB}) \times \text{AD}$$
$$= 0.5(3 + 1.5) \times 1.5$$
$$= 0.5 \times 4.5 \times 1.5$$
$$= 3.375$$

Therefore the distance between the stations is 3.375 km.

1. The velocity-time graph represents a car journey between two sets of traffic lights.

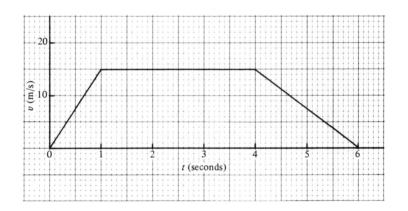

a) What is the acceleration of the car?

b) What is the deceleration of the car?

c) For how long does the car accelerate?

d) How many metres does the car travel while braking?

e) Find the distance between the two sets of lights.

2. Use the graphs for questions 1, 2 and 3 of Exercise 18h to find

a) the distance covered by the car in question 1

b) the distance travelled by the rocket in the first 3 minutes in question 2

c) the distance travelled by the train in the first 2 minutes in question 3. (Be careful with the units.)

3. The velocity–time graph represents a bullet fired into a 'wall' made up of a layer of sand followed by a layer of wood and then a layer of brick.

a) Find the deceleration of the bullet as it passes through the layer of sand.

b) Find the depth of the sand.

c) Find the deceleration of the bullet as it passes through the layer of wood

d) Find the depth of the layer of wood.

e) What retardation of the bullet does the layer of brick cause ?

f) Find the depth to which the bullet penetrates the brick.

4. The graph represents a two-minute section of a car journey.

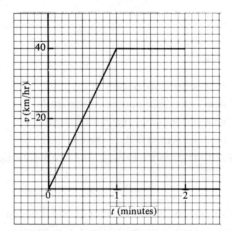

Find

a) the acceleration, in m/s², of the car during the first minute

b) the distance, in metres, travelled by the car during the 2 minutes.

5. A cross-country runner covers three sections of the course in succession. The first is a downhill sweep, then there is a level section followed by a hill climb. The graph below shows the speed, v, of the runner over the three sections.

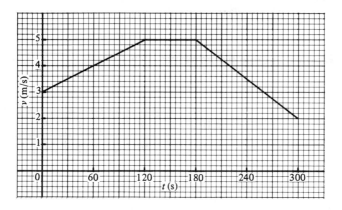

Find

a) the acceleration of the runner on the downhill section

b) the constant speed over the level section

c) the deceleration of the runner during the hill climb

d) the distance covered on the level section

e) the distance covered on the hill climb.

6. The graph represents the journey made by a bus between two bus stops.

a) What is the acceleration of the bus ?

b) What is the deceleration of the bus ?

c) What distance does the bus cover while accelerating ?

d) What distance does the bus cover while decelerating ?

e) What is the distance between the two bus stops ?

CURVED VELOCITY-TIME GRAPHS

When acceleration is not constant, the velocity-time graph is a curved line.

For example, suppose that a ball rolls along the ground in such a way that, t seconds after starting, its velocity is v m/s where

$$v = t(10-t)$$

Forming a table listing values of v for values of t from 0 to 10 gives

t	0	1	2	4	5	6	8	9	10
$(10-t)$	10	9	8	6	5	4	2	1	0
v	0	9	16	24	25	24	16	9	0

from which we draw the following velocity-time graph.

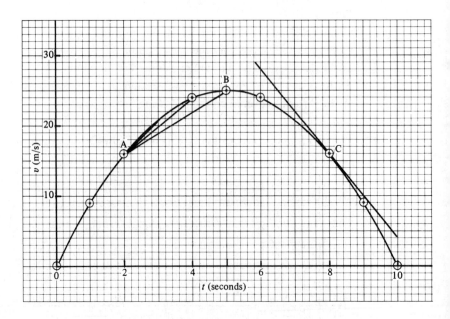

From the graph we see that the speed of the ball increases for 5 seconds, i.e. the ball accelerates for 5 seconds. Then the speed decreases for 5 seconds, i.e. the ball decelerates for 5 seconds.

The maximum speed is 25 m/s and occurs 5 seconds after the start.

The *average acceleration* over an interval of time is the steady acceleration that gives the same final velocity.

In the interval of time from $t = 2$ to $t = 5$, a steady increase in velocity is represented by the straight line AB. Hence the average acceleration over this interval of time is represented by the gradient of the chord AB.

Now consider *acceleration at an instant*. On the graph, the gradient of the tangent at the point C represents the rate at which v is changing at the instant when $t = 8$, i.e. the acceleration at the instant when $t = 8$. Hence

> acceleration at an instant is represented by the gradient of the tangent to the velocity–time curve at that instant.

Consider the *distance travelled* in an interval of time. When the acceleration is constant, the velocity–time graph is a straight line and the distance is represented by the area under the straight line. Now a curve can be represented approximately by a succession of short straight lines; the diagram shows an approximation to the curve between A and B.

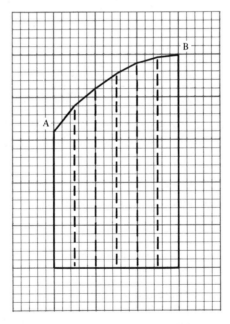

The sum of the areas under each of these straight lines gives a very good approximation for the distance covered in the interval from $t = 2$ to $t = 5$. Hence

> the distance covered in an interval of time is represented by the area under the velocity–time graph for that interval.

EXERCISE 18j

The graph represents the first five minutes of the journey of a train.

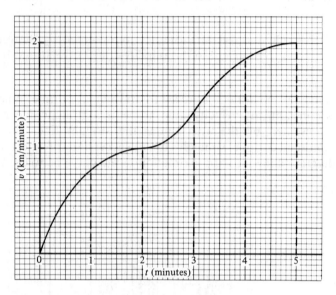

Find   a) the time at which the acceleration is zero
b) the distance covered by the train in the 5 minutes.

a)   (The tangent has zero gradient where $t = 2$)

The acceleration is zero when $t = 2$

b)   Using five strips each of width 1 unit gives five trapeziums.

Therefore the area is approximately

$$\tfrac{1}{2}(0 + 0.8)(1) + \tfrac{1}{2}(0.8 + 1)(1) + \tfrac{1}{2}(1 + 1.35)(1)$$
$$+ \tfrac{1}{2}(1.35 + 1.85)(1) + \tfrac{1}{2}(1.85 + 2)(1)$$
$$= 0.4 + 0.9 + 1.175 + 1.6 + 1.925 = 6$$

Distance covered $\approx 6\,\text{km}$.

1. The graph illustrates the motion of a ball thrown alo

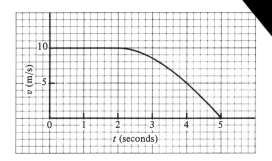

a) Find the velocity of the ball when $t = 4$

b) Is the ball accelerating or decelerating from $t = 2$ to $t = 5$?

c) Find the distance the ball moves before it stops. (Use five strips each of width 1 unit.)

2. The graph illustrates a five-second interval of a car journey.

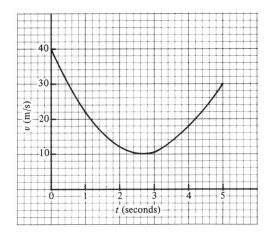

a) Find the distance covered by the car in these five seconds.

b) The following statements about this graph are either true or false. If the statement is true write T, if it is false write F.

i) The car is accelerating when $t = 4$.

ii) The car comes momentarily to rest when $t = 2.7$.

iii) The car changes direction halfway through this interval of time.

iv) The car's speed is decreasing for the first 2 seconds.

its velocity, v km/minute, t minutes after firing is given

$$v = t^3$$

following table.

0	1	2	3	4
0		8		

...ute and $1\,\text{cm} \equiv 10\,\text{km/min}$ to draw the

graph.

From your graph find

a) the acceleration 2 minutes after firing

b) the velocity after $2\frac{1}{2}$ minutes

c) the time when the velocity is 20 km/min

d) the distance covered in the first 3 minutes

e) the distance covered in the fourth minute.

4. The table shows the velocity, v m/s, of a helium filled balloon t seconds after being released in the air on a calm day.

t	0	1	2	3	4	5	6
v	0	5	8	9	8	5	0

Use scales of $1\,\text{cm} \equiv 1$ second and $1\,\text{cm} \equiv 1$ m/s to draw the velocity–time graph.

From your graph find

a) the maximum velocity of the balloon and the time when this occurs

b) the velocity after $1\frac{1}{2}$ s

c) the acceleration 1 second after release

d) the acceleration when $t = 3$

e) the distance covered by the balloon in these 6 seconds.

MIXED EXERCISE

EXERCISE 18k

Each question is followed by several alternative answers. Write letter that corresponds to the correct answer.

1.

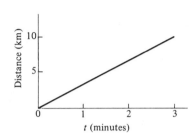

The graph shows an object moving at

A   10 km/min   **B** $3\frac{1}{3}$ km/min   **C** $\frac{3}{10}$ km/min   **D**   30 km/min

2.

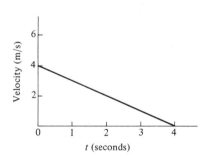

The graph shows an object which in 4 seconds covers a distance of

A   1 m   **B**   8 m   **C**   16 m   **D**   −8 m

3.   The acceleration of the object whose motion is given in question 2 is

A   1 m/s²   **B**   4 m/s²   **C**   16 m/s²   **D**   −1 m/s²

t (minutes)

covered in the thirty minutes is

⌐ 1 km **C** 2 km **D** 4 km

5.

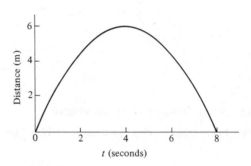

t (seconds)

The graph shows an object

A whose velocity is constant
B whose speed when $t = 0$ is zero
C which continues to move away from its initial position
D which returns to its initial position after 8 seconds.

6.

t (sec)

The average velocity from $t = 0$ to $t = 3$ is

A 2 m/s **B** 1 m/s **C** $\frac{2}{3}$ m/s **D** $1\frac{1}{2}$ m/s

7. Deducing from the shape of the graph in question 6, the acceleration when $t = 2$ could be

A -1 m/s² **B** zero **C** 20 m/s² **D** 1 m/s

8. The distance–time graph representing the motion of a stone dropped from a cliff top could be

9.

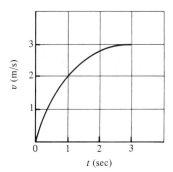

From the graph the distance covered in 3 seconds could be

A 6 m   **B** 8 m   **C** 9 m   **D** 6 km

10. A bead moves along a straight wire with a constant speed for 2 seconds and then its speed decreases at a constant rate to zero. The velocity–time graph illustrating this could be

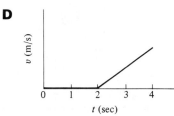

19 VARIATION

RELATIONSHIPS

Frequently, in everyday life, we come across two quantities that appear to be related to each other in some way. The amount I spend on potatoes, when they cost 60 p a bag, depends on the number of bags I buy; the distance I travel in a car, at a constant speed, depends on the length of time that I am travelling; the number of 'singles' I can buy for £10, depends on the price of one record. These are examples of quantities that are related by a simple algebraic equation.

On the other hand, there is no simple algebraic relationship between the amount a person earns and the amount that person spends on food; between our weight and our height; or between how far we travel to school and the time we get up in the morning.

The first exercise in this chapter helps us to recognise some of the simple relationships that connect sets of varying quantities.

EXERCISE 19a

Write down the equation connecting the two variables given in the table.

x	2	3	5	10	12
y	6	9	15	30	36

(We observe that in each case the value of y is three times the value of x)

$$y = 3x$$

In each of the following questions write down the equation connecting the variables.

1.

x	1	2	4	7	10
y	3	6	12	21	30

2.

p	0	1	2	3	4
q	0	1	4	9	16

3.

x	1	2	3	4	5
V	1	8	27	64	125

4.

A	0	4	9	16	25
r	0	2	3	4	5

5.

x	2	4	6	24
y	12	6	4	1

6.

r	0	2	4	6	10
s	0	0.2	0.4	0.6	1

7.

x	−3	−1	0	2	4
y	36	4	0	16	64

8.

p	−9	−6	−3	2	4
q	4	6	12	−18	−9

9. Using squared paper draw six rectangles such that, in each one the length is twice the breadth. Use the lengths given in the table and complete the table to give the area of each rectangle.
What is the equation connecting the area (*A*) and the length (*L*)?

Length of rectangle (*L*) in cm	2	4	5	6	8	10
Area of rectangle (*A*) in cm^2						

10. Copy the triangle given below on squared paper. Its base is 3 cm and its height is 2 cm.

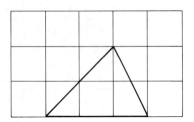

Draw three further similar triangles with bases 6 cm, 9 cm and 12 cm whose heights will be 4 cm, 6 cm and 8 cm respectively. Find the area of each triangle. Use these values to complete the following table.

Base (b) in cm	3	6	9	12
Area (A) in cm^2				

What equation connects A and b?

11. For this question imagine that you have a quantity of identical cubes. Cubes of sugar or Oxo cubes would be suitable. Use these cubes to build bigger cubes whose sides are larger than the basic cube by factors of 2, 3, 4 and 5. It will help if you draw diagrams. How many times larger is the volume of each of these cubes than the volume of the basic cube, i.e. how many of the smallest cubes are required to make each of the larger cubes? Use your results to complete the following table.

Factor by which the side of the basic cube is multiplied (x)	2	3	4	5
Factor by which the volume of the basic cube is multiplied (y)				

The questions in this exercise have illustrated several different ways in which varying quantities may be related. An increase in one quantity may lead to an increase or a decrease in the other.

DIRECT VARIATION

Consider the total cost for a group of people to attend a concert. The varying costs, depending on the size of the group, are given in the table.

Number of people (N)	5	10	15	25	35	50
Total cost in £ (C)	20	40	60	100	140	200

The two quantities C and N are connected by the equation $C = 4N$ i.e. the value of C is always four times the value of N.
This relation is called *direct proportion.*

In general, if two variables Y and X are in direct proportion then $Y = kX$ where k is the constant of proportion.

Sometimes we say that y varies directly with x. This gives exactly the same equation, i.e. $y = kx$ where k is the constant of variation.

In mathematics we are always looking for shorter ways of writing things. Instead of writing the relation 'y is directly proportional to x' or 'y varies directly as x' we sometimes write $y \propto x$, from which we can write the equation $y = kx$ where k is some constant.

EXERCISE 19b

1. Copy and complete the table so that $y \propto x$.

x	2		7	8	
y	20	40			95

What is the equation connecting x and y?

2. Copy and complete the table so that $C \propto r$.

r		3	5		8
C	6	18		36	48

What is the equation connecting C and r?

3. Copy and complete the table so that $C \propto n$.

Number of units of electricity used (n)	100	120	142	260	312	460
Total cost in pence (C)	600		852	1560		2760

What meaning can you give to the constant of proportion?

4. Copy and complete the table so that $Y \propto X$.

Number of oranges bought (X)	2	4	7	9	11	15
Total cost in pence (Y)	20	40		90		150

What meaning can you give to the constant of variation?

If y varies directly as x and $y = 2$ when $x = 3$, find
a) y when x is 9   b) x when y is 18

$$y \propto x$$

i.e. $y = kx$ where k is a constant

But $y = 2$ when $x = 3$

$\therefore$ $2 = k \times 3$

i.e. $3k = 2$

or $k = \dfrac{2}{3}$

so $y = \dfrac{2}{3}x$

a) If $x = 9$, $y = \dfrac{2}{3} \times 9$

$= 6$

b) If $y = 18$, $18 = \dfrac{2}{3}x$

i.e. $54 = 2x$

$27 = x$

$\therefore$ $x = 27$

---

5. y varies directly as x and $y = 21$ when $x = 7$.
Find   a) y when $x = 3$ b) x when $y = 48$.

6. $y \propto x$ and $y = 6$ when $x = 24$.
Find   a) y when $x = 6$ b) x when $y = 5$.

7. *s* varies directly as *t* and *s* = 35 when *t* = 5.
Find   a) *s* when *t* = 3   b) *t* when *s* = 49.

8. *y* varies as $3x - 4$ and *y* = 33 when *x* = 5.
Find   a) *y* when *x* = 2   b) *x* when *y* = 15.

9. *P* is directly proportional to *Q* and *P* = 15 when *Q* = 50.
Find   a) *P* when *Q* is 70   b) *Q* when *P* is 12.

10. *W* is directly proportional to *S* and *W* = 8 when *S* is 10.
Find   a) *W* when *S* is 30   b) *S* when *W* is 12.

11. *Y* is directly proportional to *X* and *Y* = 45 when *X* = 18.
Find   a) *Y* when *X* is 6   b) *X* when *Y* is 20.

DEPENDENT AND INDEPENDENT VARIABLES

Usually one of the quantities varies because of a change in the other. In question 3 on page 357 the total cost goes up because the number of units of electricity used goes up, i.e. the variation in the first quantity (*C*) *depends* on the change in the other (*n*). *C* is called a *dependent variable* while *n* is referred to as an *independent variable.*

Similarly, when the radius of a circle increases, the area of the circle increases. Therefore the radius is the independent variable and the area is the dependent variable.

The dependent variable is sometimes proportional to a power of the independent variable. For example, the area of a circle is directly proportional to the *square* of its radius and we can write
$A \propto R^2$ or $A = kR^2$ (*k* has a special value in this case; can you say what it stands for?)

Similarly, if the safe speed (*V*) at which a car can round a bend varies as the square root of the radius of the bend (*R*) then $V \propto \sqrt{R}$ or $V = k\sqrt{R}$.

EXERCISE 19c

1. Copy and complete the table so that $y \propto x^2$

x	0		3	4	5	
y		12	27		75	192

What is the equation connecting *x* and *y*?

2. Copy and complete the table so that $s \propto t^2$.

t	2	4			6	10
s		80	125	180		

What is the equation connecting s and t?

3. Copy and complete the table so that $y \propto x^2$

x	−3	−1	0	2	4	7
y				16		196

What is the equation connecting x and y?

If y is directly proportional to the square of x and $y = 3$ when $x = 1$, find

a) y when x is 4   b) x when y is $\frac{3}{4}$.

$$y \propto x^2$$

i.e. $y = kx^2$ where k is a constant

But $y = 3$ when $x = 1$

∴ $3 = k \times 1^2$

i.e. $k = 3$

so $y = 3x^2$

a)   If $x = 4$, $y = 3 \times 4^2$

$$= 3 \times 16$$

$$= 48$$

b)   If $y = \frac{3}{4}$, $\frac{3}{4} = 3x^2$

$$x^2 = \frac{1}{4} \qquad \text{(dividing both sides by 3)}$$

$$x = \pm \frac{1}{2}$$

4. y is directly proportional to the square of x and $y = 18$ when $x = 3$.
Find   a) y when $x = 4$ b) x when $y = \frac{1}{2}$.

5. y varies as the square of x and $y = 48$ when $x = 4$. Show that $y = 3x^2$
and find   a) y when $x = \frac{1}{2}$ b) x when $y = \frac{1}{3}$.

6. $P \propto Q^2$ and $P = 12$ when $Q = 4$.
Find   a) P when $Q = 12$ b) the positive value of Q when $P = 48$.

If y is directly proportional to the cube of x and $y = 4$ when $x = 2$ find

a) y when $x = 4$ b) x when $y = \frac{1}{2}$.

$$y \propto x^3$$

i.e. $$y = kx^3$$

But $y = 4$ when $x = 2$

$\therefore$ $$4 = k \times 2^3$$

i.e. $$8k = 4$$

$$k = \frac{1}{2}$$

so $$y = \frac{1}{2}x^3$$

a)   If $x = 4$, $y = \frac{1}{2} \times 4^3$

$$= 32$$

b)   If $y = \frac{1}{2}$, $\frac{1}{2} = \frac{1}{2}x^3$

i.e. $$x^3 = 1$$

$$x = 1$$

---

7. Copy and complete the table so that $V \propto H^3$.

H	2		6	8	10
V	2	16	54		

What is the equation connecting V and H?

8. Copy and complete the table so that $y \propto x^3$.

x	3	6	9	12	15
y		72		576	

What is the equation connecting x and y?

9. $y \propto x^3$ and $y = 3$ when $x = 2$.
Find   a) y when $x = 4$ b) x when $y = 81$.

10. If y varies directly as the cube of x and $y = 64$ when $x = 2$,
find   a) y when $x = 3$ b) x when $y = 8$.

11. W is proportional to the cube of H and $W = 32$ when $H = 4$.
Find   a) W when $H = 6$ b) H when $W = 4$.

12. Copy and complete the table so that $V \propto \sqrt{R}$.

R	0	1	4		25
V			8	12	

What is the equation connecting V and R?

13. Y varies directly as the square root of X and $Y = 1$ when $X = 100$.
Find   a) Y when $X = 400$ b) X when $Y = 3$.

14. Plot the graph of y against x for the following data.

x	1	4	9	16	25
y	1	2	3	4	5

Is the graph a straight line? If it is not, complete the following table and
plot the graph of y against $\sqrt{x}$.

$\sqrt{x}$					
y	1	2	3	4	5

Is this graph a straight line? What is the equation connecting x and y?

15. Plot the graph of y against x for the following data.

x	1	2	3	4	5
y	0.5	4	13.5	32	62.5

Is the graph a straight line? If not, plot the graphs of y against x^2
and y against x^3. What is the equation connecting x and y?

INVERSE VARIATION

When one quantity decreases as the other increases, the two are said to be inversely proportional, provided that their product always gives the same value. For example, the number of similar postage stamps I can buy for £4.80 depends on their price. At 10p each I can buy 48, at 12p each 40, at 20p each 24 and at 40p each 12. In each case the product of the number of stamps and the price of one stamp is 480p.

EXERCISE 19d

In each question from 1 to 3 complete the given table and show that the product of the varying quantities is constant. Write down the equation connecting these varying quantities.

1.

Cost of a birthday card in pence (C)	25	50	100	125
Number of cards that can be bought for £5 (N)	20		5	

2.

Number of similar magazines a boy could buy with his pocket money (N)		12	9	8	6
Cost of one magazine in pence (C)		60		90	

3.

Pressure (P)	4	5	6	8	12
Volume (V)	30		20		10

In questions 4 to 6 write down the equations connecting x and y.

4.

x	1	2	3	4	6	12
y	12	6	4	3	2	1

5.

x	36	24	18	12	8
y	2	3	4	6	9

6.

x	10	5	1	0.5	0.25
y	0.1	0.2	1	2	4

EQUATIONS FOR INVERSE VARIATION

A teacher has £120 to spend on books. The table shows the number of books of various prices that can be bought.

Cost per book in £ (c)	1	2	3	4	5	8	10
Number of books that can be bought (N)	120	60	40	30	24	15	12

As the cost per book increases the number of books that can be bought decreases. For example, if the cost per book doubles the number of books that can be bought is halved.

We say N varies inversely as C or N is inversely proportional to C, and write this $N \propto \dfrac{1}{C}$ or $N = \dfrac{k}{C}$

In this case $N = \dfrac{120}{C}$ hence $NC = 120$.

This confirms the definition on the previous page, that if two quantities are inversely proportional, their product is constant.

i.e. if $y = \dfrac{k}{x}$ then $xy = k$.

Similarly if p is inversely proportional to the square of q then

$$p \propto \frac{1}{q^2}, \quad p = \frac{k}{q^2} \quad \text{and again} \quad pq^2 = k$$

EXERCISE 19e

Copy and complete the table so that $y \propto \dfrac{1}{x^2}$

x	3	5		10	15
y	100	36	25		

If $y \propto \dfrac{1}{x^2}$

then $y = \dfrac{k}{x^2}$

But $y = 100$ when $x = 3$

$\therefore \qquad\qquad\qquad 100 = \dfrac{k}{9}$

i.e. $\quad k = 900 \qquad$ so $\qquad y = \dfrac{900}{x^2}$

(Check: when $x = 5$, $y = \dfrac{900}{25} = 36$)

If $x = 10$, $\qquad y = \dfrac{900}{100} = 9$

If $x = 15$, $\qquad y = \dfrac{900}{225} = 4$

If $y = 25$, $\qquad 25 = \dfrac{900}{x^2}$

i.e. $\qquad 25x^2 = 900$

$$x^2 = \frac{900}{25} = 36$$

$\qquad\qquad x = 6 \qquad\qquad$ (taking only the positive value)

$\therefore$ the completed table is

x	3	5	6	10	15
y	100	36	25	9	4

1. Copy and complete the table so that $y \propto \dfrac{1}{x}$

x	2	4	6	9	12	
y	18	9			3	2

What is the equation connecting x and y?

2. Copy and complete the table so that $y \propto \dfrac{1}{x^2}$

x	0.5		2	3	6	10
y		36	9			

What is the equation connecting x and y?

3. Copy and complete the table so that $q \propto \dfrac{1}{\sqrt{p}}$

p	0.25		4	9		25
q	120	60	30		15	12

What is the equation connecting p and q?

4. If y is inversely proportional to x, and $y = 8$ when $x = 5$
find   a) y when x is 10   b) x when y is 2   c) y when x is -4.

5. $y \propto \dfrac{1}{\sqrt{x}}$ and $y = 2$ when $x = 4$.
Find   a) y when $x = 9$ b) x when $y = 1$.

6. If p is inversely proportional to v, and $p = 15$ when $v = 20$
find   a) p when $v = 30$ b) v when $p = 7.5$.

7. If P varies inversely as $Q + 2$ and $P = 5$ when $Q = 4$
find   a) P when $Q = 3$ b) Q when $P = 15$.

8. If y is inversely proportional to the square of x and $y = 4$ when $x = 5$
find   a) y when $x = 2$ b) x when $y = 1$.

9. If y varies inversely as x and $y = 6$ when $x = 8$
find   a) y when $x = 12$ b) x when $y = 4$.

10. If y varies inversely as the cube of x and $y = 7$ when $x = 6$
find   a) y when $x = 3$ b) x when $y = 189$.

If y is the constant speed of a train and x is the time it takes to travel a distance k, find the value of n if x and y are related by a law of the form $y \propto x^n$.

Since   distance travelled $=$ constant speed $\times$ time

$$k = y \times x$$

i.e. $$xy = k$$

and $$y = \frac{k}{x}$$

or $$y = kx^{-1}$$

$\therefore$ $$y \propto x^n \quad \text{where} \quad n = -1$$

11. In each of the following cases, x and y are related by a law of the form $y \propto x^n$. Find the value of n.

a) y is the area of a square and x is the length of one side.

b) y is the area of a circle and x is its radius.

c) y is the volume of a sphere and x is its radius.

d) y is the length of a rectangle of constant area and x is its breadth.

e) y is the radius of a circle and x is its area.

f) y is the length of a line in centimetres and x is its length in millimetres.

MIXED EXAMPLES

EXERCISE 19f

1. p varies directly as the square of q and $p = 9$ when $q = 6$.
Find p when q is   a) 2   b) -2 c) 5.

2. A is directly proportional to L and $A = 28$ when $L = 4$.
Find   a) A when $L = 3$ b) L when $A = 42$.

3. $y \propto x^3$ and $y = 48$ when $x = 4$.
Find   a) the formula for y in terms of x b) y when $x = 2$
c) x when $y = 6$.

4. y varies inversely as x and $y = 7$ when $x = 6$.
Find   a) y when $x = 3$ b) x when $y = 14$.

5. y is inversely proportional to x^2 and $y = 4.5$ when $x = 4$.
Find   a) y when $x = 3$ b) x when $y = 8$.

6. Copy and complete the table so that $y \propto x^2$.

x	0	1		4	8
y		0.25	1		16

7. Copy and complete the table so that $t \propto \sqrt{s}$.

s			4	9		
t	0	0.5			1	2

8. Given that y varies as x^n, write down the value of n in each of the following cases:

a) y is the area of a square of side x

b) y is the volume of a cube of side x

c) y is the volume of a cylinder with constant base area A and height x

d) y and x are the sides of a rectangle with a given area.

GRAPHS FROM EXPERIMENTAL DATA

In science we often conduct experiments where one quantity (say q) is measured for various values of another quantity (say p).

If these values are plotted on a graph, the points often lie, more or less, on a straight line.

Consider the following experimental data for two quantities p and q.

p	1	2	3	4	5	6	7
q	4	6.5	7.5	10.5	12	10	16.5

Plotting these points gives this diagram.

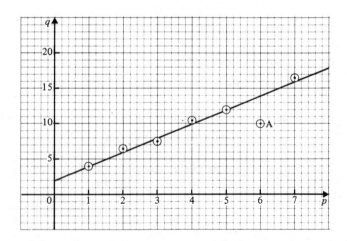

If we assume that the point marked A is the result of an error in measurement and hence ignore it, then the other points can be seen to lie roughly on a straight line. It is unrealistic to expect the points to lie *exactly* on a straight line as measurements cannot be taken so accurately.

Assuming that some measurements are high and some are low, the line that best fits these points can be drawn by positioning the line so that the sum of the distances of points above the line is approximately equal to the sum of the distances of points below the line. This is best judged by eye, using a transparent ruler.

We know that when using x and y axes, the equation of a straight line can be written as $y = mx + c$ where m is the gradient and c is the intercept on the y-axis. In the same way the equation of our line can be written in the form $q = mp + c$ and this gives the relationship between p and q.

From the graph,   the gradient of the line is 2
                               and the intercept on the q-axis is 2.

Therefore the equation of the line is

$$q = 2p + 2$$

i.e. the relationship between p and q is $q = 2p + 2$.

EXERCISE 19g

1. In a spring stretching experiment the following results were obtained.

Stretching force in newtons (F)	0	1	2	3	4	5	6
Extension of spring in mm (E)	0	8	17	25	33	42	50

Use scales of 4 cm to 10 mm and 2 cm to 1 newton to plot a graph of E against F and use it to find
a) the stretching force required to produce an extension of 20 mm
b) the relationship between E and F.

2. The table shows the results of measuring the length of a column of air at various temperatures.

Temperature in °C (T)	20°	30°	40°	50°	60°	70°	80°
Length of column in cm (l)	7	7.2	7.3	7.6	7.9	8	8.1

Use a scale of 2 cm to 10°C and 2 cm to 1 cm and plot these results. Draw the straight line that best fits these points and use it to find the temperature when the column of air is 7.5 cm long.

3. The relationship between the current, I, flowing through a tangent galvanometer is given by the formula $I = k \tan \theta$ where θ is the angle of deflection. The table shows the results obtained in an experiment.

Current in amps (I)	0.42	0.65	0.89	1.18	1.70	1.88
Mean deflection (θ)	27.6°	38.7°	43°	56.2°	64.4°	67.3°
Tan θ						

a) Copy the table and complete the last row.

b) Plot values of I against values of $\tan \theta$ using a scale of 1 cm to 0.1 units on both axes.

c) By drawing the line that best fits these points, find the value of k.

4. An athlete trained by running round a track. His coach recorded the distance covered by the athlete at various times and the results are shown in the table.

Time in seconds from start (t)	10	20	30	50	80	100
Distance from starting point in metres (d)	42	83	120	210	350	390

Use scales of 4 cm to 100 m and 1 cm to 10 seconds and plot these results on a graph.

a) If the coach made an error on one reading, which one is it?

b) Ignoring the one reading that is wrong, draw the line that best fits the other results.

c) Show that the distance varies directly as the time and hence find the speed of the athlete.

5. The magnification, M, produced by a convex lens of focal length f when the distance of the lens from the image is v is given by the equation

$$M = \frac{v}{f} - 1$$

In an experiment the following values of v and M were obtained

v (cm)	20.3	24.8	27.1	30.4	38.0	42.3	47.4
M	1	1.5	1.75	2.1	2.4	3.25	3.75

Plot a graph of M against v and draw the straight line that best fits this data. Use your graph to find the value of f.

PROBLEMS ON DIRECT AND INVERSE VARIATION

EXERCISE 19h

A stone falls from rest down a mine shaft. It falls D metres in T seconds where D varies as the square of T. If it falls 20 m in the first 2 s and takes 5 s to reach the bottom, how deep is the shaft?

$$D \propto T^2$$

i.e. $$D = kT^2$$

But $D = 20$ when $T = 2$

$\therefore$ $$20 = k \times 2^2$$

i.e. $$4k = 20$$

$$k = 5$$

$\therefore$ $$D = 5T^2$$

If $T = 5$, $D = 5 \times 5^2$

$$= 125$$

Therefore the shaft is 125 metres deep.

---

1. The mass, M kg, of a circular disc of constant thickness varies as the square of its radius, R cm. If a disc of 5 cm radius has a mass of 1 kilogram find

a) the mass of a disc of radius 10 cm

b) the radius of a disc of mass 25 kg.

2. The safe speed, V km/h, at which a car can round a bend of radius R metres varies as $\sqrt{R}$. If the safe speed on a curve of radius 25 m is 40 km/h, find the radius of the curve for which the safe speed is 64 km/h.

3. The time of swing, T s, of a simple pendulum is directly proportional to the square root of its length, L cm. If $T = 2$ when $L = 100$ find
a) T when $L = 64$ b) L when $T = 1\frac{1}{2}$.

4. The extension, x cm, of an elastic string varies as the force, F newtons, used to extend it. If a force of 4 newtons gives an extension of 10 cm find

a) the extension given by a force of 10 newtons

b) the force required to give an extension of 12 cm.

5. The cost of buying a rectangular carpet is directly proportional to the square of its longer side. If a carpet whose longer side is 3 m costs £180 find

a) the cost of a carpet with a longer side of 4 m

b) the length of the longer side of a carpet costing £405.

6. The radius of a circle, r cm, varies as the square root of its area, A cm². How does the radius change if the area is increased by

a) a factor of 4   b) a factor of 25 ?

7. Mathematically similar jugs have capacities that vary as the cubes of their heights. If a jug 10 cm high holds $\frac{1}{8}$ litre find

a) the capacity of a jug that is 12 cm high

b) the height of a jug that will hold 1 litre.

8. For a given mass of gas at a given temperature the pressure p varies inversely as the volume, v. If $p = 100$ when $v = 2.4$ find

a) v when $p = 80$ b) p when $v = 2$.

9. For a vehicle travelling between two motorway service stations the time taken is inversely proportional to its speed. If it takes $2\frac{1}{2}$ hours when its speed is 48 m.p.h. find

a) its average speed if it takes 3 hours

b) by how much its average speed must increase if the journey time is to be reduced to 2 hours.

10. By what factor does y change when x is doubled if

a) $y \propto x$ b) $y \propto \dfrac{1}{x}$ c) $y \propto x^2$ d) $y \propto x^3$

11. State the percentage change in y when x is increased by 25% if

a) $y \propto x$ b) $y \propto \dfrac{1}{x}$ c) $y \propto x^2$

20 GENERAL REVISION EXERCISES

EXERCISE 20a

1. A motorcyclist buys 20 litres of petrol at 48.7 p per litre.
   a) Find the cost of the petrol bought.
   b) Using $4\ell \approx 7$ pints, find the number of gallons bought.

2. Factorise:
   a) $2x^2 - 6x$ b) $x(x-1) - 3(x-1)$ c) $x^2 - 3x - 10$

3. Solve the equations   a) $\dfrac{3}{x} + \dfrac{1}{2} = 4$
                              b) $x^2 - 5x + 6 = 0$
                              c) $x + y = 2$
                                 $x - y = 4$

4. Simplify   a) $3(2-x) - 2(x-1)$
                   b) $\left(1\tfrac{1}{2}\right)^{-2}$
                   c) $\dfrac{x-1}{3} - \dfrac{x-4}{6}$

5. A house was bought for £20 000 on 1st January 1980. Each year the value of the house appreciates by 10% of its value at the beginning of the year. Find the value of the house on 1st January 1986.

6. Alison is twice as good as Paul at chess. They play two games. What is the probability that
   a) Alison wins both games   b) she wins only one game?

7. A and B are two points 6 cm apart. Sketch the loci that will enable you to shade the region in which every point satisfies both the following conditions.
   a) It is within 4 cm of A.
   b) It is further away from A than it is from B.

8. y varies inversely as x and $y = 8$ when $x = 18$.
   Find a formula for y in terms of x and use it to find
   a) the value of y when $x = 4$ b) the value of x when $y = 9$.

9. A ship A is 8 miles due East of a ship B. A third ship C is observed simultaneously from A and B and found to be on a bearing of 290° from A and on a bearing of 020° from B. Draw a sketch showing the positions of A, B and C. Calculate the distances of C from A and from B giving your answers correct to three significant figures.

10.

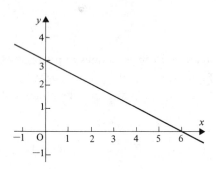

Use the diagram to find

a) the gradient of the line

b) the equation of the line

c) the area enclosed by the line, the x-axis and the ordinates $x = 2$ and $x = 4$.

EXERCISE 20b

1. An automatic cooker works on a 24-hr digital clock. To make the oven cook automatically, both the cooking time and the finishing time have to be programmed in. A casserole which needs $3\frac{1}{2}$ hours cooking-time, has to be ready at 6.30 p.m. and quarter of an hour is required for the oven to heat up. Find

a) the finishing time to be entered on the programme

b) the reading on the clock when the oven comes on.

2. A ball is thrown vertically upward from a point A with speed u m/s. Its distance, s metres, from A, t seconds after being thrown, is given by

$$s = ut - 5t^2$$

a) Find s when $u = 40$ and $t = 5$.

b) Find t when $s = 1$ and $u = 6$.

c) Interpret your answer to (b).

d) Make u the subject of the formula.

3. Simplify:　a) $5x \times 3x^2$

b) $\dfrac{x+1}{2} - \dfrac{x-1}{5}$

c) $(125)^{1/3}$

4. Use squared paper and the same scale on both axes to draw a *sketch* of the graph of $y = x^2$. On the same axes sketch the graph of $y = x + 1$.

a) Use your sketch to estimate the solution of the equation $x^2 = x + 1$.

b) Calculate the solution of the equation $x^2 = x + 1$, giving your answers to 2 decimal places.

5. The point (x, y) is mapped to the point $(2, 4)$ by the transformation matrix $\begin{pmatrix} 1 & 2 \\ 0 & 1 \end{pmatrix}$. Find x and y.

6.

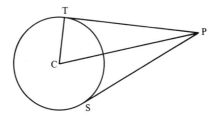

PS and PT are the two tangents from the point P to the circle centre C. P is 20 cm from the centre of the circle and the radius of the circle is 6 cm. Find

a) the lengths of the tangents PT and PS

b) the angle between the tangents.

7. In this diagram the side of each of the blocks is equal to one unit on each axis. Write down the coordinates of the corners P, Q, R, S, T, and U.

8. A racing cyclist did a trial lap of a circuit. His speed was recorded from the start at 5-second intervals of time and the results are given in the table.

Time from start, t sec	0	5	10	15	20	25
Speed, v m/s	0	6	8.2	9.3	9.9	10

Using scales of 2 cm for 5 seconds and 1 cm for 1 m/s draw a velocity–time graph showing this information. Use your graph to find, approximately

a) the speed when $t = 8$

b) the acceleration when $t = 10$

c) the distance covered in the first ten seconds.

9. Two model cars are mathematically similar. One is 8 cm long and the other is 6 cm long.

a) Calculate the width of the smaller car given that the width of the larger car is 4.8 cm.

b) If 13.5 cm³ of metal were used to make the smaller car calculate the volume of metal used to make the larger car.

10.

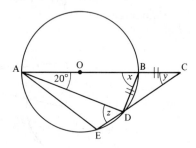

In the diagram, O is the centre of the circle, and $E\widehat{D}C$ is 180°. Find the size of each marked angle, giving reasons for your working.

EXERCISE 20c

1. A car travels from town A to town B at an average speed of 64 km/h in 1 hour 45 minutes.

a) Find the distance covered by the car.

b) Using 5 miles ≈ 8 kilometres, find the distance covered in miles.

2. Solve the equations   a) $5x = 3(8 - x)$

b) $2x - y = 5$
$x + 2y = 7$

3. A man bought x packets of butter at 50 p each and y packets of tea at 30 p each. Write down an algebraic statement describing each of the following.

a) The cost of the man's purchases was £3.20.

b) The man bought 8 packets altogether.

c) The number of packets bought was less than ten.

d) The cost of the packets was more than £5.

4. Find the value of x if   a) $x^3 = 125$ b) $2^x = \frac{1}{8}$ c) $3^x = 27$

5. Solve the equation $2x^2 - 8x + 3 = 0$ giving your answers correct to two decimal places.

6. A survey of 72 houses showed that 40 houses were owner-occupied, 5 were empty and the remainder were rented. Show this information on a pie chart, giving the angle at the centre of each slice.

7. From a year group of 90 pupils, 45 chose to study Latin, 36 chose to study Japanese. There were 10 pupils who chose to study both subjects. Draw a diagram to represent the numbers of pupils choosing the various options. Hence find the probability that a pupil chosen at random studies neither subject.

8. There are 25 pupils in a class and the ratio of girls to boys is $3:2$. What is the probability that a pupil, chosen at random for a place on a quiz team, is a girl?
What is the probability that the next pupil chosen is also a girl?

9.

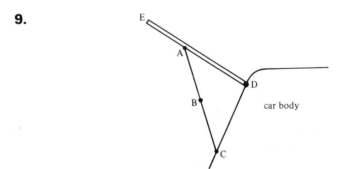

The diagram shows a section through the tailgate of a car, with the tailgate DE in its fully open position. DE is kept in this position by the stay ABC. The stay consists of two rigid bars, AB and BC which are freely hinged together at B. One end of the stay is hinged to the car body at C and the other end of the stay is hinged to the tailgate at A.
With the tailgate fully open, ABC is a straight line, 50 cm long. AD and DC are each 30 cm long.
Using a scale of 1 cm to 5 cm make a scale drawing of this section.
The stay is released by pulling the hinge B away from D. By considering the tailgate closing 20° at a time, or otherwise, draw the path traced out by the hinge B as the door closes.

10. ABCD is a rectangle with A(1, 4), B(4, 4), C(4, 8) and D(1, 8). On squared paper draw x and y axes for $-2 \leqslant x \leqslant 10$, $-10 \leqslant y \leqslant 10$.

  a) Draw ABCD and its image $A_1B_1C_1D_1$ when ABCD is reflected in the line $y = x$.

  b) Draw the image of $A_1B_1C_1D_1$ when it is rotated clockwise by 90° about O. Label the image $A_2B_2C_2D_2$.

  c) Describe the transformation that maps ABCD directly to $A_2B_2C_2D_2$.

EXERCISE 20d

1. a) Calculate, exactly, the value of $\dfrac{2.19 - 0.6753}{101 + 889}$

b) Give your answer to (a)   i) in standard form   ii) correct to 1 s.f.

2. Calculate a) $2\begin{pmatrix} 1 & 7 \\ -2 & 4 \end{pmatrix} - \begin{pmatrix} 3 & -2 \\ 1 & 5 \end{pmatrix}$

b) $\begin{pmatrix} 1 & 7 \\ -2 & 4 \end{pmatrix}\begin{pmatrix} 3 & -2 \\ 1 & 5 \end{pmatrix}$

c) Find the determinant of $\begin{pmatrix} 1 & 7 \\ -2 & 4 \end{pmatrix}$

3. A class of 30 pupils was given a test, marked out of 10. The distribution of the marks is given in the table.

Mark	0	1	2	3	4	5	6	7	8	9	10
Frequency	1	1	2	1	0	4	4	5	6	4	2

Find   a) the modal mark   b) the mean mark   c) the median mark.

4. From a point A on level ground, 30 m from the foot, B, of a tower, the angle of elevation of the top, C, of the tower is 54°. Calculate the height of the tower.

5. a) Simplify $\dfrac{5}{t+3} + \dfrac{2}{t-2}$

b) Solve the equation $5x^2 - 4x - 8 = 0$ giving your answers correct to two decimal places.

6. a) The size of each exterior angle of a regular polygon is $x°$ and the size of each interior angle is $2x°$. Find x and name the polygon.

b) In $\triangle ABC$, $\widehat{A} = 90°$, $AB = 15\,cm$ and $AC = 9\,cm$.
Find BC and angle ACB.

7.

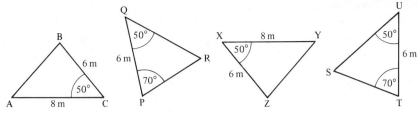

Find two pairs of congruent triangles, giving reasons for your answers.

8. Neil has twenty-two coins in his pocket and they have a total value of £8. The coins are of value £1, 50 p and 5 p. There are three times as many 50 p coins as there are £1 coins.

Let the number of £1 coins be x and write down the number of 5 p coins.

Find the value (in pence) in terms of x of

a) the £1 coins   b) the 50 p coins   c) the 5 p coins.

Form an equation in x and solve it to find the number of each kind of coin in Neil's pocket.

9.

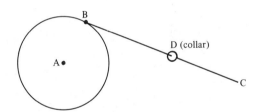

A wheel of diameter 4 cm can rotate about its centre A. A rod BC which is 8 cm long is freely pivoted to the rim of the wheel at B and passes through a fixed collar D which is 5 cm from A (i.e. AD = 5 cm). Draw, full size, the diagram when A, B, D and C are in one straight line, in that order. By considering different positions of B (let AB turn through 30° clockwise for each new position), draw the path traced out by C for each complete turn of the wheel.

10. Copy and complete the table so that $R \propto \sqrt{A}$

A	1	4	9		
R		0.4		0.8	1

What formula connects R and A? Use this formula to find A when $R = 2$.

EXERCISE 20e

1. A radio costs £56.87 including VAT at $17\frac{1}{2}\%$. Find the cost of the radio without VAT.

2. Factorise   a) $x^2 - 9$ b) $3xy - 6x^2$ c) $2x^2 - 4x - 6$.

3. A delivery company offers 'same day' delivery in the UK on parcels and packets at the following rates:

   £10 for a packet weighing up to 3 kg
   and then 50p per 500 g or part of 500 g.

   Find the charge for delivering a packet weighing
   a) 2.7 kg   b) 5.2 kg   c) 4.8 kg.

4. Given that $a = \dfrac{1}{b} + \dfrac{1}{c}$ find

   a) the value of a when $b = 3$ and $c = -4$
   b) the value of b when $a = 2$ and $c = 5$.
   c) Make c the subject of the formula.

5. 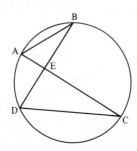 A, B, C and D are four points on the circumference of a circle. Prove that $\triangle ABE$ is similar to $\triangle DCE$.

6. a) On a map whose scale is $1 : 5000$, the area of a field is $4\,\text{cm}^2$. Find the area of the actual field.

   b)

   Triangles ABC and DEF are similar and the scale factor for reducing $\triangle ABC$ to $\triangle DEF$ is $\frac{1}{2}$.
   i)   If $AB = 8\,\text{cm}$, find DE.
   ii) If $BC = 13\,\text{cm}$, find EF.
   iii) If $DF = 4.5\,\text{cm}$, find AC.
   iv) If area $\triangle ABC = 35.5\,\text{cm}^2$ find area $\triangle DEF$.

7. The sum of the squares of two consecutive even numbers, the first of which is x, is 164. Form an equation in x and solve it to find these numbers.

8.

Paddington*	d	00 50	06 55	08 00	09 00	09 35	10 00	11 00	11 35	12 00	13 00	14 00	15 00
Slough	d		07 08			09 48			11 48				
Reading A*	d		07 23	08 24	09 24	10 03		11 24	12 03		13 24		15 24
Didcot	d		07 34			10 16			12 16				
Swindon	d	02 17	07 54			10 37			12 37			14 49	
Bristol Parkway	d		08 21	09 12	10 12	11 01		12 12	13 01		14 12	15 14	16 12
Newport	a	03 10	08 42	09 32	10 32	11 21	11 27	12 32	13 21	13 28	14 32	15 35	16 32
Cardiff Central	a	03 39	05 58	09 48	10 48	11 39	11 43	12 48	13 39	13 44	14 48	15 51	16 48

Paddington*	d	16 00	16 25	17 00	18 00	18 17
Slough	d					
Reading A*	d		16 49		18 25	
Didcot	d					
Swindon	d		17 17			
Bristol Parkway	d	17 08	17 43	18 09	19 12	19 46
Newport	a	17 28	18 04	18 32	19 32	20 08
Cardiff Central	a	17 44	18 22	18 46	19 48	20 26

Use this extract from the timetable for trains from London (Paddington) to Cardiff to find

a) the time of departure of the latest train from London to arrive in Cardiff before 4 p.m.

b) the time of departure of the fastest train and its journey-time

c) the time of departure of the slowest train and its journey-time.

9. The histogram shows the distribution of marks obtained in a test by a group of pupils.

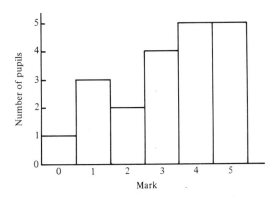

State whether each of the following statements is true or false

a) Twenty pupils took the test.

b) The median mark is $2\frac{1}{2}$.

c) More than half the pupils got a mark of 3 or more.

d) The mean mark is 3.2.

10. a) A rectangular sheet of card, 10 cm by 30 cm, is curved round to form a cylinder 10 cm high. Assuming that the straight edges of the card just meet and there is no overlap, find

    i) the radius of the cylinder

    ii) the volume enclosed by the cylinder.

b)

This net makes a triangular prism when folded along the dotted lines.

Find   i) which letter is joined to B

        ii) which letter is joined to J

        iii) the volume of the prism.